Groundwater Pollution

Groundwater Pollution

Dr. Pawan Kumar 'Bharti',
(M.Sc., Ph.D., FASEA)

Founder Member
Centre for Agro-Rural Technologies,
RIIT Campus, Barwala, Panchkula, Haryana

BIOTECH
2012
BIOTECH BOOKS®

ISBN 978-81-7622-242-6

Published by: **BIOTECH BOOKS®**
4762-63/23, Ansari Road, Darya Ganj,
New Delhi - 110 002
Phone: +91-011-23262132
E-mail: biotechbooks@yahoo.co.in

Printed at: **Chawla Offset Printers**
Delhi - 110 052

PRINTED IN INDIA

Preface

Water is not only essential for life but predominant inorganic constituent of living matter forming in general nearly three quarters of the weight of living cells. Next to oxygen, water is the most important substance for human existence and it is essential for everything on our planet to grow and prosper.

Most of our water resources are gradually becoming contaminated due to the addition of foreign materials from the surroundings. These include organic matter of plant and animal origin, land surface washing and industrial and sewage effluents. Rapid urbanization and industrialization with improper environmental planning often lead to discharge of industrial and sewage effluents into rivers. Pollution of environment with heavy metals is a serious problem. It is major concern to ecologist or researcher, because air or water pollution from point and non-point sources may contribute significantly to the load of metals on natural ecosystem.

The world is now facing water crisis of dimensions that no earlier generation has had to face. It may already be late for some water scare countries with rapid population growth to avoid a water crisis unless they take immediate and drastic steps for sustainable management of urban water resources. But a water crisis in the near future can be avoided if appropriate policies and strategies are formulated and acted upon quickly. In this regard, water conservation and its better management are the effective strategies for consideration. To avoid a catastrophe over the long term, it is also important to act to reduce the demand of freshwater by slowing the population growth. Urgent and decisive action must begin now if regional water crisis are to be avoided during the next century. There is an imperative need to change people's attitudes towards water.

Chapter 1 of this book gives an outline about the books contents. It is an introduction to all aspects described in this book.

Chapter 2 described the story of industrialization, and the percolation of heavy metal from industrial wastewater to deep Groundwater aquifer resources. Main focus of this chapter is on the main aspects of pollution including the use of chemicals in industries, and the discharge of heavy metal with effluents. This section also highlights the further impacts of industrial waste to the surrounding environmental components.

Chapter 3 highlights the role and significance of water to the human health. Water is like a medicine if it is uncontaminated and fresh, otherwise it may be dangerous to health. The chapter described the phase and forms of water on this planet. Besides, all these aspects this section has some tables related to the threshold values of heavy metal with respect to human health. Heavy metal may be harmful for human. How much concentration of particular metal can cause hazards to human, this is also important. Reference values of heavy metals are also given in this chapter.

Chapter 4 highlights the significance of heavy metals in water and their effects to the human health. Heavy metals and some other physico-chemical parameters of polluted water may cause many effects on environment. BIS, CPCB, WHO and many bodies has declared their standards for water quality. MINAS is also described and given in the tabular form in the chapter. The chapter described the various standards of water quality. Besides, all these aspects this section has some tables related to the standards of physico-chemical parameters and heavy metal in drinking water. Heavy metal may be harmful for human, so the standards are given in tabular form. Standard values of heavy metals described by various bodies are also given in this chapter.

Chapter 5 pointed out the increasing demand of water in different sector including, industrial, agriculture and domestic. This section elaborated the need of a water policy for the proper management and availability of water in various sectors. This small chapter included the main points of national water policy of India.

Chapter 6 highlighted the management plans for water resources. The available resources of water are given in this chapter in tabular form. Chapter starts with the presence of water on planet earth and the distribution of freshwater and marine water on earth. Complete water budget is presented in elaborated manner. This section also described the water demand and water crisis and the predicted requirement of water in different sectors with the help of graphs and tables. Chapter also highlighted the water supply problems and the possible solutions of water demand at various levels.

Chapter 7 is completely devoted to the Groundwater recharging techniques, benefits and status in India. Different methods of Groundwater recharging are also given in this chapter. This section pointed out the advantages and disadvantages of Groundwater recharging. Brief notes on rain water, rainwater harvesting and run-off coefficients are also given in the chapter. The text is supported with many figures and tables whenever and whatever required.

Chapter 8 focused on the modeling application in the study of Groundwater. Chapter described the movement of Groundwater in starting segment and further highlights the groundwater Flow Pattern. The mathematical formulas and equations are given as per the requirement. In the next segment of this chapter, Darcy and

Linear Velocity or Flow Velocity is described. For the prediction and modeling of toxic metals, flow of Heavy Metals in Unsaturated Soils, and the equation for the Transport Model is also given. In the last segment, the chapter described the groundwater monitoring techniques and finally the concept of groundwater modeling with the help of points and steps.

In the chapter 9, a case study is given of Groundwater pollution in Panipat city. The initial segment of chapter described the features of study area and research protocol adopted for that study. In the next segments of this chapter, the characteristics and impacts of industrial effluents on surface water, sediments of drain and pond are described. The pollution load in Groundwater of the city is elaborated and depicted in tabular form at different depth Groundwater. Separate study was executed for various depth of water table. In the last segment of chapter, the total focus is on heavy metal concentration in environment. Heavy metal analytical methodology, the use of AAS and many related requirements at the time of metal analysis are given. This chapter highlighted the heavy metal route in the environment.

In last, a glossary is given to describe the definitions of selected terms and words. The glossary will be beneficial for the researchers, students of Groundwater and Environmental Science.

(Pawan Kumar 'Bharti')

Contents

Chapter 1
Introduction

In vedic literature, water is called as a medicine for human health. Nobody can imagine life without water. Water is our basic requirement even animal and plant can't survive without water. It is common statement that ***"Life is not possible without water"***. Thus life and water are inseparable faces of the same coin. Water is not only essential for life but predominant inorganic constituent of living matter forming in general nearly three quarters of the weight of living cells. It makes some 5 percent of the body weight of an adult human and can forms as 98% of the mass of certain jellyfish. Organisms that contain relatively small amounts of water are generally in dormant state or show very slow development; seeds and certain invertebrates that live in arid environments are examples. On the other hand high rainfall over a landmass in variably means a large biomass per unit area.

Next to oxygen, water is the most important substance for human existence and it is essential for everything on our planet to grow and prosper. Freshwater rivers, lakes and groundwater are used to irrigate crops, to provide drinking water and to act as a sanitation system. Although we as humans recognize this fact, we disregard it by polluting our rivers, lakes, and oceans. Most of our water resources are gradually 7becoming contaminated due to the addition of foreign materials from the surroundings. These include organic matter of plant and animal origin, land surface washing and industrial and sewage effluents. Rapid urbanization and industrialization with improper environmental planning often lead to discharge of industrial and sewage effluents into rivers. In addition to the process of desertification, pollution is also reducing the volume of safe fishing, irrigation and drinking water.

The story of industrialization and the percolation of heavy metal from industrial wastewater to deep Groundwater aquifer resources are described in second chapter.

Main focus of this chapter is on the main aspects of pollution including the use of chemicals in industries, and the discharge of heavy metal with effluents. This section also highlights the further impacts of industrial waste to the surrounding environmental components.

The problem of water pollution due to toxic metals has begun to cause concern now in most metropolitan cities. The toxic heavy metals entering the ecosystem may lead to geo-accumulation and biomagnifications. Metals like Fe, Cu, Zn, Ni and other trace elements are important for proper functioning of biological systems and their deficiency or excess could lead to a number of disorders Food chain contamination by heavy metals has become a burning issue in recent years because of their potential accumulation in biological systems through contaminated water, soil and air.

Wastewater discharged from textile and dyestuff industries have to be treated due to their impact on the water bodies and growing public concern over their toxicity and carcinogenicity in particular.

The role and significance of water to the human health is highlighted in third chapter. Water is like a medicine if it is uncontaminated and fresh, otherwise it may be dangerous to health. The chapter described the phase and forms of water on this planet. Besides, all these aspects this section has some tables related to the threshold values of heavy metal with respect to human health. Heavy metal may be harmful for human. How much concentration of particular metal can cause hazards to human, this is also important. Reference values of heavy metals are also given in this chapter.

Groundwater may also contain soluble natural substances like arsenic, fluoride, nitrate or sulphate, which restrict or even prevent its direct use because of health concerns.

Heavy metals are introduced into aquatic system from various anthropogenic sources. Heavy metals constitute a special group of contaminants of aquatic systems and deserve special attention. Since natural degradation processes do not remove metals, they may become enriched in sediments over time. Metal contamination of sediments is an issue of growing concerns worldwide (NRC, 1989). Both natural processes and anthropogenic activities are responsible for introducing metals in to the aquatic system (Nriagu, 1989). Many contaminants discharged into surface waters rapidly become associated with the particulate matter and incorporated in sediments. Metals in aquatic systems become part of the water-sediment system and their distribution is controlled by a dynamic set of physical-chemical interactions and equilibria, largely governed by pH and type of legends and chelating agents, oxidation state of the mineral components and the redox conditions of the system. Metal contaminated sediments may release heavy metals back to the overlying water column and, thus, pose risk to aquatic life and ecosystems.

The significance of heavy metals in water and their effects to the human health are discussed in forth chapter. Heavy metals and some other physico-chemical parameters of polluted water may cause many effects on environment. BIS, CPCB, WHO and many bodies has declared their standards for water quality. MINAS is also described and given in the tabular form in the chapter.

Water is a medicine and poison as well, it depends upon the pollution load of water and concentration of heavy metal and various toxic materials in it. The chapter described the various standards of water quality. Besides, all these aspects this section has some tables related to the standards of physico-chemical parameters and heavy metal in drinking water. Heavy metal may be harmful for human, so the standards are given in tabular form. Standard values of heavy metals described by various bodies are also given in this chapter.

Most of the industries discharged their waste directly (without any treatment) into the stream, lakes and oceans as well as in the open land and that contaminate the groundwater. There are number of pollutants like fertilizers, pesticides, heavy metals, which seriously affect human like by entering into the system directly or indirectly through food material. Dyes may be harmful for living organisms because these contain toxic heavy metals. Labour and handling workers may affect by toxic metal with contact directly to soft organs, wounds or by inhalation. Heavy metals present in the dyes, may affect a community by consumption of contaminated water.

Pollution of environment with heavy metals is a serious problem. Besides causing specific toxicity symptoms, these metals may also contribute to global warming by destroying the atmosphere ozone layer like atmosphere methane, nitrous oxide and sulphur dioxide because of potentially harmful effects on human and animal health, few toxic metals (lead, cadmium, mercury, arsenic, and chromium). It is major concern to ecologist or researcher, because air or water pollution from point and non-point sources may contribute significantly to the load of metals on natural ecosystem

The increasing demand of water in different sector including, industrial, agriculture and domestic are pointed out in fifth chapter. This section elaborated the need of a water policy for the proper management and availability of water in various sectors. This small chapter included the main points of national water policy of India.

Clean groundwater is needed for more than drinking purposes. Agriculture depends highly on groundwater for irrigation; as a large number of groundwater pumps were used for crop irrigation in India. Poor or contaminated groundwater could jeopardize crops and threaten the health of livestock. Groundwater is connected to surface water in the hydrological cycle, and some aquifers actually feed area springs and rivers.

The management plans for water resourcesis highlighted in sixth chapter. The available resources of water are given in this chapter in tabular form. Chapter starts with the presence of water on planet earth and the distribution of freshwater and marine water on earth. Complete water budget is presented in elaborated manner. This section also described the water demand and water crisis and the predicted requirement of water in different sectors with the help of graphs and tables. Chapter also highlighted the water supply problems and the possible solutions of water demand at various levels.

The world is now facing water crisis of dimensions that no earlier generation has had to face. It may already be late for some water scare countries with rapid population growth to avoid a water crisis unless they take immediate and drastic steps for sustainable management of urban water resources. But a water crisis in the near future can be avoided if appropriate policies and strategies are formulated and acted upon quickly. In this regard, water conservation and its better management are the effective strategies for consideration. To avoid a catastrophe over the long term, it is also important to act to reduce the demand of freshwater by slowing the population growth. Urgent and decisive action must begin now if regional water crisis are to be avoided during the next century. There is an imperative need to change people's attitudes towards water.

The Groundwater recharging techniques, benefits and status in India are described in seventh chapter. This chapter is completely devoted to Groundwater recharging methods in India. Different methods of Groundwater recharging are also given in this chapter. This section pointed out the advantages and disadvantages of Groundwater recharging. Brief notes on rain water, rainwater harvesting and run-off coefficients are also given in the chapter. The text is supported with many figures and tables whenever and whatever required.

Artificial groundwater recharge is a process by which the groundwater reservoir is augmented at a rate exceeding the augmentation rate under natural conditions of replenishment. In some parts of India, due to over-exploitation of groundwater, decline in groundwater levels resulting in shortage of supply of water, and intrusion of saline water in coastal areas have been observed. In such areas, there is need for artificial recharge of groundwater by augmenting the natural infiltration of precipitation or surface-water into underground formations by methods such as water spreading, recharge through wells, pits, shafts, etc.

The modeling application in the study of Groundwater is focused in eighth chapter. Chapter described the movement of Groundwater in starting segment and further highlights the groundwater Flow Pattern. The mathematical formulas and equations are given as per the requirement. In the next segment of this chapter, Darcy and Linear Velocity or Flow Velocity is described. For the prediction and modeling of toxic metals, flow of Heavy Metals in Unsaturated Soils, and the equation for the Transport Model is also given. In the last segment, the chapter described the groundwater monitoring techniques and finally the concept of groundwater modeling with the help of points and steps.

Heavy metals from textile industries affected the shallow groundwater quality in shallow badly, while deep groundwater affected slightly. Vertically, heavy metals contamination decreased with the increasing depth of water table. In the case of horizontal distribution, the heavy metal concentrations decrease with increasing distance from pollution source.

A case study is given of Groundwater pollution in Panipat city in ninth chapter. The initial segment of chapter described the features of study area and research protocol adopted for that study. In the next segments of this chapter, the characteristics and impacts of industrial effluents on surface water, sediments of drain and pond are described. The pollution load in Groundwater of the city is elaborated and depicted in tabular form at different depth Groundwater. Separate study was executed for various depth of water table. In the last segment of chapter, the total focus is on heavy metal concentration in environment. Heavy metal analytical methodology, the use of AAS and many related requirements at the time of metal analysis are given. This chapter highlighted the heavy metal route in the environment.

Effective steps should be taken for improving water use efficiency, as the integrated management of water resources should be based on the treatment of wastewater as an integral part of ecosystem and as a natural resource whose quantity and quality determine the nature of its utilization. Wastewater use in turn has its impact on the water quality and therefore utilization of water has to be managed as not to contribute to the deterioration of water quality. Secondly, conjunctive use of groundwater and surface water resources needs to be planned in the irrigation project from the beginning. There is a need to take effective steps for improving wastewater use efficiency through renovation and modernization of recycling treatments of wastewater.

Different guidelines and standards limits should be immediately applied in small scale textile industries for utilization of groundwater and open discharging the effluents into surface water or on land. A regular bio-monitoring should be applied for the assessment of effluent quality of every dye house outlet.

Besides this, water supply of the industrial sector should be managed and regularly analyzed the suitability of drinking water quality. Groundwater safety measures are immediately necessary in the industrial regions.

Chapter 2
Groundwater

Contents

In modern industrialization period, the most of water resources have affected enormously by seepage, leaching and intermixing of industrial effluents in maximum metropolitan cities and industrial townships. The effluents have consisting high concentrations of heavy metals, organic pollutants and toxic colours, may alter the water quality of the region and ultimately causes the health hazards among livestock and human being. In the last two decades, the rapid growth of industrialization and urbanization has created negative impacts on the environment. The industrial, municipal and agricultural wastes containing pesticides, insecticides, fertilizers residues, organic pollutants and heavy metals in their effluents have been polluted surface and groundwater. In India, the industrial effluents have contributed a major source of pollution. In the modern industrial era, rapidly growing of industrialization and urbanization has posed adverse impacts on the environment and its all components. Air, soil and water everything on earth surface may changed its quality due to the increasing pollution. Also the underground water resources may affect after a long time by continuous pollution condition.

Water has become an essential commodity for the development of industries and agriculture. Water is one of the widely distributed and abundant substance found in the nature it covers about 75% of the earth surface therefore earth is sometimes called a "water planet" water is in sea, river, ocean, pond, streams and even in the atmosphere in the form of humidity. Most of the earth surface water is in the sea, the ocean contain about excessive quantities of salts. Freshwater is in lakes, ponds, rivers and streams. Freshwater is also available in the forms of rain, snow, dew etc. The Earth's atmosphere contains 0.02 to 4 percent water by volume, depending on the location (Kudesia, 1992). In addition to providing sources for precipitation, atmospheric water vapors intercept some of the ultraviolet radiation and intercept heat loss from the earth sand redirect part of it to the Earth.

The available natural freshwater resources today are threatened by hazard of pollution; particularly rivers are greatly polluted due to release of untreated effluents and waste material from agriculture practices and industries located around water bodies. The poor living conditions of people in settlement around water bodies or rivers, non availability of treatment from urban areas and negligence of industries for treatment of effluent before release of natural water bodies are the major reason of pollution of Indian rivers and other water bodies like ponds, lakes, etc.

Water is one of the prime necessities of life. We can hardly live for a few days without water. Drinking water are obtained from all sorts of sources, some good, some not well, some bad and some outright dangerous. These are reflected in the health, vitality and longevity of people. Since one gulp water and it is taken straight into the body its cleanliness is vitally important. It should be free from pathogens, it should not contain excessive amount of salts and toxic elements. Scientifically distilled water is the cleanest, but it is not good drinking water. Water is the mostly used for industrial, municipal and agricultural purpose. The quantity and quality of available water are very important for the purpose of industries. Each industry has its own water requirements and sometimes adequate supply of water may be very suitable for one industry but the same may be dangerous for other. It is therefore, extremely important to take into account the use of water to be carried out, its suitability based on the result of chemical analysis.

Groundwater is used by about two billion people worldwide; making it the single most used natural resource. The estimated annual production of groundwater is between 600 and 700 cubic kilometres (billion cubic metres, or billion tonnes). In comparison, the worldwide annual consumption of sand and gravel is about 18 billion tonnes, while worldwide oil consumption is a mere 3.5 billion tonnes (www.yearofplanetearth.org).

Groundwater is considered public property in many countries. Where it is scarce, groundwater could be considered an economic commodity; but in most cases no value is assigned to this. However, the costs of groundwater exploitation, supply and treatment need to be covered through water charges to maintain sustainable supplies. No figures are currently available on wealth creation resulting from providing groundwater to consumers worldwide.

2.1 Pollution

The industrial effluents and trade waste of pulp and paper, distillery, fertilizer, electroplating, asbestos, silt, alcohol, detergents, steel, tannery, textile, cane sugar, oils, pesticides and herbicides, radioactive wastes etc., play a significant contribution in pollution of water. As we know our life depends upon water and man needs water for his drinking and other domestic and industrial processes. With the fast increasing in our industrial civilization, the demand for water is increasing tremendously day by day. Although water pollution is an age old problem but in this modern age, the problems like population increase, sewage disposal, industrial waste, radioactive waste etc. have polluted our water resources so much so that about 70% rivers and streams not only in India but of all the countries contain polluted waters (Kudesia, 1992).

In India, the industrial effluents have contributed a major source of pollution. Different industries of the country contribute about 16% of the total wastewater generated. The treatment facilities have been installed in less than one third of the polluting industries (Gopal, 1994). Most of effluent treatment plants (ETP) have not performed physical and chemical treatment processes satisfactory due to economic reasons on commercial scales.

Water may pollute by many anthropogenic activities like discharge of household sewage, disposal of various industrial wastes, run off form agricultural fields, acid rain and many other man made infrastructures and activities. Different types of industries exploit the huge amount of freshwater and discharge wastewater in the form of effluents. These effluents discharged directly into any freshwater body, *viz.* pond, lake, stream or any seasonal drains.

Textile industry is one of the oldest types of industry in India, manufacturing different types of clothes. There are about 850 textile mills established in big cities of India, manufacturing approximately 11000 million meters cloth. Textile industries can be classified into three categories: cotton, woolen and synthetic fibres depending upon the used raw materials. The cotton textile industries are one of the oldest industries in our country having more than 1000 mills mainly located in Mumbai, Surat, Ahemdabad, Coimbatore, Delhi and Kanpur. The woollen mills in the country are mostly located mainly in Amritsar, Bikaner, Ludhiana and Panipat. Synthetic fibre, a comparatively new entry, has become an integral part of the textile industry and is being used to manufacture purely synthetic fabric or is mixed with cotton or wool to manufacture blended fabrics in mills throughout the country (Groff, 1993).

Textile industries in general consume large volume of water of high purity. Consequently, these units discharge large quantities of effluent that normally exhibit polluting characteristics. According to review of available literature the quantity of effluent discharged and quantity of consumed water by woollen units and composite cotton textile industries, always remain high. In the cotton industry, the solid waste generated during processing fibers and spinning amounts to be about 5 per cent of raw cotton weight. In woollen industry, about 4 per cent of the raw wool weight comes out as solid waste prior to and during spinning. Other solid waste generated in the textile industry includes rags, felts, waste piece of cloth and yarns, packaging materials, ash from coal-fired boiler.

As far as the textile mills are concerned boiler feed water should be as soft as possible and should contain least amount of nitrate and organic matter in order to prevent encrustations or corrosion of boilerplates. For the purpose of dyeing water should be free from iron and should posses little hardness only. The consumption of water in dyeing and printing mills is 3,45,000 liters/day.

2.2 Industrilization

Consumer demand for industries is ever increasing in the domestic and international market. More cotton textile processing industries are set up at a rapid rate in many Indian cities, the problem of treating wastewater generated at these industries are compounded. Small-scale units cannot afford to have their own treatment facilities because of non-availability of land and skilled manpower to operate it. A common effluent treatment plant (CETP), for the treatment of combined wastewater from a cluster of small scale units is generally designed based on primary and secondary waste treatment system, which involves screening, degreeting, primary clarifier and aerobic biological system.

In the preparation of these raw materials for spinning, weaving and finishing, liquid wastes are produced, the volume and strength of which extend over a wide range, depending not only on the type of fibre being processed but also on the source of raw product, the ultimate use, availability of process water, control of manufacture and other variables.

The industries not only add to air pollution by ejecting chimney gases into the atmosphere but also the considerable water pollution by discharging their liquid effluents into various receiving bodies like public sewer, inland surface water like ponds, rivers, *Nallas* or on irrigation land. In fact, major pollution load from the textile mills can be attributed to the liquid effluents from the various wet processing operation like scouring, bleaching, mercerizing, dyeing, etc. amount of composite effluents discharged from the textile mills varies from 1 to 10 million liters per day depending upon quantity of the cloth produced and various manufacturing processes employed. Selection of treatment methods for these waste waters will be governed by their characters, the policy of regulatory body covering the waters of receiving stream, economics of treatment and present day knowledge of method of purifications.

These industries consume substantial volume of water and chemicals in wet processing of textile. Approximately, 40,000 different dyes and pigments are used in the industry and over 7×10^5 tons of these dyes are produced annually worldwide (Zollinger, 1987). It was estimated that 10-15% of the dyes used in textile processing were lost in the effluent during the dying processes (Vaidge and Datye, 1982). These dyes include several structural varieties of dyes, such as acidic, reactive basic, disperse, azo, diazo, anthraquinone-based and metal complex dyes. The only one thing in common among them is the ability to absorb light in the visible region (Wong, 2000). The effluents from dye industries contain high amount of cation, anion, organic pollutants in the form of colour and heavy metals.

Dying is the process of applying to the fabric stock yarn or fabric. The dying is carried out with six different dye classes, vat, direct, developed, napthol, sulphur and aniline black. If aniline and sulphur dye are used, dye wastewater may contain colours, which are extremely difficult to be removed by common waste treatment methods. The water requirement for textile industry is very large for their various processes. The use of water varies from mill to mill and depends on source of water, availability and quantity and quality of fabric produced. To produce one meter of cloth 12-65 liters of water is required, as textile industry requires large volume of water, it releases large amount of wastewater after processing.

The main source of wastewaters of textile industry *viz.* preparation of yarn-slashing process waste, textile processing- desizing, kiering, slashing, bleaching, mercerizing, dying and printing waste, washing waste in each step, other waste streams- like cooling water, boiler, housekeeping, spills, leaks and sanitary wastes. The quantity of waste discharged from each mill process is very small as compared to the volume of waste generated from the washing and rinsing of cloth. The volume of wastes is highly variable from one mill to another. The pollution load in wastewater posed by textile industry is very high and affects water quality and other environmental components in many ways. These wastes are coloured due to use of dyes and dying aid agents in the different textile processing of material.

2.3 Chemicals

Interest in the pollution potential of textile dyes comes from their possible toxicity and carcinogenicity. This is because many dyes are synthesized from known carcinogens, such as benzidine or their aromatic compounds. Some azo dyes are reported to be reduced in sediments and aquatic environment to form toxic, mutagenic or even carcinogenic aromatic amines among different trophic organisms.

Synthetic dyes are major contaminants in textile wastewater and have to be removed before discharging into water bodies or on land. The presence of very small amounts of synthetic dues in water (less than 1 mg/l for some dyes) is highly visible and affects the aesthetic qualities, water transparency, and gas solubility, in lakes, rivers and other water bodies. The removal of synthetic dyes from wastewater is often more important than the removal of the soluble colourless organic substances, which usually contributes the major fraction of the biochemical oxygen demand. Methods for the removal of the BOD from most effluents are fairly well developed, synthetic dyes, however are more difficult to be degraded because of their synthetic origin and mainly complex aromatic molecular structures. Such structures are often constructed intentionally to resist fading on exposure to sweat, soap water, light or oxidizing agents (Mckay, 1979) and this renders them more stable and less amenable to biodegradation (Seshadri *et al.*, 1994).

Wastewater discharged from textile and dyestuff industries have to be treated due to their impact on the water bodies and growing public concern over their toxicity and carcinogenicity in particular. Dyes usually have synthetic origin and complex aromatic molecular structure. According to their dissociation in an aqueous solution, dye can be classified as (i) Anionic acid, direct and reactive dye (ii) Cationic, basic dye and (iii) Non ionic, dispersive dyes. Dyes such as acid, basics and direct are all water soluble but dispersive dyes have low solubility and colloidal dispersion properties, thus they are agglomerations. Physically, dyes are mostly used in the powder, liquid and pearl or granulate form. Chemically, dyes may be categories as Nitro dyes (napthol yellow), Nitroso dyes (napthol green), Azo dyes (synthetic), Di and triphenol methane dyes, Vat dyes, Anthraquinonoid dyes, Quinoline dyes, Sulphur dyes. Broadly dyes may be classified as direct dyes and developed dyes. Six main classes of dyes for cotton fabric namely vat, direct, developed, napthol, sulphur and aniline black. Many different and complicated molecular structures of dyes make dye water difficult to be treated by conventional biological and physico-chemical processes. About 6,34,900 metric tons of dyes are produce worldwide each year and nearly 10-15% of them are discharged through effluents. Generally conventional biological treatment processes have certain difficulties in degrading those dues causing high COD and colours in the wastewater. A significant portion about 40-70 % of COD and colour in textile effluents, are still remaining, and is required an advanced treatment. Studies using physical and chemical processes to further reduce COD and colour in textile wastewater have been intensively reported (Zhang *et al.*, 1994). Developing countries like India and other Asian countries discharge the effluents to the surface water without any treatment or sometimes little treatment due to technological and economical limitations. Colours affect the nature of water, inhibit sunlight penetration and reduce the photosynthetic action. Some of the dyes cause rapid depletion of dissolved oxygen affecting aquatic life adversely. Some of the dyes, especially Benzidine based dyes are toxic and carcinogenic.

Thus, uses of dyes contaminated water without any treatment may cause adverse effect on the health of human beings, domestic animals, wildlife and aquatic environment. So, it is very much essential to treat dye-contaminated wastewater before discharging in to the surface water and develop simple and economical method to treat the stream suitable for developing countries. The conventional methods of removal of dyes using alum, ferric chloride, activated carbon, lime etc. are not economical. Adsorption is a physico-chemical treatment process, which has gained a lot of attraction for the removal of dye from wastewater, since it produces a high quantity treated effluent. The most widely used adsorbent is activated carbon for industrial wastewaters application. But the cost of the activated carbon is high and it increases with its quality. Agricultural solid waste such as coir, pitch, banana pitch, coconut husk, biogas slurry, rice husk, bagasse and paddy straw, saw dust etc. have been investigated for the removal of dye from wastewater.

Polluted groundwater can be decontaminated only by expensive long-term procedures. In the worst cases, complete abandonment for a very long time is the only available course of action. These facts are becoming more widely recognised by the international community, and science and technology are increasingly engaged in helping to avoid the worst effects. Precious groundwater resources increasingly need to be protected and well managed to allow sustainable long-term use.

In some areas groundwater may contain enhanced levels of natural substances that can restrict its use. For example, seawater may invade the aquifer. Groundwater may also contain soluble natural substances like arsenic, fluoride, nitrate or sulfate, which restrict or even prevent its direct use because of health concerns. Suitable treatment processes can usually be found to diminish or remove harmful substances, but this often entails financial cost. In general, therefore, the groundwater quality must, in all cases, be controlled both before and during its use.

In most cases, groundwater is cleaner than surface water. Groundwater is usually protected against contamination from the surface by soils and covering rock layers. This is why most drinking water in many areas of the world is groundwater. However, rising world population, changes in land use and rapid industrialisation (or de-industrialisation) increasingly place groundwater in jeopardy. Polluted water can transmit diseases and carry poisonous chemicals. Such water can make people sick and even kill. Clean water is therefore an important cross-cutting theme within the United Nations' Millennium Development Goals (www.un.org).

2.4 Heavy Metals

Heavy metals are introduced into aquatic system from various anthropogenic sources. Heavy metals constitute a special group of contaminants of aquatic systems and deserve special attention. Since natural degradation processes do not remove metals, they may become enriched in sediments over time. Metal contamination of sediments is an issue of growing concerns worldwide (NRC, 1989). Both natural processes and anthropogenic activities are responsible for introducing metals in to the aquatic system (Nriagu, 1989). Many contaminants discharged into surface waters rapidly become associated with the particulate matter and incorporated in sediments. Metals in aquatic systems become part of the water-sediment system and their distribution is controlled by a dynamic set of physical-chemical interactions and equilibria, largely governed by pH and type of legends and chelating agents, oxidation state of the mineral components and the redox conditions of the system. Metal contaminated sediments may release heavy metals back to the overlying water column and, thus, pose risk to aquatic life and ecosystems. Due to their particle reactivity, heavy metals tend to accumulate in sediment as a result may persist in the environment long after their primary sources have been removed (Forstner and Wittman, 1981).

Heavy metals are chemical elements with a specific gravity that is at least 5 times the specific gravity of water. The specific gravity of water is 1 at 4°C (39°F). Simply stated, specific gravity is a measure of density of a given amount of a solid substance when it is compared to an equal amount of water. Some well-known toxic metallic elements with a specific gravity that is 5 or more times that of water are arsenic, 5.7; cadmium, 8.65; iron, 7.9; lead, 11.34; and mercury, 13.546. In small quantities, certain heavy metals are nutritionally essential for a healthy life. Some of these are referred to as the trace elements (e.g., iron, copper, manganese, and zinc). These elements or some form of them are commonly found naturally in foodstuffs, in fruits and vegetables and in commercially available multivitamin products. Heavy metals are also common in industrial applications such as in the manufacture of pesticides, batteries, alloys, electroplated metal parts, textile dyes, steel and so forth. Twentieth century industrialization has led to an increased exposure to heavy metals for everyone. Certain people suffer a lot due to toxic exposure because of where they live, their occupation, or their lifestyle. Others may be genetically predisposed to heavy metal accumulation due to poor detoxification systems in their bodies.

Heavy metals are usually present in trace amounts in naturally waters but many of them are toxic even at very low concentration. Although many of the metals are essential components of the biological system yet some of these are potentially toxic. Metals such as arsenic, lead, cadmium, nickel, mercury, chromium, cobalt, zinc and selenium are highly toxic even in minor quantity. Increasing quantity of heavy metals in aquatic resources is currently an area of greater concern especially since a large number of industries are discharging their metal containing effluents in to freshwater with out any adequate treatment (Canter, 1987).

Heavy metals become toxic when they are not metabolized by the body and accumulate in the soft tissues. Heavy metals may enter the human body through food, water, air, or absorption through the skin when they come in contact with humans in agriculture and in production of different industrial products, pharmaceutical, biotechnogical or residential settings. Industrial exposure accounts for a common route of exposure for adults and children. Ingestion is the most common route of exposure in children. Children may develop toxic levels from the normal hand-to-mouth activity of small children who come in contact with contaminated soil or by actually eating objects that are not food (dirt or paint chips).

Most of the industries discharged their waste directly (without any treatment) into the stream, lakes and oceans as well as in the open land and that contaminate the groundwater. There are number of pollutants like fertilizers, pesticides, heavy metals, which seriously affect human like by entering into the system directly or indirectly through food material. Pollution of environment with heavy metals is a serious problem. Besides causing specific toxicity symptoms, these metals may also contribute to global warming by destroying the atmosphere ozone layer like atmosphere methane, nitrous oxide and sulphur dioxide because of potentially harmful effects on human and animal health, few toxic metals (lead, cadmium, mercury, arsenic, and chromium). It is major concern to ecologist or researcher, because air or water pollution from point and non-point sources may contribute significantly to the load of metals on natural ecosystem (Mani *et al.*, 2005). Environmental contamination and exposure to heavy metals such as mercury, cadmium and lead is a serious growing problem throughout the world. Human exposure to heavy metals has risen dramatically in the last 50 years as a result of an exponential increase in the use of heavy metals in industrial processes and products.

The most common heavy metal pollutants are As, Cd, Cr, Cu, Ni, Pb, and Hg. There are different types of sources of metal pollutants; such as, point sources (localized pollution). The second types of pollutant sources are non-point sources, where pollutants come from dispersed (and often difficult to identify) sources. There are only a few examples of localized metal pollution, like the natural weathering of ore bodies and the little metal particles coming from coal burning power plants via smokestacks in air, water and soils around the factory. The most common metal pollution in freshwater comes from mining operations. They usually use an acid mine drainage system to release heavy metals from ores, because metals are very soluble in an acid solution. After the drainage process, they disperse the acid solution in the groundwater, containing high levels of metals (www.lenntech.com).

In the recent years there has been a growing concern with environmental protection. This can be achieved either by decreasing the afflux of pollutants to the environment or by their removal from contaminated media. The former is a feasible choice only for pollutants of anthropogenic origin, whereas, the latter is unavoidable for those of natural origin (Gomez-Serrano *et al.*, 1998). The presence of heavy metals in the aquatic environment has been of great concern to scientists and engineers because of their increased discharge, toxic nature, and other adverse effects on receiving waters.

2.5 Groundwater

The Earth's freshwater resources consist mostly of ice, snow and groundwater. Rivers and lakes constitute a tiny part of the total global freshwater volume. Earth's total resources of fresh groundwater are estimated at about 10,000,000 cubic kilometres–more than two hundred times the global annual renewable water resource provided by rain. This is because most groundwater resources have accumulated over centuries–or even millennia. In some places they bear witness to wetter climates in the past. These unique freshwater resources can be found even in present-day desert areas. The overwhelming freshwater resource is the annually renewed input of precipitation around the globe. Rivers are of prime importance in distributing this water.

Groundwater, although second to rivers as a distributor of freshwater, is much the largest regulator of freshwater resources. Groundwater forms the invisible, subsurface part of the natural water cycle, in which evaporation, precipitation, seepage and discharge are the main components. The "visible" components are all strongly affected by weather and climate, and although they can be contaminated quickly, they generally recover quickly too. By contrast, the subsurface processes of groundwater are much slower and longer lasting, ranging from years to millennia. However, with careful management, these different timescales can be used to create an integrated system of water supply that is robust in the face of drought.

People's lives and livelihoods depend on water. Demand for clean water increases continually in line with world population growth. People in many areas of the world lack the fresh, drinkable water essential to their survival; if they are to prosper, more secure and low cost water supplies are needed. Maintaining secure water supplies for drinking, industry and agriculture would be impossible without groundwater, the largest and most reliable of all freshwater resources. In many areas most drinking water is groundwater–up to 80 % in Europe and Russia, and even more in North Africa and the Middle East.

Unlike other natural resources or raw materials, groundwater is present throughout the world. Possibilities for its abstraction vary greatly from place to place, owing to rainfall conditions and the distribution of aquifers (rocks, sand layers and so on, in whose pore spaces the groundwater sits). Generally, groundwater is renewed only during a part of each year, but can be abstracted year-round. Provided that there is adequate replenishment, and that the source is protected from pollution, groundwater can be abstracted indefinitely. The groundwater involved in the present day water cycle is comparatively small compared to the volume of groundwater 'in stock', stored in porous or fractured strata down to a depth of a few thousand metres below the surface.

Clean groundwater is needed for more than drinking purposes. Agriculture depends highly on groundwater for irrigation; as a large number of groundwater pumps were used for crop irrigation in India. Poor or contaminated groundwater could jeopardize crops and threaten the health of livestock. Groundwater is connected to surface water in the hydrological cycle, and some aquifers actually feed area springs and rivers. Sometimes contamination occurs naturally by mixing the sallow aquifers with other contaminated sources of water table. Saline water from deeper aquifers may reach aquifers that provide water for human beings, livestock and others agricultural activities. Some groundwater may have naturally high levels of nitrates, metals, iron, sulfate, or chloride, all of which provides an odd odor, color, or taste in water. Groundwater contamination has become a major problem in recent decades due to exploring industrialization. Groundwater, as a wide resource for irrigation in most part of country, may contaminate the soil quality by repeated irrigation of agricultural fields. Bed quality of groundwater used in irrigation may alter the characteristics of agriculture soils of the area.

Groundwater is used for domestic supply, industries, and agriculture in most part of the world as it is a replenishable resource and has inherent advantage over surface water. There has been a tremendous increase in the demand of freshwater due to growth in population, advanced agriculture practices and industrial usages (Bachmat, 1994). In the last two decades, the rapid growth of industrialization and urbanization has created negative impacts on the environment. Due to industrial, municipal and agricultural wastes containing pesticides, insecticides, fertilizers residues and heavy metals with water; groundwater has been polluted by leaching process of pollutants present in effluents (Sastry and Rathee, 1999).

In Haryana, about 90% of the population of rural areas utilizes groundwater for drinking, washing and other daily uses. But groundwater in Haryana is very saline and large variation in salinity can be observed over a short distance. Water table is also very high. Therefore, scarcity of drinking water is very big problem faced by population of this state. Panipat district of Haryana is well known for the textile industries. A large number of small-scale industries mainly textile printing and textile dying have been established in Panipat city. These industries discharge their effluent openly into pond or other water bodies. The seepage of effluents posed serious threat to the groundwater resources (Groff, 1993). So, groundwater must be managed and protected carefully for the most beneficial use in the future.

Water plays a vital role in sustaining the existence of all living things. The importance of managing the different aspects of the water, including its quantity, quality, transport processes, utilization, and management becomes apparent when the supply of water, especially potable water, is limited. This article is intended to be an introduction of the subject of groundwater. It includes a historical perspective of development, well hydraulics, the quality aspect, and a number of remediation technologies. It has been estimated that approximately 300 million cubic miles of water exist on the earth at different locations and in different states phases. From Table 2.1, it can be seen that the ocean forms about 97% of the earth's water as saline water. The remaining 3% is total freshwater. This freshwater supply would be quickly depleted if it were not for its endless interaction and exchange with the ocean. This movement of the earth's waters, known as the *hydrologic cycle*. Due to the complexity of the hydrologic cycle, not all of the components can be determined easily. A detailed discussion on the subject is presented by the United Nations Educational, Scientific, and Cultural Organization (UNESCO) (USSR National Committee for the International Hydrological Decade, 1978). On a long-term average basis, the total freshwater supply is to be considered constant (Pfafflin and Ziegler, 2006). Therefore, the budget equation for freshwater can be expressed as:

$$[\text{Total precipitation}] = [\text{Evaporation}] + [\text{Transpiration}]$$

Table 2.1: World Water Distribution (Pfafflin and Ziegler, 2006)

Form of Water	*Share of World Reserves (%)*			
	Area Covered (km²)	*Volume (km³)*	*of Total Water Reserves*	*of Freshwater Reserves*
World ocean	361,300,000	1,338,000,000	96.5	–
Groundwater	134,800,000	23,400,000	1.7	–
Predominantly fresh				
Groundwater	134,800,000	10,530,000	0.76	30.1
Soil moisture	82,000,000	16,500	0.001	0.05
Glaciers and permanent snow cover	16,227,500	24,064,100	1.74	68.7
Antarctica	13,980,000	21,600,000	1.56	61.7
Greenland	1,802,400	2,340,000	0.17	6.68
Artic islands	226,100	83,500	0.006	0.24
Mountain areas	224,000	40,600	0.003	0.12
Ground ice in zones of permafrost strata	21,000,000	300,000	0.022	0.86
Water reserves in lakes	2,058,700	176,400	0.013	–
Freshwater	1,236,400	91,000	0.007	0.26
Saltwater	822,300	85,400	0.006	–
Marsh water	2,682,600	11,470	0.0008	0.03
Water in rivers	148,800,000	2,120	0.0002	0.006
Biological water	510,000,000	1,120	0.0001	0.003
Atmospheric water	510,000,000	12,900	0.001	0.04
Total water	510,000,000	1,385,984, 610	100	–
Total freshwater	148,800,000	35,029,210	2.53	100

Here, the freshwater is found in the atmosphere as water vapour; on the land as water, snow, dew, and ice; and in the ground usually in the form of water. Approximately 99.5% of all the Earth's water is in a form or location unavailable for use (see Table 2.1), leaving only about 0.5% of the earth's water remaining for consumption. The largest source of available water is groundwater, which forms an important part of the water supply for municipalities, agriculture, and industry. For instance, in the United States, approximately 50% of the total water usage is from groundwater, while over 90% of the world's potable water supply is derived from groundwater (Pfafflin and Ziegler, 2006).

Thus, groundwater is one of the most important natural resources. Groundwater occurs in the saturated zone of water bearing soils. However, it may also be found in sedimentary deposits, fissures in igneous rocks, limestone caverns, and other water-bearing sources, which may lie near the surface or hundreds of feet beneath the surface. The subject of groundwater is addressed by a variety of disciplines, including hydrology, geology, and hydraulics. In general, hydrologists and engineers are concerned with the long-range yield from watersheds and aquifers. Yield is a function of watershed storage capacity and the supply, which fluctuates with time. It is of paramount importance to ensure enough supply to last through drought periods. Currently, accurate prediction of drought phenomena is difficult and unavailable, as indicated by the National Research Council. The subject is still an active research in water-resource engineering. Because of the cost of well drilling, it is desirable to have some assurance that the water-supply well will reach a satisfactory aquifer. In order for the hydrologist or engineer to obtain an appreciation of groundwater flow, he/she must understand that the notion of 'safe yield' in groundwater is the quantity of groundwater that can be withdrawn without impairing its quality.

2.6 Effect on Environment

Undergroundwater is one of the major water resources for domestic, agricultural and industrial uses. Pollutants are being added to the groundwater and soil system through various human activities and rapid growth of industrialization, which affects the human health directly or indirectly. This study would provide baseline data on status and management of industrial effluent pollution as well as its impact on groundwater potability and agricultural uses and suggest remedial and preventive measures in future for remediation studies of pollutants removal from groundwater and agricultural soil system.

The sediments existing as the bottom of the water column play a major role in the pollution scheme of an aquatic system by heavy metals (Forstner, 1985). They reflect the current quality of the water system and can be used in detecting the presence of contaminants that do not remain soluble after discharge into surface water. As a result of complex physical, chemical and biological processes a major fraction of heavy metals (contributed naturally as well as through various anthropogenic activities) is found to be associated with bottom sediments (Baruah *et al.*, 1996). Bed sediments in surface water systems thus act both as a sink and source of metals. Metal accumulation in sediments provides a record of the spatial and temporal history of pollution (Martin and Whitfield, 1983). Hence, sediment monitoring can provide important information on various pollution events.

Discharges of textile waste on land and used for agricultural purpose have also affected the crop and soil productivity due to high dissolved salts. The suspended solids, which are present in the waste, may carry out clogging of soil pores. The sodium, which is present in the waste, may lead to hardening of texture of soil, thereby preventing penetration of roots in soil.

Agricultural soils require sufficient irrigation for high production and irrigation water with poor quality can result in a buildup of soil salts and high soil pH. The chief minerals in irrigation water are chloride, sulfate, bicarbonate, sodium, calcium, and magnesium. These minerals contained in the irrigation water can build up in the soil and cause problems. Sodium, bicarbonate, and chloride are the three minerals that contribute most to soil salinity and alkalinity. More frequent irrigations become necessary to keep up with increasing soil salinity levels. Plants are most sensitive to saline soils during germination. Once established, they have the ability to tolerate higher soil salinity levels. Soil acidity affects a plant's ability to absorb nutrients.

Textile effluent pollution may also alter the characteristics of sediment and soil of industrial area directly or indirectly. Composite effluents from textile industries and dye houses of Panipat industrial area normally discharged openly into a common effluent drain without any adequate treatment and commences in a large pond near Binjhole village near to industrial area, which may change the quality of bottom sediments of drain, pond sediment quality and also the physico-chemical characteristics of surrounding agricultural soil.

Dyes may be harmful for living organisms because these contain toxic heavy metals. Labour and handling workers may affect by toxic metal with contact directly to soft organs, wounds or by inhalation. Heavy metals present in the dyes, may affect a community by consumption of contaminated water. These are harmful aspects of textile industries regarding the loss of properties and human health hazards, while the rest negative impacts of textile industries are on environment and its all components, living and non-livings, such as water, soil, agriculture plants, cattle, human beings.

Chapter 3
Water and Human Health

Content

Water is the most Essential commodity for all living creatures. Man needs it for his physiological existence water is the elixir of life It is the source of energy and govern the evaluation and function of the universe on the earth 97.3% of the worlds water *i.e.* 1.4 billion cubic kilometer ocean salty water cannot be used for agriculture domestic and industries purposes. Out of it 2.7% freshwater *i.e.* 73 x 10^6 cubic in the form of streams, lakes, wells and tube wells *i.e.* 0.6% 8.5 x $10^{15}m^3$ is groundwater which oceans at the depth of 80 meter below the ground surface (Bolen back 1983, Kataria 1994).

The origin of water on earth is not clear so far. However, the current presumption is that the primordial earth had no oceans and perhaps very little atmosphere. It is believed that the volatile constituents bound in the earth crust, oozing to the surface through volcanoes, rock movements and hot springs, condensed to form the ocean, atmosphere and mountains. This way perhaps this remarkable combination of hydrogen and oxygen called water come into being and eventually became an indispensable component of earth's environments.

In Vedic Literature water is mainly called, as *Apha* we all know that waters is the elixir of life. All living organisms, plants and animals are structurally 30-98% water.

Besides being a structural component of body water is essential environmentally too. Water is the medium through which nutrients of soil underneath and above on the surface move horizontally as well as vertically water has great power of dissolving most of the inorganic components in mixture form and in the pure elemental and ionic form. Water provides a medium for interaction among different compounds water is a great nurture for plants as well as for animals water helps in conducting of energy the form of heat helps in maintaining a soothing climate, water acts as a rejuvenator and medicament it self (Rig 1.23.19).

Chemically, water is the mono-oxide of Hydrogen *i.e.* (H.O.H). It freely disassociated into hydrogen and hydroxyl ions. The ionization product (H^+) and (OH^-) is about 10^{-14}. Water is a colourless liquid and possesses a high dielectric constant (81), and there for salts gets highly ionized when dissolved in water but not so in the other solvents. Due to this property, water is known as universal solvent present on the earth that is why the natural water contains many salts in dissolved form. On the basis of amount these slats dissolved in the earth only 3% of the total water (approximately 1.4 billion cubic kilometer) is fresh and suitable for human consumption of this, less than 0.01% is associated with rivers and streams (Water Resources 1980).

3.1 Water and Human Health

In vedic literature, water is called as a medicine for human health. Nobody can imagine life without water. Water is our basic requirement even animal and plant can't survive without water. It is common statement that ***"Life is not possible without water"***. Thus life and water are inseparable faces of the same coin. Water is not only essential for life but predominant inorganic constituent of living matter forming in general nearly three quarters of the weight of living cells. It makes some 5 percent of the body weight of an adult human and can forms as 98% of the mass of certain jellyfish. Organisms that contain relatively small amounts of water are generally in dormant state or show very slow development; seeds and certain invertebrates that live in arid environments are examples. On the other hand high rainfall over a landmass in variably means a large biomass per unit area.

Next to oxygen, water is the most important substance for human existence and it is essential for everything on our planet to grow and prosper (Girma, 2005). Freshwater rivers, lakes and groundwater are used to irrigate crops, to provide drinking water and to act as a sanitation system. Although we as humans recognize this fact, we disregard it by polluting our rivers, lakes, and oceans. Most of our water resources are gradually becoming contaminated due to the addition of foreign materials from the surroundings (Lokeshwari and Chandrappa, 2006). These include organic matter of plant and animal origin, land surface washing and industrial and sewage effluents. Rapid urbanization and industrialization with improper environmental planning often lead to discharge of industrial and sewage effluents into rivers. In addition to the process of desertification, pollution is also reducing the volume of safe fishing, irrigation and drinking water.

The problem of water pollution due to toxic metals has begun to cause concern now in most metropolitan cities. The toxic heavy metals entering the ecosystem may lead to geo-accumulation and biomagnifications. Metals like Fe, Cu, Zn, Ni and other trace elements are important for proper functioning of biological systems and their deficiency or excess could lead to a number of disorders (Ward, 1995). Food chain contamination by heavy metals has become a burning issue in recent years because of their potential accumulation in biological systems through contaminated water, soil and air. Therefore, a better understanding of heavy metal sources, their accumulation in the soil and the effect of their presence in water, soil and on plant systems seem to be particularly important issues of present day research on risk assessment. The main sources of heavy metals to vegetable crops are their growth media (soil, air, nutrient solutions) from which these are taken up by the roots or foliage.

Water is a resource circulated throughout all ecosystems and is one of the most important factors of them (Odum 1971). From the point of view of eco-hydrology, for the main elements of an ecosystem including inorganic and organic compound, producers and consumers both the quantity and the chemistry of water have a decisive impact on its biomass and biotic composition. Information obtained from current hydro-chemical analyses of water specimens is very important but it is sometimes difficult to Ganga the overall situation especially the occurrence of nutrient, which may be very important to an ecosystem.

Everything originated in the water and everything is sustained by water all life on earth depends on water. Water is very essential for the survival of all living organism there is a wide variety of beneficial uses of water. Man uses water for many purposes, drinking, irrigation, fisheries, industrial purposes, transportation and waste disposal. The origin of water on the earth is not clear so far. However, the current presumption is that the primordial earth had no oceans and perhaps volatile constituents bound in the earth crust oozing to the surface through volcanoes rock movements and hot springs, condensed to form the ocean and the atmosphere. This way come into being and eventually become an indispensable component of earth' environment.

Water quality includes all physical, chemical and biological factor that influence the beneficial use of water, Lotic habitats are those exiting in relatively fast running streams, springs, river and brooks. The lakes represent lentic habitats; marshes and swamps represent ponds and wetland. The above classification of freshwater environment is based on currents and ratio of the depth of surface area.

3.2 Sources of water:

1. Rainfall
2. Groundwater
   - ☆ Dug wells
   - ☆ Bore wells
   - ☆ Tube wells
   - ☆ Hand pumps

3. Surface water
   (*a*) Freshwater:
      (*i*) Lentic (still water)
         ✰ Ponds
         ✰ Lakes.
         ✰ Wetlands
      (*ii*) Lotic water (running water)-
         ✰ Rivers
         ✰ Springs
         ✰ Streams
         ✰ Brooks
   (*b*) Marine water
      ✰ Ocean
      ✰ Sea.

3.3 Phases of Surface Water

1. Permafrost
2. Hail
3. Fog
4. Water vapour
5. Dew
6. Ice
7. Aquifer
8. Sleet
9. Frost

Groundwater is one of the major water resources for domestic, agricultural and industrial uses. Pollutants are being added to the groundwater and soil system through various human activities and rapid growth of industrialization, which affects the human health directly or indirectly.

Environmental assessment in this context is concerned with groundwater concentrations of cadmium, zinc, lead and arsenic, the levels of which are often increased by the effects of human activity. Metals are spread via the atmosphere from smelters and other metal industrial plants. Significant increases in groundwater concentrations of metals from such sources may occur within a local radius of ca. ten kilometers; but their distribution through the atmosphere extends over far greater areas. Large quantities of lead have also been released into the atmosphere through the use of leaded petrol. Such releases have declined in recent years, but the greater portion of airborne lead pollution from previous years is still present in the surface layers of earth. Levels of cadmium, lead, zinc and arsenic in groundwater are often related to pollution or other human activities. Cadmium, lead and arsenic are dangerous to human health even in fairly low concentrations.

Metals have also entered land and water by more direct routes. In some areas, the use of cadmium-contaminated phosphate fertilizer has led to a doubling of cadmium levels in cropland during the past fifty years. Since zinc is often used for anti-corrosion purposes, it may enter the soil via galvanized steel products embedded in the ground. Both arsenic and zinc are included in many wood preservatives, and can be spread via waste spill at impregnating facilities or via the wood products themselves. Waste sites are another source of zinc and arsenic, which may leach out from discarded materials that include those metals. Still greater quantities of polluting metals may leach from dumps of mining waste.

Naturally high levels of cadmium and arsenic can occur in areas where the bedrock contains high concentrations of metals; this applies to many types of shale and slate. Lowering the water table, for example by pumping out water, may lead to increases in the amounts of naturally-occurring metals that enter the groundwater. This is because metals in bedrock are often bound in sulfide minerals. The addition of oxygen results in oxidation of the sulfide compounds and the release of their metallic components. In some cases, however, arsenic may also be released as the result of a rise in the water table. It is with redox class 3 that the risk of water-soluble arsenic is greatest.

The solubility of cadmium and zinc increases significantly with a decline in pH value, which means that acidification, can lead to increased levels of those metals in groundwater. Normally, lead is very tightly bound to humus and clay, but it may dissolve more readily if the pH value declines. In the case of arsenic, the reverse usually applies: Solubility increases concurrently with rising pH values. Zinc is an element that is essential to life for most organisms, and humans can tolerate high concentrations. Aquatic organisms, on the other hand, are much more sensitive to zinc. Increased levels in groundwater indicate that concentrations of other metals may be above normal. This is especially true of cadmium, which is often present concurrently with zinc. In most cases, cadmium levels are, at most, one percent higher than those of zinc; but cadmium can be harmful even at such low concentrations. Lead is another heavy metal, which is toxic at low concentrations. If pregnant women are exposed to lead concentrations above medically established threshold levels, there is an increased risk of birth defects. The toxicity of arsenic is comparatively moderate, but over longer periods of time it may produce changes in skin tissue, even at levels below medically established thresholds.

3.4 Threshold Levels of Heavy Metals

Table 3.1: Threshold Levels of Heavy Metals

Class	*Level*	*Cadmium µg/l*	*Zinc µg/l*	*Lead µg/l*	*Arsenic µg/l*
1	Very low	< 0.05	< 5	< 0.2	< 1
2	Low	0.05-0.1	5-20	0.2-1	1-5
3	Moderate	0.1-1	20-300	1-3	5-10
4	High	1-5	300-1000	3-10	10-50
5	Very high	> 5	> 1000	> 10	> 50

In several cases, the limits for the above five classes correspond with those of the National Food Administration's threshold levels (see table below). For all metals, the boundary between class 2 and class 3 is defined as the level at which effects on organisms in lakes and watercourses begin to occur.

Table 3.2: Different Types of Threshold Levels of Heavy Metals

Type of Threshold Level	*Cadmium µg/l*	*Zinc µg/l*	*Lead µg/l*	*Arsenic µg/l*
Warning based on technical grounds; survival of aquatic organisms is affected even with brief exposure		> 300		
Warning based on technical and aesthetic grounds; risk of taste changes and turbidity		> 1000		
Medically-established threshold; use with caution	> 1			> 10
Medically-established; unsuitable for drinking	> 5		> 10	> 50

Source: National Food Administration.

3.5 Reference Values

Reference values have been set so high that uncontaminated groundwater has low concentrations of metals in the majority of cases. Such water may, however, include pollutants that have traveled lengthy distances through the atmosphere.

Table 3.3: Reference Values of Heavy Metals

Metal	*Reference value, µg/l*
Cadmium	0.1
Zinc	100
Lead	1
Arsenic	1

Table 3.4: Deviations from Reference Values of Heavy Metals

Class	*Extent of Deviation*	*Cadmium µg/l*	*Zinc µg/l*	*Lead µg/l*	*Arsenic µg/l*
1	None or insignificant	< 0.1	< 100	< 1	< 1
2	Moderate	0.1-0.5	100-200	1-1.5	1-2
3	Significant	0.5-2	200-400	1.5-2.5	2-5
4	Large	2-5	400-700	2.5-5	5-10
5	Very large	> 5	> 700	> 5	> 10

The five classes indicate the extent to which measured levels of metals in groundwater deviate from the reference values, which are relatively unaffected by non-natural causes. The upper limit of class 1, separating it from class 2, is the same as the reference value. The values of class 5 indicate the strong possibility of a local source of contamination. But in isolated cases, there may be another cause of the unusually high levels, for example: Class 5 levels of cadmium may occur naturally in extremely acid water ($pH < 5$); likewise, high arsenic levels occur naturally at a number of locations in the regions of Bergslagen and Skellefteå, as well as other parts in certain deep-drilled wells with high levels of iron (redox class 3) and high pH values.

Chapter 4

Water Quality Standards

Contents

Modern civilization is dependent upon the water for irrigation, domestic need, industrial and for power generation. So we can say that life and water are inseparable faces of the same coin. The intensity of human activities and the diversity and magnitude of wastes introduced into environment as a consequence are increasing at an accelerating rate with improvements in technology, advancing industrialization and create a significance impact on environment and effect all living beings including man himself. The increasing rate of population growth and progress of human beings in different fields is creating an alarming condition of environmental pollution.

Pollution is the release of substances or energy into the environment by man in quantities that damages either his health or resources (Edwards, 1972). Municipal sewage, domestic wastes, industrial wastes and effluents, synthetic chemicals like pesticides, detergents and toxic metals of fertilizer have polluted maximum water bodies. Water pollution by radioactivity and thermal pollution are also noteworthy. Sewage can be regarded as the water borne waste products of man. Sewage consists of discharge of water from bathrooms, kitchen and laboratories.

The increased contamination of aquatic environment by domestic sewage and industrial effluents has focused attention on the behavior and interaction of many rare and neglected elements in the biosphere. Bioaccumulation of heavy metals in living organisms occurs due to their property of persistence and non-degradability of the complex organic compounds. Aquatic plants in general are more sensitive to environmental dangers. Sensitive aquatic macrophytic species can serve as indicators and those resistances to pollution as accumulators. In the present study, *Eichhornia crassipes,* an aquatic weed has tremendous capacity to remove the pollutant from the water and also to grow and multiply rapidly in sewage containing aquatic environment.

Raw sewage consists of 99.9% water and 0.1% solids, which include 70% organic and 30% inorganic compounds. Sewage is an excellent medium for growth of pathogenic bacteria, viruses and protozoa. Domestic sewage, which is primary compost of, spent water containing wine, faeces, soapy waste, food materials and paper makes the water extremely anesthetic. Water becomes totally unfit for drinking and domestic use.

Sewage containing oxidizable and fermentable matter causes depletion of dissolved oxygen in the receiving water bodies affecting the aquatic flora severely. Oxygen deficiency also leads to the production of objectionable odours in water. Highly organic suspended matters, which purify the water, get deposited on riverbeds, behind weir or sludge. Suspended matter present in sewage has a tendency to blenket the stream thereby interfering with the spawning of fish and reduction of aquatic biota. Accumulation of sewage and domestic waste in water bodies retards the self-regulatory capabilities of aquatic organisms. Discharge of nutrient rich effluents, sewage and domestic waste in combination with industrial wastes poses serious health problem in man.

Every community produces both liquid and solid wastes. The wastewater is essentially the water supply of the community after it has been fouled by a variety of uses. Wastewater is commonly classified as domestic, industrial or agricultural according to its source. Sewage water originates from domestic sources and contain varying amount of industrial wastewater of occasionally rainwater. The quantity of sewage water is about 80% of the total consumption and varies between 100 to 300 capita per day depending upon the standard of living and season of the year. Most city jewelers are unable conceive that individual produces about 150 liter of sewage per day of it simply does not disappear underground.

The wastewater collected from cities and towns must ultimately be returned to the receiving water or on the land after the containments have been removed to protect the environment depending upon the local needs of the end use of the treated water.

4.1 Remediation

Bioremediation is the use of living organisms (primarily microorganisms) to degrade environmental pollution or to prevent pollution through waste treatment. Research projects are being modified to expand the range of microorganisms used for bioremediation. There is search for naturally occurring microbes that have better pollutant degradation kinetics, attack a wider range of microbial growth condition and could grow under extreme environmental condition, such as tolrance to organic solvents, growth under extremely alkaline substrate or high temperatures.

Phytoremediation is the process of recovery of hazardous substances from soil and wastewater by using plants. Aquatic macrophytes such as species of *Salvina, Lemna, Azolla, Eichhornia, Sedeges* and even tree species are also known to tolerate, uptake and even accumulate heavy metals and other toxicants in their cell.

In rural and small urban localities, the volume of sewage generated is low. It is very expensive to treat such low volumes by conventional technology because according to the economics of scale, lower the quantity of waste to have treated by any technology, higher is the cost of treatment per litre. This is one of the reasons why most villages and small town in developing countries don't have any sewage treatment facility. This leads to wide spread water and soil pollution and frequent outbreaks of water born diseases. Against the background, the emerging technology of using aquatic macrophytes especially water hyacinth, which enable cost effective treatment of sewage, assumes greater significance and promise.

To minimize the pollution load of water bodies various guidelines, quality standards and maximum permissible limits of pollutants have been set up in different countries. However, WHO standards are being applied in most countries of the world as they are considered as ideal. The Indian standards (BIS) or CPCB standards show relatively high deviation from the WHO standards for environmental quality. Maximum permissible limits for some water quality parameters are different than those of WHO. Limits for toxic metals (Cd, Cu, Hg, Mn, Ni, Pb, Zn) in drinking water are high in BIS or CPCB standards compared to WHO standards. Heavy metals are highly toxic and cause various health problems in humans and also affect cattle and vegetation. Thus, it is essential to control their migration to the unpolluted environment for the safety of human health and livestock (Bharti, 2007).

In modern era of industrialization, the water pollution is always a big problem among human beings. Polluted water may harms to animals, soil productivity, agriculture crop, aquatic biota, material and properties in different way. It may cause some severe health problems also, so it is essential to keep water clean and adopt some strategies against polluted water for remedial process. Chemical or other advance techniques are very expensive, so phytoremediation is the only way to protect and purify the polluted water without any more expense. Phytoremediation using *Lemna minor* and *Pistia stratiotes* aquatic plants may absorb a huge concentration of metals from the conducted laboratory experiment. Similarly Ceratophyllum, Vallesneria and many other aquatic macrophyte may be use to combat against pollutants in a modern fashion.

Water–the most abundant and vital natural resource is extremely essential for survival of all living organisms, but today clean water has become a precious commodity and its quality is threatened by numerous sources of pollution. Water pollution creates physical, chemical and biological changes in the water, and further affects the water quality for a long time of period. As the heavy metals enter in the food chains of aquatic ecosystem, ultimately affect the health of higher animals of that particular ecosystem. Different heavy metals like Mercury, Lead, Chromium, and Nickel, Cadmium etc. release from various sources like agriculture, urban and industrial uses, and these factors degrade the water quality.

The aquatic macrophytes are of considerable ecological and economic importance and contribute significantly to enhancing the biological productivity of water bodies, mobilize mineral element from the bottom sediment and provide shelter and food to aquatic fauna. They also respond to the changes in water quality and have been used as an indicator of pollution in several cases. The aquatic plants are commonly found in shoreline of lakes, rivers and water logged areas

In recent past, there has been great emphasis on the importance of macrophytes in removing nutrient from the polluted water and their use in upgrading waste water quality. Aquatic plants posses tremendous potential to reduce the level of toxic metals, nutrients, BOD and to improve other physico-chemical characteristics of waste water. However, use of these plants in designing a low cost treatment system is still at the experimental stage and is considered to be a potentially important area of environmental management. Keep this in view; phytoremediation technique is adopted in which two macrophytes *Lemna* and *Pistia* were used for waste water treatment as a clean and cheap technology for special reference to Indian sub-continent.

4.2 Quality Standards

The first sets of standards were published as Indian Standard, 2490 in 1963. These standards set the tolerance limits for Industrial Effluent discharged into inland surface water. The Indian Standard 2296 was also published in 1963, which set the tolerance limits for inland surface water subject to pollution.

Table 4.1: Standards for Effluent from Textile Industry by CPCB
MoEF Notification, New Delhi, 25th september, 2000
Bharat Ka Rajpatra- Bhaag –II, Khand 3 (i)
(For large scale industries)
Standards for effluents from textile industry

Parameter	*Concentration not to Exceed, mg/l, except pH*
pH	5.5-9.0
Total suspended solids	100
BOD	30
COD	250
Total residual chlorine	1
Oil and grease	10
Total chromium as Cr	2
Sulphide as S	2
Phenolic compounds as C_6H_5OH	1

1. Where the treated effluent is discharged into municipal sewer leading to terminal treatment plant, the BOD may be relaxed to 100 mg/l and COD to 400 mg/l.
2. The quantity of effluent (l/kg of product) shall not exceed 100, 250 and 80 in composite cotton textile industry, composite woolen textile industry and textile processing industry, respectively.

Table-4.2: Standard for the Textile Effluent According to Bureau of Indian Standard (BIS)

Parameter	*BIS (IS : 3307, 1965) (IS : 3306, 1965)*
pH	5.5-9.0
Temperature °C	40.0
Colour Co-pt (mg/l)	0.0
Total Solids (mg/l)	-
Total Dissolved Solids (mg/l)	-
Total Suspended Solids (mg/l)	100
Biochemical Oxygen Demand (mg/l)	30.0
Chemical Oxygen Demand (mg/l)	250
Oil and Grease (mg/l)	10
Ammonical Nitrogen (mg/l)	50

The first attempts of water pollution control thus approached the problem using two independent concepts, one dealt with the control of pollution through specification of various parameters and their maximum concentration in the effluent itself. These could be referred to as 'Effluent Standards'. The other approach was to set standards for the receiving water body presumply after a reasonable opportunity for dilution. These standards could be called 'Receiving Water Body Standards' and were related to identified beneficial use to the receiving water body. It is extremely significant that the very first attempt of control of water pollution was through setting of standards simultaneously adopting the above two approaches.

Table 4.3: Standards for Small Scale Industries (*i.e.* total discharge upto 25 KL/day) Notified Under the Environmental (Protection) Act, 1986

Parameter	*Cotton Textile Industry (Composite)*	*Woolen Mill (Composite and Processing)*
Common		
pH	5.5-9.0	5.5-9.0
SS	100	100
BOD	150	150
Oil and Grease	10	10
Bio-assay Test	90% survival of fish after 96 hours	90% survival of fish after 96 hours
Special		
Total Chromium (as Cr)	2	2
Sulphide (as S)	2	2
Phenolic Compounds (as C_6H_5OH)	5	5

Table 4.4: Environmental Standards (cpcb.nic.in, 2006)
Dye and Dye Intermediate Industry: Wastewater Discharge Standards

Parameter	*Concentration not to exceed, mg/l (except pH, colour and bio-assay test)*
pH	6.0 to 9.0
Colour, hazen unit	400
Suspended solids	100
BOD (27oC, 3 days)	100
Oil and Grease	10.0
Phenolics as C_6H_5OH	1.0
Cadmium as Cd	0.2
Copper as Cu	2.0
Manganese as Mn	2.0
Lead as Pb	0.1
Mercury as Hg	0.01
Nickel as Ni	2.0
Zinc as Zn	5.0
Chromium as Cr	
Hexavalent	0.1
Total	2.0
Bio-assay test	90 per cent survival in 96 hours

Table 4.5: WHO's Guidelines for Drinking Water Quality, 2006, are the International reference point for standard setting and drinking-water safety.

Element/ Substance	*Symbol/ Formula*	*Normally found in Freshwater/Surface Water/Groundwater*	*Health Based Guideline by the WHO*
Aluminium	Al		0.2 mg/l
Ammonia	NH_4	< 0.2 mg/l (up to 0.3 mg/l in anaerobic waters)	No guideline
Antimony	Sb	< 4 μg/l	0.02 mg/l
Arsenic	As		0.01 mg/l
Asbestos			No guideline
Barium	Ba		0.7 mg/l
Beryllium	Be	< 1 μg/l	No guideline
Boron	B	< 1 mg/l	0.5 mg/l
Cadmium	Cd	< 1 μg/l	0.003 mg/l
Chloride	Cl		No guideline
Chromium	Cr^{+3}, Cr^{+6}	< 2 μg/l	0.05 mg/l

Contd...

Table 4.5–*Contd...*

Element/ Substance	*Symbol/ Formula*	*Normally found in Freshwater/Surface Water/Groundwater*	*Health Based Guideline by the WHO*
Colour			Not mentioned
Copper	Cu		2 mg/l
Cyanide	CN^-		0.07 mg/l
Dissolved oxygen	O_2		No guideline
Fluoride	F	< 1.5 mg/l (up to 10)	1.5 mg/l
Hardness	mg/l $CaCO_3$		No guideline
Hydrogen sulfide	H_2S		No guideline
Iron	Fe	0.5–50 mg/l	No guideline
Lead	Pb		0.01 mg/l
Manganese	Mn		0.4 mg/l
Mercury	Hg	< 0.5 μg/l	0.006 mg/l
Molybdenum	Mb	< 0.01 mg/l	0.07 mg/l
Nickel	Ni	< 0.02 mg/l	0.07 mg/l
Nitrate and nitrite	NO_3, NO_2		50 mg/l and 3 mg/l
Turbidity			Not mentioned
pH			No guideline
Selenium	Se	< 0.01 mg/l	0.01 mg/l
Silver	Ag	5 – 50 μg/l	No guideline
Sodium	Na	< 20 mg/l	No guideline
Sulfate	SO_4		No guideline
Inorganic tin	Sn		Not mentioned
TDS			No guideline
Uranium	U		0.015 mg/l
Zinc	Zn		No guideline

Source: www.who.in.

Effluent Standards versus Receiving Water Body Standards

As the Indian Standards were evolved, a choice between Effluent Standards and Receiving Water Body Standards emerged, considering the fact that most of the Indian rivers are not perennial and hence carry only the effluents during major period of the year, the choice generally favoured the Effluent Standards. Effluent Standards are also relatively easy to enforce. This has generally led the various Pollution Control Boards to favoured Effluent Standards. In specific cases however, such as deep marine outfall disposal, it is necessary that the receiving water body standards be considered.

Table 4.6: Drinking Water Quality Standards

Parameters	*BIS*	*CPCB*	*UPPCB*	*WHO*
Temperature	40 ºC	±5ºC than receiving water	40 ºC	–
SS	100 mg/l	100 mg/l	100 mg/l	5–25 mg/l
pH	5.5–9.0	5.5–9.0	5.5–9.0	7.0–8.5
BOD_5 at 20ºC	30 mg/l	30 mg/l	30 mg/l	–
COD	250 mg/l	250 mg/l	250 mg/l	–
Cl	–	–	–	75–200 mg/l
Ca	–	–	–	75–200 mg/l
Mg	–	–	–	30–150 mg/l
Cd	2.0 mg/l	2.0 mg/l	2.0 mg/l	0.1 mg/l
Cu	3.0 mg/l	3.0 mg/l	3.0 mg/l	0.05–1.5 mg/l
Fe	–	3.0 mg/l	–	0.1–1.0 mg/l
Pb	0.1 mg/l	0.1 mg/l	0.1 mg/l	0.1 mg/l
Mn	–	2.0 mg/l	–	0.05–0.5 mg/l
Ni	2.0 mg/l	3.0 mg/l	2.0 mg/l	–
Zn	5.0 mg/l	5.0 mg/l	5.0 mg/l	5–15.0 mg/l

Table 4.7: Recent Standards for Heavy Metals (in mg/l)

	Inland Surface Water		*Drinking Water*		
	BIS/CPCB	*WHO*	*WHO, 1993*	*WHO, 2006*	
			Drinking Water	*Normal*	*Health Based*
Cd	2.0	0.1	0.003–0.005	<1µg/l	0.003
Cu	3.0	0.05–1.5	2.0	–	2.0
Fe	3.0	0.1–1.0	0.2	0.5–50	–
Mn	2.0	0.05–0.5	0.5–0.05	–	0.4
Ni	2.0	–	0.02	0.02	0.07
Pb	0.1	0.1	0.01	–	0.01
Zn	5.0	5.0–15.0	3.0	<20	–

Source: www.lenntech.com.

4.3 MINAS

Around 1976, the CPCB developed the concept of evolving industry specific effluent standards based on a comprehensive study of the problems of that particular industry relevant polluting parameters, their pollution potential, best pollution control technology available in the country and the cost of such a technology.

From these, comprehensive documentation evolved the idea of Minimal National Standards (MINAS). These standards were considered to be the minimum standards for specified industries. In the Environmental Protection Act (EPA), 1986, some of these standards were incorporated. Since these are the Minimal National Standards, the State Boards are only permitted to make them more stringent and in no case can relax them. It is essential that effluent standards satisfy three basic criteria namely Necessity, Implement ability and Enforceability. The stipulation of standards for a specific parameter is necessary when the effect of the parameters on the environment were thoroughly studied and established. No compromise, therefore, can be made with regard to concentration of toxic pollutants. By implement ability it should mean that with best pollution control technology currently available in this country, these parameters could be brought down to the specified limits. Enforceability means either the industry or the concerned authorities have the expertise to analyze, to monitor the wastewater discharged from the industry. Each of the parameters included in the MINAS must satisfy each of these three fundamental criteria. At the same time, the set of parameters chosen must ensure the primary objective of protection of environment. Keeping in mind the basic criteria, major polluting parameters from the industries and the performance of the treatment plants, the standards are evolved.

Chapter 5

National Water Policy

Contents

Land, water and energy are the basic need for any development of the region. Out of this water has become the matter of concern in almost all the countries. The central theme in the "decade of 80" was water, because of the major droughts faced by many countries. This period has paradoxically coincided with the International Decade of drinking water. The rapidity with which the water crisis occupied the center stage of Indian planning warns that water resources should not be taken for granted any more.

Water is not automatically available because the ecological process that gives stability to the water cycle governs its renewability. The seasonal rains in most parts of India, lasting hardly for 90 days, have made the agriculture and social life adapt to seasonability. Frequent droughts have made it necessary to employ various water conservation methods, including traditional ones.

The water logging and subsequent salinity problems which have become common phenomenon in most of the surface irrigation project, the increasing concentration of nitrates, phosphates, fluoride and potash in intensely cultivated areas and major urban areas point out that groundwater management and conservation of groundwater as a precious national resources should be taken up seriously by the planners and by the general public. Otherwise, the unplanned exploitation coupled with contamination and salinity ingress would cause damage to the entire groundwater system. Such damage has already been noticed in certain coastal areas and in parts of the Lakshadweep and Andman-Nicobar Islands in the Arabian Sea and Bay of Bengal Islands respectively.

5.1 Water Demand

India is the wettest country in the world, should consider itself singularly blessed as it is one of the few countries which is self sufficient in water resources. It receives an average yearly rainfall of 1170 mm while central west America which is supposed to be the food bowl of the world, gets a more 200 mm annual rainfall.

It is estimated that in our country about 19 million kiloliters of freshwater is trappable but we utilize only fraction of this amount. It is estimated that by the turn of the 21st century, we will be able to utilize only about 10.9 million kiloliters of water, that is, just a little more than half the amount available. Out of this available supply, 79.59 per cent will be used for irrigation, 13.75 per cent for the production for electric power, 3.2 per cent in industries and 3.47 percent for domestic purposes.

In our country, piped or organized water supply was given a thrust in 1970s and in the beginning three metropolitan cities "Calcutta, Bombay and Madras (now Kolkata, Mumbai, and Chennai) were covered". Still by 1991, about 44 per cent of the population had access to piped water supply. Out of the beneficiaries so covered 71 per cent live in the urban areas and 29 per cent in rural areas. If the current trend continues for another three years, India will suffer an acute drinking water crisis. The present crisis is due to mismanagement in the storage of rainwater. At present India utilizes only about 10 per cent of the available rainfall and, according to some projections at the current rate we will use a maximum of 25 per cent of available annual rainfall in the next 30 years. About one-third of the villages in the country have been declared water deficient, the main reason for within is rapid industrialization. In the last 10 years, the urban population has risen by 46.2 per cent.

Today, India is not the only country which is facing crisis but there are 26 another countries, collectively home of 230 million people, in this category. The lack of water becomes a severe constraint in food production, economic development and protection of natural systems. In many reasons as demand continue to rise and water supply projects get more difficult to built, water budgets are becoming badly imbalanced. Water that is reliably available to the human population is about 9000 cubic kilometers per year or about 1800 cubic meters per person. This may sound like a lot of water but the available resource are neither distributed evenly nor used efficiently. More than 600 million people live in the world arid and semi-arid areas where they face chronic water scarcity. It is a serious problem in these areas because about 47 per cent of rain fed crop land is affected by desertification.

Africa has the largest number of water scare countries *i.e.* eleven and the Middle East is the world's worst affected region, with nine of its 14 countries facing shortages. Chine with 2 per cent of the world's people and just 8 per cent of its freshwater faces severe constraints. Water labels beneath Beijing have been dropping one of two meters a year, and a third of its wells have gone dry. Some 100 Chinese cities and town, in the northern and coastal regions, have suffered severe shortage in the last few years.

Paris of Mexico, Thailand and the western United States also suffer from a declining water table.

5.2 Need for Policy

Water is a prime natural resource, a basic human need and a precious national asset. Planning and development of water resources must take into account interalia, the national water resource position and financial and material aspects of explotation and sustenance of water resources under an integrated national prospective.

It has been estimated that out of the total precipitation of around 400 million hectare meters in the country, the surface water availability is about 178 million hectare meters. Out of this, about 50% can be put to beneficial use because of topographical and other constraints. In addition, there is a groundwater potential of about 42 million hectare meters. The availability of water is highly uneven in terms of both space and time. Precipitation is confined to only about three or four months in the year and varies from 10 cm in the western parts of Rajasthan to over 1000 cm at Cherrapunji in Meghalaya. Further, water does not respect state boundaries. Not merely rivers but even underground aquifers often cut across state boundaries. Water as a resource is one and indivisible: rainfall, river waters, surface ponds and lakes and groundwater are all part of one system. Similarly, water is also a part of a large ecological system.

Flood sand droughts affect vast areas of the country, transcending state boundaries. Almost one third of the country is drought-prone. Floods affect an average area of around 9 million hectares per year. According to the National Commission on Floods, the area susceptible to floods is around 40 million hectares. The approach to the management of drought and floods has to be coordinated and guided at the national level. Even the planning and implementation of individual irrigation of multi-purpose projects, though done at the State level, involve a number of aspects and issues such as environmental protection, rehabilitation of project affected people and livestock, public health consequences of water impoundment, dam safety, etc.

On these matters integrated approaches and guidelines are necessary. Moreover certain problems and weaknesses have affected a large number of projects all over the country. There have been substantial time and cost overruns on projects. In some irrigation commands, problems of water-logging and soil salinity have emerged, leading to the degradation of good agriculture land. There are also complex problems of equity and social justice in regard to water distribution. The development and exploitation of the country's groundwater resources also give rise to questions of judicious and scientific resource management and conservation. All these question need to be tackled on the basis of common policies and strategies. The growth process and the expansion of economic activities inevitably lead to increasing demands for water for diverse purposes like domestic, industrial, agricultural, hydro-power, navigational and recreational use.

Domestic and industrial water needs have largely been concentrated in or near the principal cities, but the demand from rural society his expected to increase substantially as the development programme improve economic conditions in the rural areas. The demand for water for hydro and thermal power generation and for other industrial uses is also likely to increase substantially. As a result water which is already a scare resource will become even most scare in future.

The emphasized the need for the utmost efficiency in water utilization and a public awareness of the importance of its conservation. Another important aspect is water quality. Improvements in existing strategies and the innovation of new techniques based on strong research and developmental activities in science and technology will be needed to eliminate the pollution of surface and groundwater resources, to improve water quality and to set up the recycling and re-use of water. Science and technology and training have also important roles to play in water resources development in general.

Water is one of the most crucial elements in developmental planning. The need for a national water policy is thus abundantly clear that water is a source and precious national resource to be planned, developed and conserved on an integrated and environmentally sustainable basis, keeping in view the needs of the states concerned.

5.3 National Water Policy

As it is necessary to plan and develop this prime natural resource carefully under the given national perspectives, the Ministry of Water Resources drafted the National Water Policy in 1987. a brief outline of the chief contents of the policy is as follows:

1. A standard national information system should be established with a network of data banks to collect information about resource's availability and their utilization.
2. Comprehensive and reliable projections of future demands for water for diverse purposes.
3. Maximum utilization of water resources with the help of conservation augmentation and prevention of losses.
4. Establishment of organizational set up for the planned development and management of a river basin as a whole with the help of appropriate legislations.
5. Transfers of surplus water from one river basin in other having shortage of the same.
6. Recycling and reuse of water.
7. Water resources projects should be multipurpose projects with priority for drinking water use, the other uses being irrigation flood control, power generation, navigational, piscicultural, industrial and recreational.
8. Study of environmental socio-economic impacts of the projects during construction and later stages should be an essential component of project planning. The adverse impact if any should be minimized and off-set by adequate compensatory measures.
9. Integrated multi-disciplinary approach with more attention to needs of tribal and scheduled castes or weaker sections of the populations.

10. Appropriate provision should be made for periodic maintenance of the systems and structures created.
11. Continuous surveillance and monitoring of the system created.
12. Periodic reassessment of groundwater resources.
13. Periodic quality monitoring in case of surface water and groundwater.
14. Strict control on groundwater exploitation to ensure social equity and to avoid adverse effects like salinity ingress.
15. Integrated and co-ordinated development of surface and groundwater their conjunctive use.
16. Water rates should be such as to convey the scarcity value of the resources to the users and to foster the motivation for economy in water use.
17. Efforts should be made to involve people in various aspects of management especially distribution of water and collection water rates.
18. Water zoning: Industrial, agricultural and urban development should be planned on the basis of water availability in a particular zone.
19. Drought prone areas should be made less vulnerable to nature's vagaries through:
    (*a*) Soil moisture conservation measures;
    (*b*) Rain water harvesting;
    (*c*) Minimization of evaporation losses; and
    (*d*) Full development of groundwater and surface water potential.
20. Adequate training facilities for personnel engaged/involved in the discipline of water management.

Base on the National Water Policy document, the conference of "State Secretaries connected with groundwater exploitation work and concerned officials from the Government of India", gave recommendations as follows (June 1989, New Delhi):

1. Establishment of block wise and district wise computerized data storage and retrieval system.
2. Periodic assessment of groundwater potential.
3. Continuous monitoring of water quality and mapping of protection zones were considered to be of paramount importance for urban, industrial and agricultural areas with intensive chemical inputs. The States should arrange follow up action in areas identified as potentially hazardous from groundwater pollution angle.
4. The designs of groundwater structures should be on the basis of the recommendations of the District Development Plans prepared by Central Groundwater Board (which is the apex Government organization in the field of groundwater management commonly known as CGWB), so that they could withstand the vagaries of the monsoon.

5. Based on predicted level of the monsoon rainfall, management of the total resource would be worked out to ensure fulfillment of the needs of domestic water supply followed by needs of agricultural production.
6. Area specific methodologies would be developed for artificial recharge of groundwater. These projects would be prioritized and implemented in a phased manner.

Chapter 6
Water Resources Management

Contents

World's available freshwater supply is not distributed uniformly around the globe throughout the seasons or from year to year. Nearly three quarters of the worlds annual rainfall comes down in areas inhabited by less than one third of the world's population, while two third of the world's population lived in areas receiving only one quarter of the world's annual rainfall. A water crisis, which has come about because rain–as a source of water has been ignored. The potential of rain to meet water demand is tremendous. Theoretically, the average rainfall of 100 mm of rain falling on one hectare of land in arid regions like Jaisalmer can yield up to one million liters of water.

Despite several initiatives taken by Government and public bodies, in 1995 some 20% of the world's population of 5.7 billion people still lacked safe, fresh and reliable water supply, while more than 50% were without adequate sanitation system. Today, thirty-one countries having nearly 8% of the total population face water shortages, affecting more than 2.8 billion people, which is more than one third of the world's projected population.

6.1 Water on Earth

The amount of freshwater available on Earth today is no more than that was available 2,000 years ago when the Earth's population was less than 3% of its current size. Rising demands of water in agriculture, domestic (municipal) consumption and industry are forcing stiff competition over the distribution of scare water resource, both amongst different regions and types of use. Water is likely to play the same role in world economy in the 21st century that oil played in the 20th century and will be source of conflicts world over to pose a major threat to human security if proper preventive measures are not taken globally. Growing water scarcity has become a very real obstacle to sustainable development.

Water is not only essential for life but predominant inorganic constituent of living matter forming in general nearly three quarters of the weight of living cells. It makes some 5 percent of the body weight of an adult human and can forms as 98% of the mass of certain jellyfish. Organisms that contain relatively small amounts of water are generally in dormant state or show very slow development; seeds and certain invertebrates that live in arid environments are examples. On the other hand high rainfall over a landmass in variably means a large biomass per unit area.

India is a rich country in natural resources. One has to realize the need and importance of water conservation. Conservation and management of water resources was advocated even in ancient times when there was not much pressure on this resource. This is evident from this verse as quoted from the Atharva Veda:

आपो यद् वस्तपस्तेन तं प्रतितपत यो।

स्मान द्वेष्टि यं वयं द्विष्मः।।

—अथर्व0 2: 23: 1

i.e. water of river, well, pond etc, if used and managed efficiently will reduced the intensity of drought and water scarcity. Some such strategies of water conservation/ management are described in his pamphlet. Water is used in everything people do; for irrigation, for industry, for power generation, for navigation, drinking, cooling, waste disposal and recreation.

Water conservation basically aims at matching demand and supply. The strategies for water conservation may be either demand oriented or supply oriented. The strategies may vary depending upon the field of water use domestic, irrigation or industrial. Some of the supply oriented strategies such as creation of storage; long distance transfer and control of water loss through evaporation are generally common to all the fields of water use, whereas the others may be applicable only to specific field.

Storage of water by construction of various water resources projects has been one of the measures of water conservation. A reference from Vrahat Sanhita (550 A.D.) as quoted below describes utility of ponds for effective storage of water.

पाली प्रागणरायताम्बु सुचिरंधत्ते न याम्योन्तरा।

क्ल्लौलैख दारमेति मरूता सा प्रयषः प्रेरितैः।।

तां चेदिच्छति सारदारूमिरपा सम्पातमावांरयेत,

पाशाणदिभिरेव वा प्रतिचयं क्षुश्णं द्विपा वादिभि।

वृहत संहिता– 54: 118

i.e. a pond laid East to West remains water for a long time while one from North to South is spoilt invariably by the waves raised by the winds. To render it stable the walls have to be lined with timber or with stone and the adjoining soil strengthened by stamping and tramping of elephants, horses etc.

For centuries, streams and rivers have provided a convenient place to dump wastes. Today, water pollution comes from many different sources. These include untreated sewage, industrial discharge, leakage from oil storage tanks, mine drainage and mine drainage and pesticides. Water pollution varies in severity in one region to the next depending on the density of urban development, agricultural and industrial practices and the presence or absence of system for collecting and treating the wastewater. The large industrial cities of the world produce huge amount of sewage, both from households and industries, causing problems not only for human health but also for ecosystems.

Industry is also highly water-intensive. For example, making one tonne of steel can consume as much as 300 tonnes of water. Driven by stiffer regulations and the need to cut costs, such water-intensive industries as chemicals, iron and steel, and pulp and paper have made impressive strides in reducing the amount of water in current production processes. Some of these industries have also redesigned production processes, which require less water per unit of production.

Conserving water for personal use in cities (including use by households and municipalities) requires managing both the supply of and demand for water. Much of the municipal water supply is lost before it can reach consumers, leaking out of water mains, pipes, and faucets, or disappearing through illegal tapes. Moreover, when they have convenient access to running water, consumers often use much, more water than they actually need. In India over 40% of the total municipal water supply is lost in transit, before it reaches the consumers. In most cities, nothing more than tightening the joints in the water pipes and fixing leaky community standpipes and household connections could save more than one third of the water that is currently wasted. Many cities could manage the water supply better if they could eliminate illegal water taps. Beside, treated wastewater can be used for purposes where the quality standard requirements are not very high, for example, flushing toilets, washing cars, cleaning floors, gardening, etc.

Since agriculture accounts for nearly 70% of all water withdrawn from rivers, lakes and underground aquifers for human use, large potential for conservation lies with increasing irrigation, efficiencies. Typically, only about 45% of water withdrawn for irrigated agriculture ever reaches the crops. Even when sufficient irrigation water reaches agriculture fields, it can spoil much of the land unless drained properly.

Also, poorly drained irrigation water can raise the groundwater table until it reaches the root zone, thereby water logging and drowning crops. Globally some 80 million hectares of farmland have been degraded by a combination of salinization and waterlogging. Efficient irrigation techniques not only save water but also protect the land. Drip irrigation is one such technique. It consists of a network of perforated piping, usually installed on the surface or just below ground, which delivers water directly to the root zone of crops. This technique keeps evaporation losses low, at an efficiency rate of 95%. Drip irrigation systems can cut water use by an estimated 50% compared with gravity systems.

Another promising conservation technique – low-energy precision application (LEPA) – offers substantial improvements over conventional sprinkler systems that spray water in to air. Instead the low-energy precision application method delivers water to the crops from drop tubes that extend from the sprinkler's arm. When applied together with appropriate water-saving farming techniques, this method also can achieve efficiencies as high as 95%. Since this method operates at low pressure, it results in 20% to 50% energy savings as compared to conventional systems.

Apart from leakage and pilferage, another major reason for large-scale wastage of municipal water in cities is the nominal cost or no cost charged for it. Water should be treated as a commodity and sold to consumers at rates that reflect its value in order to encourage conservation. With higher cost recovery, utilities in developing countries could improve the quality and availability of water even in low-income areas. Water supply projects require huge capital investments, yet cities are faced with diminishing funds for urban water supply to provide for the burgeoning urban populations.

According to a recent analysis of a World Bank financed project, in developing countries, consumers play only about 35% of the costs of supplying water. Recovering a greater percentage of these costs could provide city managers with funds to expand coverage to new areas or to maintain and improve existing facilities. Other measures that could reduce municipal demand include: building codes that require installation of low flush toilets, low water use landscaping – known as xeriscaping – in arid and semi arid areas. Such measures could be adopted in both developed and developing countries.

6.2 Distribution of Water

About 30% of the area of the continents (except Antarctica) is underlain by relatively homogeneous aquifers containing important groundwater reserves. About 19% is endowed with groundwater, some of which is extensive, in geologically complex regions. Half of the continental area contains generally minor occurrences of groundwater that are restricted to near-surface unconsolidated gravels, sands, and rock debris; but these groundwater resources are still sufficient to sustain small to medium-sized population centres. Fifteen percent of the world's land area receives less than 200mm average annual precipitation (c. 200 litres per square metre). In these low rainfall regions there is normally very little groundwater recharge, so groundwater used will not generally be replaced for hundreds–perhaps thousands of years. Extraction in these areas must therefore be considered as "mining" a limited resource, rather than tapping a continuous supply. The geological conditions and hydro-geological characteristics of the rocks are

critical controls on groundwater quantity, quality and flow regime. According to the UN, Planet Earth's mean annual renewable volume of water is 43,000 cubic kilometres. This is about half of all the freshwater contained in all the Earth's natural lakes and about ten times the volume of all man-made reservoirs. Groundwater recharge accounts for about 10,000 cubic kilometres annually, (c. 0.1% of all groundwater resources). Thus, only a tiny proportion of the total volume of groundwater reserves is recharged each year, compared to the large volume in stock (www.yearofplanetearth.org).

Some groundwater systems are non-renewable under current climatic conditions because they formed under much wetter climates that prevailed perhaps 1000 or 10,000 years ago. These groundwater reservoirs are being increasingly "mined" in the arid zones of the world. For example, in the north-eastern Sahara, the Nubian Sandstone Aquifer System underlies an area of more than two million square kilometres in Chad, Egypt, Libya and Sudan, and contains huge amounts of fresh groundwater. It is thought to contain about a hundred times the present annual global water consumption. Giant groundwater deposits of comparable size and limited recharge are thought to exist on nearly all continents, but the amount of groundwater that can be pumped out is unknown. Information about the age, travel times and flow of the water underground, and other features such as chemical characteristics and processes are needed.

Water covers nearly 70% of the globe, but most of it is salt water that fills the oceans. By volume, less than 3% of all the water on earth is freshwater, most of which lies frozen in Antarctica and Greenland in Polar ice and is unavailable to humanity. Less than 1 % of the all water on earth is easily accessible in the form of surface freshwater, found in lakes, rivers and underground in shallow aquifers. This amount of water is regularly renewed by precipitation in the form of rain and snowfall or by melt by glaciers in the mountains and supplemented by dew and fog drip in some locations.

Atmospheric water is about % of the total estimated distribution of world's water resources taking part in the hydrological cycle. It is also estimated that the freshwater resources is about 3%, 77.2% of this is in cold storage, frozen in the ice caps and glaciers. Most of the remaining supply of freshwater *i.e.* 22.4% is groundwater and soil moisture. This leaves only a very small amount of fresh surface water *i.e.* 0.35% contained in lakes and swamps and less than 0.01% in rivers and streams. The freshwater resources with their estimated volumes in km^3 with average residence time in the earth environment are:

Atmospheric water	113,000 (8 to 10 days)
Oceans and open seas	1,370,000,000 (4000 + years)
Freshwater lakes and reservoirs	125,000 (from days to years)
Saline lakes and inland seas	104,000
River channels	1,700 (2 weeks)

Swamps and marshes	3,600 (years)
Biological waters	65,000 (1 week- used by plants)
Moisture in soil and unsaturated zone	65,000 (2 week to 1 year- zones of aeration)
Groundwater (10 days to thousands of years)	4,000,000 to 60,000,000
Frozen water (Glaciers and ice caps)	30,000,000 (10 days to thousands of years)

The total quantity of water on our planet is fixed and its distribution is highly uneven. Almost 95% of the total water present on the earth is chemically bound in to rocks and does not cycle. Of the remainder, about 97.3% is in the ocean, about 2.15 exists as ice in the polar caps and permanent glaciers and the rest is freshwater present in the form of atmospheric water vapour, groundwater, and inland surface water. Thus, less than one percent of the total freshwater precipitates in the hydrological cycle.

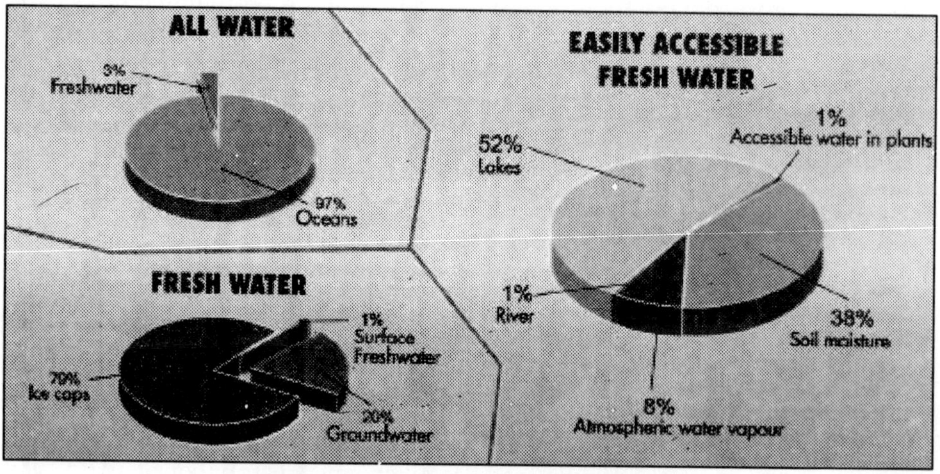

Figure 6.1: Global Distribution of Water
(*Source*: Prakash and Prakash, 2001)

6.3 Water Demand and Crisis

A water crisis that has come about, because rain, as a source of water has been ignored. The potential of rain to meet water demand is tremendous. Theoretically, the average rainfall of 100 mm of rain falling on one hectare of land in arid regions like Jaisalmer can yield up to one million litres of water.

The demand for water is continually growing globally at an accelerated pace. The demand for water in various sectors including domestic use, irrigation, energy and industry etc, during year 1990 and projections four years 2000 and 2025 are given in Table 6.2. The total quantum for water available on the average may be enough to meet all our demands put together. But its availability is highly irregular.

It is not available in places where we want it, at times when we want it and in which we want it – hence the need for conservation.

Table 6.1: Total Estimated Water Resources on Earth

Sl.No.	*Reserves*	*Volume Km³*	*Percentage*
1.	Oceans	1,32,20,00,000	92.200
2.	Ice caps and Glaciers	2,92,00,000	2.150
3.	Underground	41,70,000	0.625
4.	Freshwater Lakes	1,25,000	0.009
5.	Saline Lakes and Inland Seas	1,04,000	0.008
6.	Soil Moisture	67,000	0.005
7.	Atmosphere	13,000	0.001
8.	Rivers	1,250	0.001
	Total	1,35,56,80,250 Km³	100%

Table 6.2: Demands for Various Sectors

Purpose	*Demand (km³)–in the Year*		
	1900	*2000*	*2025*
Domestic use	25	33	52
Irrigation	460	630	770
Energy	19	27	71
Industrial use	15	30	120
Others	33	30	37
Total	552	750	1050
Surface water	362	500	700
Groundwater	190	250	350

Conservation is defined as preservation against loss of waste. Technically conservation of water implies the same meaning in a much wider perspective. Briefly stated it means putting the water resources of the country for the best beneficial use with all the technologies at our command. In other words, surface water running down to sea should be stored to the maximum extant, evaporation and other losses minimized and benefits spread with the sole criteria of maximum benefit to maximum number having due regard to the properties like drinking, irrigation, industrial use, navigation etc.

World's available freshwater supply is not distributed uniformly around the globe throughout the seasons or from year to year. Nearly three quarters of the worlds annual rainfall comes down in areas inhabited by less than one third of the world's population, while two third of the world's population lived in areas receiving only one quarter of the world's annual rainfall.

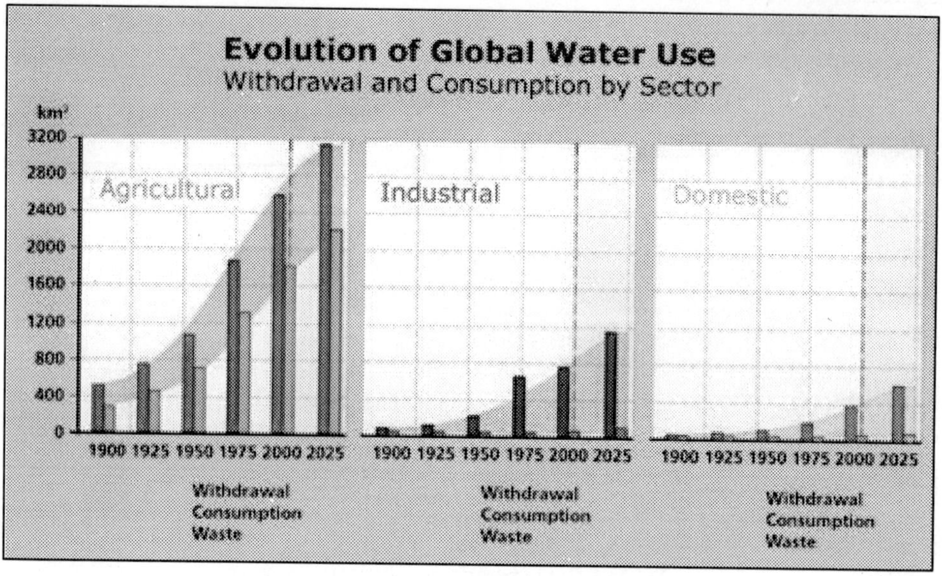

Figure 6.2: Water Requirement for Various Sectors
(*Source*: www.yearofplanetearth.org)

Despite several initiatives taken by Government and public bodies, in 1995 some 20% of the world's population of 5.7 billion people still lacked safe and reliable water supply, while more than 50% were without adequate sanitation system. Today, thirty-one countries having nearly 8% of the total population face water shortages, affecting more than 2.8 billion people, which is more than one third of the world's projected population.

Among the country likely to run short of water in the next 25 years are India, Ethiopia, Kenya, Nigeria, Peru, China, Bangladesh. Now more than 25 countries already facing chronic water problems. Groundwater, which now accounts for 80% of rural and 60% of the urban water supply in India, is depleting at an alarming rate. In fact, today 19 major cities of India already face chronic water shortage.

Many rivers are already dead or dying. All the 13 great river systems in India are endangered. They are fought over and dammed in discriminately by states to provide water for irrigation and industrial use. A typical example of dying river is the Yamuna in Delhi. Because of overuse, there is no original water left in the Yamuna at Delhi. Instead it carries only narrow streams of urban and industrial wastewater. The result of tests conducted by a reputed institute of Delhi on Yamuna water is alarming. For example, the biochemical oxygen demand (BOD), which is a measure of the burden of organic waste from industries and sewage, was found to have a value between 4-75 mg/l in Yamuna water at different sites in Delhi. The permissible level of BOD is 3 mg/l or less for human consumption. Similarly dissolved oxygen, which is essential for aquatic life and measures the amount of oxygen dissolved in water, was found to be much below the required level of 5 mg/l in Yamuna water at most test sites in

Delhi. This indicates that no aquatic life can survive in the Yamuna along its entire stretch in Delhi. The only exception being the water at the Wazirabad barrage, the point where Yamuna enters Delhi.

The public sector has often failed to deliver sustainable water supply and adequate sewage treatment systems. Although officially 70% of Delhi's sewage is treated, in realty, due to the malfunctioning of ill-maintained sewage treatment plants, half that volume comes out as raw sewage. The polluted water, improper sewage disposal, and poor water management combined together cause serious public health problems. The coliform count, which is an indicator of contamination by bacteria coming mainly through domestic sewage, is found to be between 23,000 and 1,40,000 in most of the Yamuna water in Delhi. The upper level of safe level of coliform count is 500. Once again, Yamuna water only at Wazirabad is found to be safe in terms of coliform count, with a value of only 28.

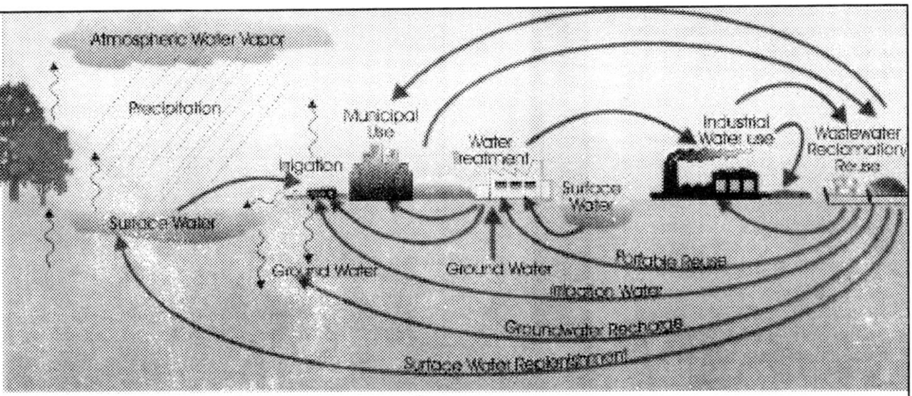

Treatment, reclamation and reuse of water in hydrologic cycle

Figure 6.3: Water Uses and Water Cycle
(*Source*: Prakash and Prakash, 2001)

The world is now facing water crisis of dimensions that no earlier generation has had to face. It may already be late for some water scare countries with rapid population growth to avoid a water crisis unless they take immediate and drastic steps for sustainable management of urban water resources. But a water crisis in the near future can be avoided if appropriate policies and strategies are formulated and acted upon quickly. In this regard, water conservation and its better management are the effective strategies for consideration. To avoid a catastrophe over the long term, it is also important to act to reduce the demand of freshwater by slowing the population growth. Urgent and decisive action must begin now if regional water crisis are to be avoided during the next century. There is an imperative need to change people's attitudes towards water. Water must be an environmental issue at the top of the agenda of Governments, institutions and individuals alike. Because knowledge of water resources and availability is the key to development, access to reliable water data needs to be given high priority by governments. At local level, everyone must use water more efficiently without wasting it. At the national level, especially in water scare-regions with dense population, adopting a watershed or river basin management perspective or harvesting of rainwater is required as an alternative to uncoordinated water-management policies. At the international level, countries that share river basins can design workable policies to manage water resources more equitably.

Ancient techniques of water harvesting, like digging of deep underground chambers for storing rainwater from the wet season for use during the dry season, or placing of long lines of stones along the contours of gently sloping ground to slow runoff and spread the water across a wider area, are prevalent in some societies. These practices when applied together have been known to increase crop production by as much as 50%. Treated urban wastewater from towns and cities, often referred to as 'brown water', may be channeled onto nearby farms for growing vegetables and fruits. In Calcutta, much of the raw sewage is channeled into a system of natural lagoons, where fish are raised. The city's hectares of lagoons produce about 6,000 metric tons of fish a year for urban consumers. However, there is a need to be cautions as unless urban wastewater receives some pre-treatment, either from natural wetlands or sewage treatment plants, it can transfer disease organisms to vegetables and fruits or fish and endanger human health.

Watershed management, which refers to managing an entire land area served by all the rivers and aquifers that drain into a particular body of water, such as a semi-enclosed bay, has assumed great importance as a water conservation measure. A river or a lake must be seen along with its entire watershed and all its physical, chemical, and biological elements, as part of a complex, integrated system. People living in most of these watersheds have radically altered the natural drainage systems around them. Tempering with watershed has proved ruinous for many developing countries, where hillsides, denuded of vegetation, empty tonnes of soil into watercourses every year, causing floods during the wet seasons and suffocating aquatic life during the dry seasons. Deforestation has ruined land and altered climates, causing less rain in some areas. In others, rainwater runs off so fast that little can be collected for use later. Watershed management is generally complicated and can be contentious because watershed boundaries do not coincide with those of political or administrative jurisdictions. It involves many levels of Government and many different communities, each with its own constituencies and concerns. Balancing the multitude of interests involved which is time consuming and troublesome, is the key to the success of watershed management. But if we carried out properly, watershed or river basin management pays multiple benefits.

Every year India gets an estimated rain and snowfall spread over 400 million hectares of land. Even if rain is captured from just one to two percent of India's land area, it can provide a population of one billion as much as 100 litres of water per person per day. Harvesting rainwater is one of the most effective ways of tackling water crisis. The basic principle is to collect the rainwater where it falls, us it and let it seep into the ground. In fact, India has had a long tradition of water harvesting. Aizawl in Mizoram meets most of its water needs through rooftop harvesting. In 1994 a law was promulgated for the residents of Chennai making it mandatory for new buildings to harvest rainwater if they wanted municipal water connection. This has also resulted into a few business ventures devoted exclusively to artificial recharge.

As a result of rainwater harvesting, the coastal aquifers in Tamilnadu are healthy again after several years.

Check dams can be built to store monsoon flows and recharge aquifers. Rainwater can also be stored in wells by channeling it through pipes from the rooftop terrace. Further, percolation tanks may be built to allow slow percolation and collection of rainwater into the ground. It is efficient both for soft and hard ground. Recharge wells or injection wells are just like tube wells but have the provision for pumping in water from the surface after treatment.

According to some projections, the city of Delhi can actually retrieve around 720 million liters of water every year by artificial recharge. Installing a rooftop harvesting system can cost nearly Rs. 100,000 to Rs. 150,000 for a suitably sized apartment. A rooftop recharge can provide nearly 300 litres a minute at the time of good rain. Delhi's master plan for the year 2001 projects per capita need of 400 litres of water every day and this demand can be met by adopting these new ways of harvesting water. Rainwater can not only provide much needed drinking and irrigation water but can also increase groundwater discharge, reduce urban floods and overloading of sewage treatment plants and sea water ingress in coastal areas.

One solution proposed and already being adopted around the world is to set a price of water to cover its 'real costs'; a price which would take into consideration all of the associated services such as treatment, infrastructure, distribution. Placing a price of water might attract big companies to invest in remote areas where their profit margin – because of a high consumption potential – could be high. It would also 'make it possible to reduce the burden of expenditures which up until now were met by public funds.' But what happens when people simply cannot pay? Or when they live in small, poor communities, which don't interest the big water companies? In such cases, voluntary agencies and NGOs can pay a key role. In Cambodia, for example, NGOs have helped create local drilling teams and encouraged self-management of water projects.

Nowadays, due to water crisis, state/centre dispute occur on water requirement like Kavery river in between Tamilnadu and Karnataka; Yamuna–Satluj in between Haryana, Punjab and Delhi; Sharda river in between Nepal and India; Brahmaputra river in between Bangladesh and India.

6.4 Global Supply and Demand for Water

Total Water Supply

Water supply depends on several factors in the water cycle, including the rates of rainfall, evaporation, the use of water by plants (transpiration), and river and groundwater flows. It is estimated that less than 1% of all freshwater is available for people to use (the remainder is locked up in ice sheets and glaciers). Globally, around 12,500 cubic kilometres (km^3) of water are considered available for human use on an annual basis. This amounts to about 6,600 m3 per person/year.

Total Water Demand

Today, the quantity of water used for all purposes exceeds 3,700 km^3 per year.

Agriculture is the largest user, consuming almost two-thirds of all water drawn from rivers, lakes and groundwater. While irrigation has undoubtedly contributed significantly to world agricultural production, it is extremely water intensive. Since 1960, water use for crop irrigation has risen by 60-70%. Industry uses about 20% of available water, and the municipal sector uses about 10%. Population growth, urbanization and industrialization have increased the use of water in these sectors.

Access to Water

The previous section examined the gross supply of and demand for water on a global basis. However, the world's available freshwater supply is not distributed evenly around the globe, throughout the seasons, or from year to year. About three-quarters of annual rainfall occurs in areas containing less than one-third of the world's population, whereas two-thirds of the world's population live in the areas receiving only one-quarter of the world's annual rainfall. For instance, about 20% of the global average runoff each year is accounted for by the Amazon Basin, a vast region with fewer than 10 million people. Similarly, the Congo River and its tributaries account for about 30% of the entire African continent's annual runoff, but the basin contains only 10% of Africa's population. Throughout much of the developing world freshwater supply comes in the form of seasonal rains, such as the monsoons in Asia. Such rains often run off too quickly for efficient use. India, for instance, gets 90% of its rainfall during the summer monsoon season – at other times rainfall over much of the country is very low. Because of the seasonal nature of the water supply (without storage), many developing countries can use no more than 20% of their potentially available freshwater resources.

Water supplies can also vary from year to year, depending on variations in the weather. For example, monsoons may fail in some years. Also natural phenomena such as the El Nino Southern Oscillation can lead to significant differences in rainfall in the southern Pacific Ocean, affecting south-east Asia and south and Central America. (www.parliament.uk/).

6.5 Possible Solutions

It is estimate that more than more than one billion people drink unsafe water and 2.4 billion, that is, 40% of the human race does not have access to adequate sanitation, and 3.4 million people, mostly children, die every year of water-related diseases (more than one million from malaria alone), the majority of them unnecessarily (Prakash and Prakash, 2001).

But the picture is neither gloomy nor hopeless, says the World Health Organization (WHO) in a report on water and sanitation. "Clearly, a problem of this magnitude cannot be solved overnight, but simple, inexpensive measures, both individual and collective, are available that will provide clean water for millions and millions of people in developing countries – now, not in 10 or 20 years," said Dr. Gro Harlem Brundtland, Director-General of WHO. "We do not have the luxury of waiting around for large infrastructure investments to provide water supplies and basic sanitation services for all who need them. It makes no sense, and it is not acceptable, to ignore the immediate priorities of the most needy. "

Optimistic but realistic, the WHO report, entitled *Water for Health – Taking Charge,* strongly urges several basic measures, including purifying water and improving hygiene, as immediate means of improving people's water supply in developing countries. Chlorination, for example, is, "a proven means of ridding water of disease causing microorganisms in piped water," according to the report. Moreover, research carried out at the Centers for Disease Control and Prevention in Atlanta, Georgia, and by the Pan American Health Organisation, supports chlorination in households without piped water, even through the prevailing wisdom is that chlorination should follow and not precede the creation of water and sanitation services. Even in conditions of very poor sanitation and hygiene, where people collect whatever water is available to use for their household water supply, if the water is chlorinated, the water quality is improved microbiologically, and there are statistically significant decreases in diarrhoel diseases.

A good example of successful chlorination can be found in the Maltheves where a national control programme used it in wells. Rainwater was also collected for drinking. Twenty years after the programme started, the entire populations of the Maltheves islands have their own community rainwater collection tanks, and deaths from diarrhea are virtually unknown.

Another easy, small-scale, and cost-effective technique for providing safe water, individually or collectively, is still little known but highly effective solar thermal technique. It is called SODIS and was promoted by the Swiss Federal Institute for Environmental Science and Technology near Zurich. SODIS, an acronym for SOlar water DISinfection, is a nearly cost free system because sunlight costs nothing, and the only other elements are throw-away transparent plastic soft-drink bottles or used mineral water bottles and a black surface. The transparent bottles are filled with water and placed horizontally on a flat surface for about five hours. The disease-causing microorganisms (pathogens) in the polluted water succumb to the killing effect of the ultraviolet light in solar radiation. The process is enhanced when the solar water disinfection is combined with a 'solar thermal water treatment' which makes use of the fact that black colour absorbs light and heat more efficiently. This is accomplished by painting the bottom half of the bottle black or placing it on black-painted corrugated iron or plastic sheets. Field studies in Bolivia, Burkina Fasco, China, Colombia, Indonesia, Thailand and Togo show that the process works.

A third recommendation of the report calls for 'changing behaviour'. Studies of diarrhea show that the simple act of washing hands with soap and water reduces incidence of the disease by 35%. Elsewhere, good water management has almost eradicated guinea worm, a disfiguring, disabling disease which afflicted 50 million people in Africa and Asia in the mid-1900s. By 1999 that number had fallen to below 10,000. But poor irrigation water management, in sharp contrast, had let to a huge spread of schistosomiasis (snail fever) to areas of the world where it never existed before. An estimated 200 million people are infected today with schistosomiasis, according to WHO.

What should be done differently to prevent water-related diseases and to ensure that everyone access to at least some safe water and sanitation? For one thing, says the WHO report, the health sector must get fully involved in water management. It can no longer be left to water management authorities or to environment ministries. Just as major development projects always have environment impact assessment, they should also require health impact assessments. Those involved in water management should be made responsible for its effects on people's health.

During the past 50 years there has been a strong emphasis on medical interventions including, for example, drug therapy, to tackle water-borne and sanitation related diseases and this has tended to reduce the attention and priority given to safe water supply and adequate sanitation. With the increasing resistance to antibiotics, insecticides and standard drugs, health authorities now understand the limitations of a strictly medical approach. That makes safe water and sanitation more important than ever before.

Interlinking of Rivers

A familiar phenomenon in human history is the fight to secure natural resources. This essay shall examine how one country, India, is seeking to solve its water problems via the interlinking of all its rivers. River interlinking is a project that is both visionary and controversial in claiming to cure all of the country's water problems. The goal of the project is to interlink all the country's rivers together. This, allegedly, will provide water to all by diverting water from areas that have a 'surplus' to those that don't and "by preventing the unnecessary spillage of water into the sea." Furthermore, such water transfers would also be aimed at flood control during the erratic monsoon ıson, where floodwaters could simply be diverted away. However, Interlinking at the same time has the potential to become another grand, large-scale project of the sort that creates more problems than it proposes to solve. To assess the risk of this fate, the author provides comparisons with other countries that have undertaken similar projects. These comparisons will show that such large-scale projects typically tend to run into difficulty and usually fail. The goal of this essay is to evaluate why, in spite of these historical precedents against large projects, governments nonetheless tend to follow through with them. Two possible answers come to mind. The first is that governments believe that these are genuinely beneficial projects based on some explicit or implicit calculation of costs and benefits. The second is that government officials are acting self-interestedly, prompted by the influence of special interest groups. The author believes that the answer lies in examining the nature of the benefits and costs involved, and the distribution of these benefits in relation to political power and government self interest. Therefore, in this essay begins with an examination of the cost-benefit procedure, and then examines Interlinking using a qualitative cost-benefit analysis. It follows with possible reasons behind the motivation of Interlinking based on the distribution of costs and benefits and the interests of government leaders, and ends with questioning whether such a project would pass through the legislature regardless (Dev Goel, 2005).

India is on the brink of executing a stupendous hydrological phenomenon of inter basin transfer of water, not of one or two river basins as has been done hither to over different parts of the world, but interlinking of all the major rivers *viz.* Ganges and Brahmaputra and connecting them with the southern rivers of Mahanadi,

Godavari, Krishna and Kaveri. The scheme, after completion will perhaps be a hydrological marvel of the world. The project, at an estimated cost of 100 billion US dollars, on completion is expected to contribute significantly to food production, water, energy and transport needs and to mitigate drought and floods in the country. Many arguments supporting and otherwise of the concept were discussed with scientific basis.

Drinking Water Problems in SAARC Countries

The drinking water problems of SAARC countries were discussed at a special colloquium. The presentations indicate that South Asia remains a region divided-divided between the hopes of the rich and despair of the poor. The rural people in almost all the SAARC countries has still to walk at least 3 – 4 km every day to fetch a pot of drinking water. Contamination from arsenic, fluoride and anthropogenic sources add fuel to fire.

Most of the presentations are focused around a pragmatic approach with peoples' participation on a local scale complemented by proactive government response.

Recommendations

1. While appreciating the existing programmes of water harvesting by government and non-government agencies, it is suggested that a systematic scientific approach should be made mandatory in the selection and the location of the harvesting structures followed by a systematic monitoring of its utility aspects.
2. The persons engaged in watershed management should have an easy access to the data on all aspects of water resources available with government, professional and academic institutions.
3. The basic data may be supplemented with standard field practices, measuring and analysis techniques, models addressed to the local problems.
4. The technocrats have agreed the concept of interlinking of rivers' in principle.

The limitations and impractical propositions raised by the members, as well as the huge costs involved may be subjective for further discussion at governmental level with various sections of people concerned. (www.appliedhydrology.org)

Negative Impacts of River Linking

The Rs. 4000 crore Ken-Betwa river linking project which includes a dam on the river Ken and a 231 km. canal linking it to the Betwa will submerge significant forest areas including parts of the Panna Tiger Reserve. The feasibility report of the project says that the project will submerge some 100 sq. km. in Panna, Chatarpur and Damoh districts – including 19 villages and about 37.5 sq. km. of forestland as well as 30 km. stretch of the Gangau-Shahpura road in Madhya Pradesh. The agreement for the project was recently signed by the Madhya Pradesh and Uttar Pradesh Chief Ministers, Babulal Gaur and Mulayam Singh Yadav, and Union water resources Minister Priya

Ranjan Das Munshi in New Delhi in the presence of Prime Minister Manmohan Singh (PAU, 2005).

Leading scientists of India have a doubt that the interlinking of rivers may affect the local weather, monsoon cycle and contribute to Climate change.

Chapter 7
Groundwater Recharging

Contents

7.1 General

Artificial groundwater recharge is a process by which the groundwater reservoir is augmented at a rate exceeding the augmentation rate under natural conditions of replenishment. In some parts of India, due to over-exploitation of groundwater, decline in groundwater levels resulting in shortage of supply of water, and intrusion of saline water in coastal areas have been observed. In such areas, there is need for artificial recharge of groundwater by augmenting the natural infiltration of precipitation or surface-water into underground formations by methods such as water spreading, recharge through wells, pits, shafts, etc. The choice of a particular method is governed by local topographical, geological and soil conditions; the quantity and quality of water available for recharge; and the technological-economical viability and social acceptability of such schemes (Bhattacharya, 2010).

In most low rainfall areas of the country the availability of utilizable surface water is so low that people have to depend largely on groundwater for agriculture and domestic use. Excessive groundwater pumping in these areas, especially in some of the 91 drought prone districts in 13 states has resulted in alarming lowering of the groundwater levels (CGWB, 2000). The problem has been further compounded due to large-scale urbanization and growth of mega cities, which has drastically reduced open lands for natural recharge. In hard rock areas there are large variations in groundwater availability even from village to village. In order to improve the groundwater situation it is necessary to artificially recharge the depleted groundwater aquifers. The available techniques are easy, cost-effective and sustainable in the long term. Many of these can be adopted by the individuals and village communities with locally available materials and manpower.

Water enters the hydrologic system as precipitation, in the form of rainfall or snowmelt. It leaves the system as stream flow or runoff, and as evapotranspiration, a combination of evaporation from open bodies of water, evaporation from soil surfaces, and transpiration from the soil by plants. Precipitation is delivered to streams on the land surface as overland flow to tributary channels, and in the subsurface as interflow or lateral subsurface flow and base flow following infiltration into the soil.

A portion of the infiltrated water enters the groundwater or aquifer system by passing through the vadose or unsaturated zone, and it exits to the atmosphere, surface water, or to plants. The flowlines deliver groundwater from the highlands towards the valleys, or from the recharge areas to the discharge areas. As the figure also shows, in a recharge area there is a component to the direction of groundwater flow that is downward. Groundwater recharge is the entry to the saturated zone of water made available at the water table surface (Sophocleous, 2004). Conversely, in a discharge area there is a component to the direction of groundwater flow that is upward. Groundwater discharge is the removal of water from the saturated zone across the water table surface. The patterns of groundwater flow from the recharge to the discharge areas form groundwater flow systems, which constitute the framework for understanding recharge processes.

The groundwater can be recharged by different ways, like:

1. *Diversion of runoff to dried-up/defunct wells*: As most of the open wells are dried up, the groundwater can be recharge by using these wells. The technology to diverting run off towards dry wells is cost effective (less than one paisa per litre per filling), eco-friendly and socially acceptable, easy to construct and replicate, useful in harvesting maximum runoff (about 80%), effective utilization of defunct wells for recharge, provide scope for life-saving irrigation during dry spells and helpful in creating awareness on water resource management issues and participatory hydrological monitoring (CRIDA, 2011).
2. *Making a series of farm ponds from ridge to valley*: This is a small water harvesting structures dug in the gullies/waterways where the flow of water exists for considerable period of time. The purpose is: to collect and store

water in a cost effective way, to recharge the groundwater depending on geology, to address drinking water needs of the cattle and to use for supplemental irrigation when stored water is available for longer period.

3. Construction of check dams etc.

7.2 Groundwater Recharging

Groundwater recharging is the replenishment of an aquifer with water from the land surface. It is usually expressed as an average rate of mm of water per year, similar to precipitation. In addition to precipitation, other sources of recharge to an aquifer are stream and lake or pond seepage, irrigation return flow (from both fields and canals), inter-aquifer flows, and urban recharge. In contrast to natural recharge; artificial recharge is the use of water to replenish artificially the water supply in an aquifer. Of all the factors in the groundwater resources evaluation, the rate of recharge is one of the most difficult to derive with confidence. Estimates of recharge are normally subject to large uncertainties and spatial and temporal variability.

Rainwater harvesting contributes in groundwater conservation as well as our daily needs. Taking more attention we can restore it in to groundwater for beneficial uses of human being in future. The artificially restoration of groundwater is generally known as 'Groundwater recharging'. In this process, rainwater should be primarily treated or passed through sediment beds for removal of particle loads by the different methods *viz.* dug well method, bore well method, soakaway and stretch methods etc.

Nowadays, both of the 'cheap and best' processes of water conservation is currently very popular in the field of water technology. In these processes we can save groundwater as well as artificial recharging is also possible.

Advantage and demerits are the two faces of the same coin, so if we have some advantages of these techniques, definitely we have some negative impacts also.

Collection of rainwater by harvesting conserves some amount of groundwater. So this method combats against groundwater depletion. Groundwater recharging helps to raise the groundwater label of the region.

Groundwater recharging has a fear to contamination of groundwater by microbial infection. Different pollutants, present in collected water may reach in the groundwater.

Domestically used Pesticides and heavy metal contents may reach in groundwater if it was in contact with this water. These residue contents migrate immediately towards the exploitation point of groundwater and further may persist in food chain.

Detailed knowledge of geological and hydrological features of the area is necessary for adequately selecting the site and the type of recharge structure. In particular, the features, parameters and data to be considered are: geological boundaries; hydraulic boundaries; inflow and outflow of waters; storage capacity; porosity; hydraulic conductivity; transmissivity; natural discharge of springs; water resources available for recharge; natural recharge; water balance; lithology; depth of the aquifer; and tectonic boundaries.

The upper 3 m of the unsaturated zone is not considered for recharging, since it may cause adverse environmental impact *e.g.* water logging, soil salinity, etc. The postmonsoon depth to water level represents a situation of minimum thickness of vadose zone available for recharge which can be considered vis-a-vis surplus monsoon run off in the area (CGWB, 2000). The artificial recharge techniques inter relate land integrate the source water to groundwater reservoir. Two effects are generated by artificial recharge in groundwater reservoir namely–(a) Rise in water level and (b) increment in the total volume of the groundwater reservoir.

The increasing demand for water has increased awareness towards the use of artificial recharge to augment groundwater supplies. Stated simply, artificial recharge is a process by which excess surface-water is directed into the ground – either by spreading on the surface, by using recharge wells, or by altering natural conditions to increase infiltration – to replenish an aquifer. It refers to the movement of water through man-made systems from the surface of the earth to undergroundwater-bearing strata where it may be stored for future use. Artificial recharging or planned recharging is a way to store water underground in times of water surplus to meet demand in times of shortage.

Some factors to consider for artificial recharge are (O'Hare *et al.*, 1986):

- ☆ Availability of waste water
- ☆ Quality of source water available
- ☆ Quantity of source water available
- ☆ Resultant water quality (after reactions with native water and aquifer materials)
- ☆ Underground storage space available
- ☆ Clogging potential
- ☆ Depth to underground storage space
- ☆ Transmission characteristics of the aquifer
- ☆ Applicable methods (injection or infiltration)
- ☆ Legal/institutional constraints
- ☆ Costs
- ☆ Cultural/social considerations

Advantages of Artificial Groundwater Recharge

Following are the main advantages of artificially recharging the groundwater aquifers:

- ☆ Enhance the dependable yield of wells and hand pumps.
- ☆ No large storage structures needed to store water. Structures required are small and cost-effective.
- ☆ No adverse effects like inundation of large surface areas and loss of crops.
- ☆ Negligible losses as compared to losses in surface storages.

- Improved water quality due to dilution of harmful chemicals/salts.
- No displacement of local population.
- Utilizes the surplus surface runoff which otherwise drains off.
- Reduction in cost of energy for lifting water especially where rise in groundwater level is substantial.

7.3 Recharging of Groundwater: Indian Scenario

The development of technologies in well construction and pumping methods has resulted in large-scale exploitation of groundwater in India and elsewhere. In many parts of India, due to the vagaries of the monsoon, and, in the arid and semi-arid regions, due to the lack or scarcity of surface-water resources, dependence on groundwater has increased tremendously in recent years. Thus, given the possibility of the available groundwater resources to be over-exploited in these areas, it is essential that proper storage and management of available groundwater resources be instituted.

Groundwater replenishment by artificial recharge of aquifers in the arid and semi-arid regions of India is essential, as the intensity of normal rainfall is grossly inadequate to produce any moisture surplus under normal infiltration conditions. Although artificial groundwater recharge methods have been extensively used in the developed nations for several decades, their use in developing nations, like India, has occurred only recently. Techniques such as canal barriers, construction of percolation tanks, and of trenches along slopes and around hills, et cetera, have been used for some time, but have typically lacked a scientific basis (e.g., knowledge of the hydrological, geological and morphological features of the areas) for selecting the sites on which the recharge structures are located.

Various techniques for groundwater recharging have been employed in the states of Gujarat, Maharashtra, Tamil Nadu and Kerala. In Maharashtra, studies were carried out on seven percolation tanks in the Sina and the Main River basins. The average recharge volume of these tanks was 50 percentage points of the capacity of the tank, provided the tank bottom was maintained by removing accumulated sediment and debris prior to the annual monsoon. Best results were obtained from systems located in areas of vesicular or fractured basalt. Canal barriers, where the recharge structure was situated within the course of the canal, was found to be most effective and economical as the surface area exposed to evaporation was, on average, 10 percentage points of that of an average-sized percolation tank. Within canal barriers, the rate of infiltration varied from 50 percentage points to 70 percentage points of the capacity of the reservoir. Infiltration was aided by a connector well linking the phreatic, alluvial aquifer at 6 metre depth with the deeper, confined basaltic aquifer at 63 metre depth, allowing the free flow of water by gravity from phreatic aquifer to the confined aquifer at the rate of 0.19 million cubic metres per year. The water level in the phreatic aquifer, which was saturated due to infiltration from the surface reservoir, was 3 metre below ground level, and the piezometric level in confined aquifer was 30 metre below ground level (Bhattacharya, 2010).

In Tamil Nadu and Kerala, studies were carried out on nine percolation tanks in the semi-arid regions of the Noyil Ponani and Vattamalai River basins. Rates of percolation were as high as 163 mm per day at the beginning of the rainy season, but diminished thereafter mainly due to the accumulation of silt in the bottoms of the tanks. Periodic de-silting, therefore, was determined to be an essential element in the maintenance of these tanks. In contrast, sub-surface dykes of 1 metre to 4 metre in height were found effective in augmenting groundwater resources, particularly in the hard rock areas underlain by fractured aquifers.

Artificial recharge studies using injection wells were carried out in the Ghaggar River basin, using canal water as the primary surface-water source. The injection rate was initially 43.8 litres per second at an injection pressure of one atmosphere. The pressure was increased to two atmospheres after 5 hours, and was kept constant thereafter, although the recharge rate gradually diminished to 3.5 litres per second after a few days. The reproducible recharge rate obtained using the pressure injection system was found to be about 10 times greater than the rate obtained using gravity flow (Bhattacharya, 2010). The increase in pressure during injection was due to clogging of the interstitial spaces within the aquifer, which can be minimised by careful control of the quality of source water. Periodic cleansing of well was also required, whenever the pressure increased beyond six atmospheres or showed a sudden rise. Further studies were conducted on induced recharge from the Ghaggar River using a well field, with individual wells spaced at 200-metre intervals, within 100 metre of the riverbank. As with the injection wells, periodic removal of the clay film deposited in the floodplain above the natural recharge areas of the aquifer was required to improve recharge efficiency.

In Gujarat, artificial recharge studies were carried out in the two areas. In the Central Mehsana area of North Gujarat, artificial recharge was carried out using injection wells, connector wells, and infiltration channels and ponds. Surplus groundwater from the floodplain aquifers of the major rivers in Mehsana area and tail end releases from the Dharoi Canal System were utilised as the water sources. In addition, the injection of water from the phreatic aquifers into the deeper, overexploited aquifers was investigated in the Central Mehsana area. In the coastal areas of Saurashtra, artificial recharge was carried out using injection wells and recharge basins. Storm-water run-off and tail-end releases from the canal system of the Hiran Irrigation Project were used as the water sources, and the studies included an evaluation of the effectiveness of the existing tidal regulators and check dams, designed to limit the extent of seawater intrusion. Also in Gujarat, studies of sub-surface storage were carried out. In the Jamnagar District, naturally occurring basaltic dykes were known to retain groundwater. However, it was also known that the surface soils in the District were not waterlogged. The studies indicated that, while the lower portion of the dyke acted as a barrier to the passage of groundwater, the top few metres of the dyke, composed of fractured basalt, allowed the passage of groundwater through the soil profile, preventing water logging in the aquifer area. This design feature was subsequently incorporated into the specifications of sub-surface dykes.

Elsewhere in India, watershed management practices adopted in some states to minimise soil loss in erosion gullies also contribute to groundwater recharge. Check dams not only store surface-water during portions of the year, but also encourage infiltration into the surface aquifers, providing a threefold benefit to communities (*i.e.*, prevention of soil loss, provision of water for livestock watering and human use, and groundwater recharge). Such works have been implemented on an extensive scale in Gujarat, Maharashtra, Madhya Pradesh, and Rajasthan since 1960.

7.4 Methods of Artificial Recharging

These can be classified as:

- ✰ Spreading Method
  - Spreading within channel
  - Spreading stream water through a network of ditches and furrows
  - Ponding over large area
    (*a*) Along stream channel *viz.* Check Dams/Nala Bunds
    (*b*) Vast open terrain of a drainage basin *viz.* Percolation Tanks
    (*c*) Modification of village tanks as recharge structures.
- ✰ Recharge Shafts
  - Vertical Shafts
  - Lateral Shafts
- ✰ Induced Recharge
- ✰ Injection Wells
- ✰ Improved Land and Watershed Management
  - Contour Bunding
  - Contour Trenching
  - Bench Terracing
  - Gully Plugging

Artificial recharge methods can be classified into two broad groups (*i*) direct methods, and (*ii*) indirect methods (Bhattacharya, 2010):

Direct Methods

(a) Surface Spreading Techniques

The most widely practised methods of artificial recharge of groundwater employ different techniques of increasing the contact area and resident time of surface-water with the soil so that maximum quantity of water can infiltrate and augment the groundwater storage. Areas with gently sloping land without gullies or ridges are most suited for surface-water spreading techniques.

Flooding

The technique of flooding is very useful in selected areas where a favourable hydro-geological situation exists for recharging the unconfined aquifer by spreading the surplus surface-water from canals/streams over large area for sufficiently long period so that it recharges the groundwater body. This technique can be used for gently sloping land with slope around 1 to 3 percentage points without gullies and ridges.

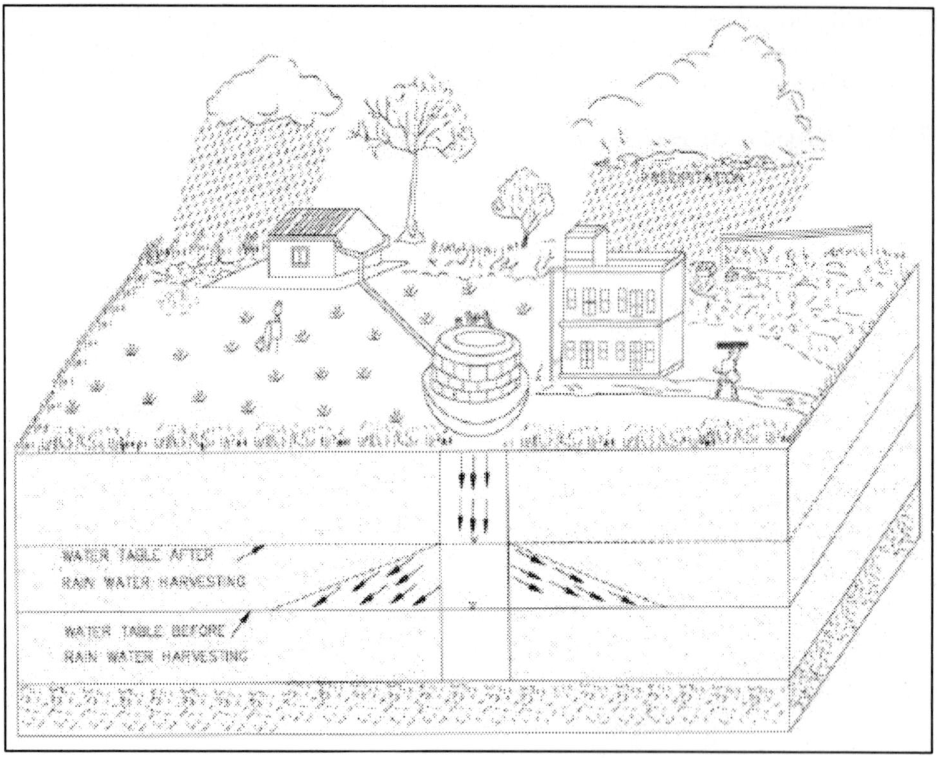

Figure 7.1: Recharge Scheme of Dug Wells through Roof Top Rain Water Harvesting

Recharge Basins

Artificial recharge basins are either excavated or enclosed by dykes or levees. They are commonly built parallel to ephemeral or intermittent stream-channels. The water contact area in this method is quite high which typically ranges from 75 to 90 percentage points of the total recharge area. In this method, efficient use of space is made and the shape of basins can be adjusted to suite the terrain condition and the available space.

Ditches and Furrows

In areas with irregular topography, shallow, flat-bottomed and closely spaced ditches and furrows provide maximum water contact area for recharging water from the source stream or canal. This technique requires less soil preparation than the recharge basin technique and is less sensitive to silting.

Run-off Conservation Structures

In areas receiving low to moderate rainfall, mostly during a single monsoon season, and not having access to water transferred from other areas, the entire effort of water conservation is required to be related to the available "*in-situ*" precipitation.

Gully plugs are the smallest run-off conservation structures built across small gullies and streams rushing down the hill slopes carrying drainage of tiny catchments during rainy season. Usually, the barrier is constructed by using local stones, earth and weathered rock, brushwood, and other such local materials.

Sloping lands with surface gradients up to 8 percentage points having adequate soil cover can be levelled through ***bench terracing*** for bringing under cultivation. It helps in soil conservation and holding run-off water on terraced area for longer duration giving rise to increased infiltration recharge.

Contour barriers involve a watershed management practice so as to build up soil moisture storages. This technique is generally adopted in areas receiving low rainfall. In this method, the monsoon run-off is impounded by putting barriers on the sloping ground all along contours of equal elevation. Contour barriers are taken up on lands with moderate slopes without involving terracing.

In areas where uncultivated land is available in and around the stream-channel section, and sufficiently high hydraulic conductivity exists for sub-surface percolation, small tanks are created by making stop dams of low elevation across the stream. The tanks can also be located adjacent to the stream by excavation and connecting them to the stream through delivery canals. These tanks are called "***percolation tanks***" and are thus artificially created surface-water bodies submerging a highly permeable land area so that the surface run-off is made to percolate and recharge the groundwater storage. Normally, a percolation tank should not retain water beyond February in the Indian context. It should be located downstream of a run-off zone, preferably towards the edge of a piedmont zone or in the upper part of a transition zone (land slope between 3 to 5 percentage points). There should be adequate area suitable for irrigation near a percolation tank.

Stream-channel Modification

The natural drainage channel can be modified with a view to increase the infiltration by detaining stream flow and increasing the stream-bed area in contact with water. This method can be employed in areas having influent streams (stream-bed above water table) which are mostly located in piedmont regions and areas with deep water table (semi-arid, arid region and valley fill deposits). stream-channel modification methods are generally applied in alluvial areas.

Surface Irrigation

Surface irrigation aims at increasing agricultural production by providing dependable watering of crops during gaps in monsoon and during non-monsoon period. Wherever adequate drainage is assured, if additional source water becomes available, surface irrigation should be given first priority as it gives a dual benefit of augmenting groundwater resources.

(b) Sub-Surface Techniques

When impervious layers overlie deeper aquifers, the infiltration from surface cannot recharge the sub-surface aquifer under natural conditions. The techniques adopted to recharge the confined aquifers directly from surface-water source are grouped under sub-surface recharge techniques.

Injection Wells

Injection wells are structures similar to a tube well but with the purpose of augmenting the groundwater storage of a confined aquifer by "pumping in" treated surface-water under pressure. The aquifer to be replenished is generally one that is already over exploited by tube well pumping and the declining trend of water levels in the aquifer has set in. Artificial recharge of aquifers by injection wells is also done in coastal regions to arrest the ingress of seawater and to combat the problems of land subsidence in areas where confined aquifers are heavenly pumped. Due to higher well losses caused by clogging, the injection wells display lower efficiency (40 to 60 percentage points) as compared to a pumping well of similar design in the same situation. The source water and the water in the aquifer should be compatible to avoid any precipitation, causing clogging of well. Injection-cum-pumping wells are more efficient because the well can be cleaned during pumping operation.

Gravity-Head Recharge Wells

In addition to specially designed injection wells, ordinary bore wells and dug wells used for pumping may also be alternatively used as recharge wells, whenever source water becomes available. In certain situations, such wells may also be constructed for effecting recharge by gravity inflow. In areas where water levels are currently declining due to over-development, using available structures for inducing recharge may be the immediately available economic option.

Connector Wells

Connector wells are special type of recharge wells where, due to difference in potentiometer head in different aquifers, water can be made to flow from one aquifer to other without any pumping. The aquifer horizons having higher heads start recharging aquifer having lower heads.

Recharge Shafts

In case, poorly permeable strata overlie the water table aquifer located deep below land surface, a shaft is used for causing artificial recharge. A recharge shaft is similar to a recharge pit but much smaller in cross-section.

Recharge Pits

Recharge pits are structures that overcome the difficulty of artificial recharge of phreatic aquifer from surface-water sources. Recharge pits are excavated of variable dimensions that are sufficiently deep to penetrate less permeable strata. A ***canal trench*** is a special case of recharge pit dug across a canal bed. An ideal site for canal trench is influent stretch of a stream that shows up as dry patch. One variation of recharge pit is a ***contour trench*** extending over long distances across the slope and following topographical contour. This measure is more suitable in piedmont regions and in areas with higher surface gradients. As in case of other water spreading methods, the source water used should be as silt free as possible. In case of hard rock terrain, a canal bed section crossing permeable strata of weathered fractured rock or the canal section coinciding with a prominent lineament or intersection of two lineaments, form ideal sites for canal trench.

Indirect Methods

(a) Induced Recharge

It is an indirect method of artificial recharge involving pumping from aquifer hydraulically connected with surface-water, to induce recharge to the groundwater reservoir. In hard rock areas, the abandoned channels often provide good sites for induced recharge. The greatest advantage of this method is that under favourable hydro-geological situations, the quality of surface-water generally improves due to its path through the aquifer materials before it is discharged from the pumping well.

Collector Wells

For obtaining very large water supplies from river-bed, lake-bed deposits or waterlogged areas, collector wells are constructed. The large discharges and lower lift heads make these wells economical even if initial capital cost is higher as compared to tube well. In areas where the phreatic aquifer adjacent to the river is of limited thickness, horizontal wells may be more appropriate than vertical wells. Collector well with horizontal laterals and infiltration galleries can get more induced recharge from the stream.

Pumping Wells

Induced recharge system is installed near perennial streams that are hydraulically connected to an aquifer through the permeable rock material of the stream-channel. The outer edge of a bend in the stream is favourable for location of well site. The chemical quality of surface-water source is one of the most important considerations during induced recharge

Infiltration Gallery

Infiltration galleries are other structures used for tapping groundwater reservoir below river-bed strata. The gallery is a horizontal perforated or porous structure (pipe) with open joints, surrounded by a gravel filter envelope laid in permeable saturated strata having shallow water table and a perennial source of recharge. The galleries are usually laid at depths between 3 to 6 metres to collect water under gravity flow. The galleries can also be constructed across the river-bed if the river-bed is not too wide. The collector well is more sophisticated and expensive but has higher capacities than the infiltration gallery. Hence, choice should be made by the required yield followed by economic aspects.

(b) Aquifer Modification

These techniques modify the aquifer characteristics to increase its capacity to store and transmit water. With such modifications, the aquifer, at least locally, becomes capable of receiving more natural as well as artificial recharge. Hence, in a sense these techniques are artificial yield augmentation measures rather than artificial recharge measures.

Bore Blasting

These techniques are suited to hard crystalline and consolidated strata. Through hydro-geological investigation, suitable sites are fixed where the aquifer displays limited yield that dwindles or dries in winter or summer months. All the blast holes reach the depth of the aquifer required to be benefited, whether unconfined or confined. All the charges of row or circle are exploded at a time.

Hydro-Fracturing

In many cases, blasting has given indifferent results. Hydro-fracturing is a recent technique that is used to improve secondary porosity in hard rock strata. Hydro-fracturing is a process whereby hydraulic pressure is applied to an isolated zone of bore wells to initiate and propagate fractures and extend existing fractures. The water under high-pressure break up the fissures cleans away clogging and leads to a better contact with adjacent water bearing strata. The yield of the bore well is improved. In hydro fracturing, vertical fractures are initiated which inter-connects aquifers at different levels in addition to extension of existing fractures. This leads to better conditions for artificial recharge. The technique may be applied at bore well sites located in hard crystalline rock or other massive consolidated strata including metamorphic and sedimentary formations. Generally, a bore well giving low or poor yield is treated, but the technique can also benefit other wells.

(*c*) Groundwater Conservation Structures

The water artificially recharged into an aquifer is immediately governed by natural groundwater flow regime. It is necessary to adopt groundwater conservation measures so that the recharged water remains available when needed.

Underground Barriers/Groundwater Dams

A groundwater dam is a sub-surface barrier across stream that retards the natural groundwater flow of the system and stores water below ground surface to meet the demands during the period of greatest need. The main purpose of groundwater dam is to arrest the flow of groundwater out of the sub-basin and increase the storage within the aquifer. The sub-surface barriers need not be only across the canal bed. In some micro watersheds, sub-surface dykes can be put to conserve the groundwater flow in larger area in a valley. Sites have to be located in areas where there is a great scarcity of water during the summer months or there is a need for additional water for irrigation. Technical possibilities of constructing the dyke and achieving large storage reservoirs with suitable recharge conditions and low seepage losses are the main criteria for sub-surface dyke. It directly benefits up-gradient area and hence care should be taken that a large number of users are not located immediately downstream.

Fracture-Sealing Cementation Technique

In many hard rock areas, the groundwater circulation to deeper levels is governed by shear, fault or fracture plane indicated by lineaments. The boreholes located on such zones prove productive but due to dissipation of the limited storage along preferred flow planes, in case of adverse topographical situation, these become dry by the end of winter or summer. Fracture-sealing cementation is a suitable water conservation measure in such situations. This measure can also be used to prevent ingress of saline or polluted water from a known source. The groundwater flow system at the site should be adequately known to establish the outflow direction and the preferred fracture planes along which the flow occurs under the influence of the natural hydraulic gradient. Under certain hydro-geological conditions, a combination of several surface recharge and sub-surface recharge methods and groundwater conservation techniques, can be used in conjunction for optimal recharge of groundwater.

7.5 Advantage of Groundwater Recharging

- ☆ Groundwater recharge stores water during the wet season for use in the dry season, when demand is the highest.
- ☆ The quality of the aquifer water can be improved by recharging with high-quality injected water.
- ☆ Recharge can significantly increase the sustainable yield of an aquifer.
- ☆ Recharge methods are environmentally attractive, particularly in arid regions.
- ☆ Most aquifer recharge systems are easy to operate.
- ☆ The use of aquifers for storage and distribution of water and removal of contaminants by natural cleansing processes that occur as polluted rain and surface-water infiltrate the soil and percolate down through the various geological formations.
- ☆ The technology is appropriate and generally well understood by both the technologists and the general population.
- ☆ Very few special tools are needed to dig wells.
- ☆ In rock formations with high structural integrity, few additional materials may be required (concrete, soft stone or coral rock blocks, metal rods et cetera) to construct the wells.
- ☆ In many river basins, control of surface-water run-off to provide aquifer recharge reduces sedimentation problems.
- ☆ Recharge with less-saline surface waters or a treated effluent improves the quality of saline aquifers, facilitating the use of the water for agriculture.

7.6 Disadvantage of Groundwater Recharging

- ☆ Recharge can degrade the aquifer unless quality control of the injected water is adequate.
- ☆ Unless significant volumes of water are injected in an aquifer, groundwater recharge may not be economically feasible.
- ☆ In the absence of financial incentives, laws, or other regulations to encourage landowners to maintain drainage wells adequately, the wells may fall into disrepair and ultimately become sources of groundwater contamination.
- ☆ There is a potential for contamination of the groundwater from injected surface-water run-off, especially from agricultural fields and road surfaces. In most cases, the surface-water run-off is not pre-treated before injection.
- ☆ The hydrogeology of an aquifer should be investigated and understood before any future full-scale recharge project is implemented. In karst terrain, dye-tracer studies can assist in acquiring this knowledge.

☆ During the construction of water-traps, disturbance of soil and vegetation cover may cause environmental damage to the project area.

7.7 Rainwater Harvesting

It is forgotten that rain is the ultimate source that feeds all these secondary sources and remain ignorant of its value. Water harvesting means to understand the value of rain, and to make optimum use of rainwater at the place where it falls. Rivers, lakes and groundwater are all secondary sources of water while rain is the first form of the water that we know in the hydrological cycle, hence is a primary source of water for us.

Water harvesting refers to collection and storage of rainwater and also other activities aimed at harvesting surface and groundwater, prevention of losses through evaporation and seepage and all other hydrological studies and engineering interventions, aimed at conservation and efficient utilization of the limited water endowment of physiographic unit such as a watershed (CSE, 2001).

Water harvesting is the activity of direct collection of rainwater. The rainwater collected can be stored for direct used or can be recharged into the groundwater.

It's a water collection method is normally 'Wealth from waste' formula based technique. In this technique we collect the available surface rainwater form the suitable catchments areas. After collection the water, we can utilize it in minor daily uses, but if we don't do so, all water will be drain away in different water bodies by run-off process or get percolate a little or more – depending upon the soil texture of the region. So we can utilize the rainwater as an extra resource for minor daily purposes. Rainwater harvesting as an excellent tool of sustainable development may be an alternative of water supply in emergency. Consumption of rainwater has a great advantage in to groundwater conservation, as well as has some limitations or negative aspects related to human health hazards, water quality, groundwater contamination, water supply and sanitation.

Traditional rainwater harvesting, which is still prevalent in rural areas, was done in surface storage bodies like lakes, ponds, Kunds, Kul irrigation, bamboo method, irrigation tanks, temple tanks etc. In urban areas, due to shrinking of open space, groundwater recharging is the best method, depending upon the soil texture.

In ancient times, houses in parts of western Rajasthan were built so that each has a rooftops was directed into underground tanks. This system can be seen even today in all forts, places and houses of the region. Underground baked earthen pipes and tunnels to maintain the flow of water and transport it to distance places, are still functional at Burhanpur at Madhya Pradesh, Golkunda and Bijapur in Karnatka, and aurangabad in Maharashtra (Ruhela *et al.*, 2005).

Rainwater

Rainwater harvesting is a traditional method for collecting the water without any more expense or investment.

Collected water may be used in:

1. Clothes washing/floor washing.
2. Vehicle washing.
3. In toilet flushes.
4. In flowerpots.
5. Cattle bathing.
6. Horticulture.
7. Aquaculture etc.

Pits, tanks, small ponds, kunds of different size may be used for storage and collection purposes. We directly collect the rainwater from the roofs, hut shades and other catchments area depending upon the topography of the region. Different types of contamination agents and pollutants may occur in that water, so this water is not for direct consumption purpose. This rainwater may contain:

1. Dust particles.
2. Fungus spores.
3. SO_2.
4. Allergents.
5. Other pollutants present in air.
6. Surface contamination (silt, dust)

The annual rainfall over India is computed to be 1170 mm (46 inches). This is higher compared to the global average of 800 mm or 32 inches (Pisharoty, 1986). Because of high intensities and short duration of heavy rain, most of the rain falling on the surface tends to flow away rapidly, leaving very little water for the recharging of groundwater. This makes most parts of India experience lack of water even for domestic uses.

Ironically, even Cherrapunji, which receives about 11000 mm of rainfall annually, suffers from acute shortage of drinking water. This is because the rainwater is not conserved and allowed to drain away. Thus it does not matter how much rain we get, if we don't capture or harvest it. This highlights the need to implement measures to ensure that the rain falling over a region is tapped as fully as possible through water harvesting, either by recharging it into the groundwater aquifers or storing it for direct use.

7.8 Harvesting Potential

The total water amount, received in the form of rainfall over an area is called the rainwater endowment of the area. Out of this, the amount that can be effectively harvested is called the water harvesting potential.

$$\text{Water harvesting potential} = \text{Rainfall (mm)} \times \text{collection efficiency}$$

The collection efficiency accounts for the fact that all the rainwater falling over an area cannot be effectively harvested, because of evaporation, spillage etc. Factors like runoff coefficient and first flush wastage are taken into account when estimating the collection efficiency.

Consider a building with a flat terrace area of 100 sq. m. The average annual rainfall in Delhi is approximately 600 mm (24 inches). Simply, this means that if the terrace floor is assumed to be impermeable, and all the rain that falls on it is retained without evaporation, then in one year, there will be rainwater on the terrace floor to a height of 600 mm.

Area of plot	= 100 sq. m. (120 sq. yd.)
Height of rainfall	= 0.6 m (600 mm or 24 inches)
Volume of rainfall	= Area of plot × Height of rainfall
Over the plot	= 100 sq. m. × 0.6 m.
	= 60 cu. m. (60000 litres)

Assuming that only 60% of total rainfall is harvested effectively,

Volume of water harvested = 36000 litres (60000 litres × 0.6)

This volume is about twice the annual drinking water requirement of a family having five members. The average daily drinking water requirement per person is ten litres (IS:1172).

Area of catchment's (sq. m.) × Amount of rainfall =
Volume of water received (cu. m.)

There are some factors, which are essential for knowledge and design of storage tank. Depending upon area, these may vary place-to-place or time-to-time. Design parameters for tanks are average annual rainfall, size of the catchment and drinking water requirement.

If the system has to be designed for meeting drinking water requirement of a family of five members living in a building with a rooftop area of 100 sq. m. Average annual rainfall in the region is 600 mm (average annual rainfall is 611 mm in Delhi). Daily drinking water requirement per person is 10 litres for drinking and cooking. We shall first calculate the maximum amount of rainfall that can be effectively harvested from the rooftop, whereas, following details are available:

Area of catchment (A) = 100 sq. m.

Average annual rainfall = 611 mm (0.61 m)

Runoff coefficient (C) = 0.85

Annual water harvesting potential from 100 sq. m. roof

= A × R × C

= 100 × 0.6 × 0.85

= 51 cu. m. (51000 litres)

The tank capacity has to be designed for the dry period, means the period between the two consecutive rainy seasons. With a monsoon extending over four months, the dry season will of 245 days. Drinking water requirement for the family in dry season:

$= 245 \times 5 \times 10$

$= 12250$ litres

The tank should be built 20 % larger than required, *i.e.*, 14700 litres, as a safety factor. This tank can meet the basic drinking water requirement of a family having five members for the dry period.

7.9 Runoff Coefficient

Runoff coefficient is a factor, which accounts for the fact that all the rainfall falling on a catchment cannot be collected. Some rainfall will be lost from the catchment by evaporation and retention on the surface itself.

Table 7.1: Runoff Coefficient for Various Surfaces (CSE, 2001)

Type of Catchment	*Coefficients*
Roof catchments –	
✰ Tiles	0.8 – 0.9
✰ Corrugated metal sheets	0.7 – 0.9
Ground surface covering –	
✰ Concrete	0.6 – 0.8
✰ Brick pavement	0.5 – 0.6
Untreated ground treatment –	
✰ Soil on slope less than 10 per cent	0.0 – 0.3
✰ Rocky natural catchments	0.2 – 0.5

Conclusion

Frequently maintenance of artificial recharge structures is essential because infiltration capacity is rapidly reduced because of silting, chemical precipitation, and accumulation of organic matter. In the case of injection wells and connector wells, periodic maintenance of the system consists of pumping and/or flushing with a mildly acidic solution to remove encrusting chemical precipitates and bacterial growths on the well tube slots. By converting the injection or connector wells into dual-purpose wells, the time interval between one cleansing and another can be extended, but, in the case of spreading structures, except for sub-surface dykes constructed with an overflow or outlet, annual de-silting is necessary.

Artificial recharge of groundwater should be licensed and controlled by competent authorities according to specific requirements laid down in an appropriate permit system that should be flexible to adapt to site-specific conditions. The question of ground-water exploitation should be clarified on a case-by-case basis, taking into account all relevant aspects, including ecological ones. Authorisation for artificially recharging the aquifer should be granted only, if the hydro-geological situation, environmental condition and the recharge-water quality permit injection, percolation or infiltration of water by artificial means into aquifers for storage and retrieval. Appropriate measures should be taken to combat saline water encroachment into coastal aquifers. The cost of a recharge scheme, in general, depends upon the degree of treatment of the source-water, the distance over which the source-water needs to be transported, and the stability of the recharge structure, and resistance to clogging and silting.

Chapter 8
Groundwater Modeling

Contents

In the last two decades, the rapid growth of industrialization and urbanization has created negative impacts on the environment. Due to industrial, municipal and agricultural wastes containing pesticides, insecticides, fertilizers residues and heavy metals with water; groundwater has been polluted (Sastry *et al.* 1999). Groundwater is used for domestic supply, industries, and agriculture in most part of the world as it is a replenishable resource and has inherent advantage over surface water.

There has been a tremendous increase in the demand of freshwater due to growth in population, advanced agriculture practices and industrial usages (Bachmat, 1994). Industries are discharging their metal and hazardous substances containing effluents in to freshwater with out any adequate treatment (Canter, 1987). The seepage of effluents posed serious threat to the groundwater resources (Groff, 1993).

In water cycle, rainfall is the main source that provides water for all living organisms in different ecosystems. Water from rain, enters in to soil and then flow vertically and down slope through the soil profile. Water flow may vary at place to place according to the physical conditions of soil of a particular area. Flow of heavy metals and groundwater movement beneath the earth may be measured by using various forms of formulas according to the physico-chemical and geographical conditions of soil and soil profile of the particular area.

8.1 Movement of Groundwater

Contamination of groundwater is more complex than surface water pollution mainly because of difficulty in its timely detection and slow movement, which requires special expertise to predict the path and rate of groundwater movement.

Generally, it is believed that movement of groundwater flows according to ground elevation or the general topography of the area. Groundwater in its natural state is invariably moving and this movement is governed by established hydraulic principle and can be expressed by Darcy's Law. According to Darcy's Law "flow rate through porous media is proportional to the head loss and inversely proportional to the length of the flow path".

$$Q = \frac{K(h_1 - h_2)}{L}$$

where,

Q: Specific discharge,

K: Hydraulic conductivity,

h_1-h_2: Head loss and

L: Distance of travel by groundwater.

In addition the complex geo-chemical reactions taking place in the subsurface between myriad contaminants and earth materials are not always well-understood. Ideally speaking contamination should be prevented from occurring. After several contaminants are found in groundwater, a decision must be made on whether to rehabilitate the aquifer or find alternative groundwater resources. So, groundwater must be managed and protected carefully for the most beneficial use in the future.

8.2 Groundwater Flow Pattern

Geology offers control on the rate of groundwater movement. The size of the pores and their relative connectivity (permeability) determine the rate at which water moves in to, though and out of aquifer.

The flow of groundwater in saturated soil is described well by Darcy's law, which, for steady flow in one dimension (linear), may be given by (Wainwright and Mulligan, 2004):

$$q = -K\frac{dH}{dx}$$

where,

q is the discharge per unit area, K is the hydraulic conductivity; H is the hydraulic head and x is the distance in the direction of flow.

To make q positive, a minus sign appears before K. this correction is necessary because water flows down the hydraulic gradient, *i.e.* it flows along a negative gradient from areas of higher H to areas of lower H (Fetter, 1994).

Richards Equation

The water flow through unsaturated soil also be described by modified Darcy's law, where K is assumed to be a function of water content (θ), *i.e.*:

$$q = -K(\theta)\frac{dH}{dx}$$

L.A. Richards was the first person to realize that the Darcy's law could be applied to unsaturated flow, so the equation may be called as Richards equation.

Where flow is unsteady such as in natural conditions, water content will change and so will K. Thus, in unsaturated flow, unlike saturated one, K is time-variant, except for some very simple cases.

The simplest of this class of model ignore or greatly simplify flow in the unsaturated zone and assume that flow in the soil is parallel with the soil surface, and that the hydraulic gradient at any point with in the saturated zone is equal to the slope (Beven, 2000). Thus, the Darcy's law becomes:

$$Q = Kh\sin\beta$$

Where, Q is the discharge per unit width of hill slope in the down slope direction, h is the depth below the water table measured orthogonally to the impermeable plane at the base of the soil and b is the slope of the plane and soil surface (Masters, 1998).

Groundwater moves more quickly in coarse sand sometimes as much as several meters per day while in case of clay which are generally impermeable the movement may seldom move not more than an inch per year (CPCB, 2003).

The general direction of groundwater flow can be established on the basis of the local topography using topographical maps or aerial photos and the presence of stream or river which act as groundwater discharge boundaries. The near surface groundwater flow generally follow surface drainage pattern. If the flow direction can not be established, three small diameter wells are temporarily installed in the aquifer (CPCB, 2003). Relative water level in these wells reveals the direction of flow. Other methods of delineating groundwater flow pattern include electromagnetic induction, earth resistivity survey, radioactivity and temperature logging.

8.3 Darcy and Linear Velocity/Flow Velocity

If we combine the usual relationship between flow rate, velocity and cross section area, than:

$$Q = Av$$

With Darcy's law we can calculate velocity,

$$\upsilon = \frac{Q}{A} = \frac{KA(dH/dL)}{A} = K\frac{dH}{dL}$$

Where, v is known as the Darcy velocity, not a real velocity because much of the cross section area is made up of solids, the actual area through which all of the flow takes place is much smaller, so the real groundwater velocity is considerably faster than the Darcy velocity (Masters, 1998). A represent the cross section area, and A' being the area of voids filled with water, than v' be the actual average linear velocity, as

$$Q = A\upsilon = A\upsilon'$$

$$\upsilon' = \frac{Q}{A'} = \frac{AL\upsilon}{A'L} = \frac{Total\ volume \times \upsilon}{Void\ volume}$$

The actual average linear velocity through the aquifer is the Darcy velocity divided by porosity, so:

$$\upsilon' = \frac{Darcy\ velocity}{Porosity} = \frac{\upsilon}{\eta}$$

$$\upsilon' = \frac{K(dH/dL)}{\eta}$$

Where, v' is the average linear velocity of groundwater, v is Darcy velocity and η is the porosity of soil medium, which is the important physical factor may influence the groundwater movement.

Retardation Factor

If a contamination moves at the same speed as the groundwater, some contaminants are absorbed on the soil particles, which reduce the overall solute flow rate relative to that of the groundwater itself (Masters, 1998). This reduction in speed is called the retardation factor,

$$\text{Re}\,tardation\ factor = R = \frac{\upsilon'}{\upsilon_s} \geq 1$$

Where, v' is the average linear velocity of groundwater, v_s is the average linear velocity of retarded constituent.

8.4 Flow of Heavy Metals in Unsaturated Soils

Equations for the Flow Model

The flow model is formulated using Richards equation for unsaturated movement of water in one dimension with the inclusion of root water uptake. The equations governing vertical water movement are

$$q = -K\left(\frac{\partial \psi}{\partial z} - 1\right) \qquad (1)$$

$$\frac{\partial \theta}{\partial t} = \left(\frac{\partial q}{\partial z} - S\right) \qquad (2)$$

where, θ is water content by volume (cm^3/cm^3), q is the water flux (cm/h), S is the sink term for root water extraction (cm^{-1}), K is the hydraulic conductivity (cm/h), Ψ(<0) is the soil matrix potential (cm), z is the vertical coordinate direction taken positive downward, and t is time (h) (Nedunuri *et al.*, 1995). The two equations can be combined to yield the Richards equation in terms of ss as

$$\frac{\partial \theta}{\partial t} = -\frac{\partial}{\partial z}\left[K(\theta)\left(\frac{\partial \psi}{\partial z} - 1\right)\right] - S(\psi) \qquad (3)$$

where, the sink term depends on S which controls the water availability to roots. The K(θ) and Ψ(θ) are non-linear functions, and have been described by Brooks and Corey. The pore water velocity at any depth is given by

$$v(z) = \frac{q(\theta)}{\theta} \qquad (4)$$

The equation describing the root water uptake is expressed as

$$S(\psi) = \alpha(\psi)\, S_{\max} \qquad (5)$$

where, α(Ψ) determines the proportion of the maximum possible root extraction rate Smax for a particular value Ψ. The expression for α(Ψ) is given as

$$\alpha(\psi) = \exp\left[-\delta\,|\psi - \psi_b|\right], \psi \le \psi_b \qquad (6)$$

where, Ψb is the air entry pressure head. Equation 6 indicates an exponential reduction in rate of availability of water to the roots as the soil becomes drier.

8.5 Equation for the Transport Model

The equation describing the movement of contaminants is:

$$\frac{\partial C_k}{\partial t} = \frac{\partial}{\partial z}\left[D\frac{\partial C_k}{\partial z}\right] - \frac{\partial}{\partial z}\left(v(z)C_k\right) + R_k \qquad (7)$$

k =1, 2,...Nc

where, Ck is the concentration of the k-th component at any spatial location z at any time t, D is the dispersion coefficient, and Rk is the chemical source/sink term representing the changes in aqueous component concentrations (www.engg.ksu.edu).

8.6 Groundwater Monitoring Techniques

Groundwater monitoring involves various investigations prior to the actual assessment of groundwater quality. The topography, geology, soil profile, aquifer characteristics, source of pollution, land-use pattern and above all the extent of groundwater development are some of the important pre-requisites to decide the scheme of groundwater monitoring. For representative information on groundwater quality the first information to look for is the movement of groundwater.

Monitoring of groundwater quality involves collection of representative sample and simultaneous collection of hydro-geological information or data about the location of sampling station. The sampling and hence the groundwater quality data may adversely affect if one or more of the following factors are not appropriately looked into (CPCB, 2003).

1. Samples are not taken at appropriate time intervals, seasonally and at improper locations
2. Sample was taken from stagnant water in the open dug well or suddenly in case of bore well without removing the casing storage effect. The error can be largely overcome if three to ten well bore volumes are removed, and in case of hand pumps sufficient water is pumped out before taking the sample.
3. Contamination due to entrained sediment.
4. Hydraulic characteristics of the soil formation near the screen, resulting in possible dilution of the contaminant.
5. Release of carbon dioxide during pumping and hence increase in pH which may cause many metallic ions to come out of solution.
6. The sample preservation is not properly done and analyzed without considering the parameter- specific prescribed period of retention time.

8.7 Concept of Groundwater Modeling

According to many instances of groundwater monitoring, the ability to predict how the contaminant plume will behave in future can be done by using the mathematical modeling techniques to estimate the spread of a contaminant and its strength at any point in the plume. A model is a device that represents an approximation of a field situation and provides a frame work for synthesizing field information and for testing of ideas about how the system works.

The concept of groundwater modeling is chiefly based on following factors:

1. Advection of the constituent with the water flowing through the aquifer.
2. Dispersion of the constituents.
3. Characteristics of recipient medium.
4. Sources of pollution.

Water chemistry data also provided a more reliable spatial measure of hyporhiec/groundwater interface seasonal fluctuation (Fraser and Williams, 1998)

The steps to build the model are shown in the structure given below:

Factors > Processes > Model > Prediction > Assessments

Table 8.1: The Basic Step of Groundwater Monitoring and Modeling

Step 1 *Factors*	*Step 2* *Processes*	*Step 3* *Model*	*Step 4* *Prediction*	*Step 5* *Assessments*
Hydrology/ Hydraulics	Dispersion/ Dilution	Attenuation and Convection	Contaminant concentrations in space and time	Comparison of model results with field data.
Physical and chemical soil characteristics	Precipitation			
	Adsorption			
Waste leachate properties.	Biological activity etc.			

Chapter 9
A Case Study: Panipat

Contents

9.1 Industrial Area and Research Protocol

9.1.1 History of Panipat

The Shivalik range rises in the North and the ancient Aravalli hills slope in the South. Haryana displays four main geographical features:

The Shivalik Hills: Altitude varying between 900 to 2300 meters. These hills are the source of the rivers like Ghaggar, Tangri and Markanda, parts of Panchkula, Ambala and Yamunanagar districts are in these hills.

The Ghagger-Yamuna plain: This is divided into higher and lower plain. The higher one is called 'Banger' and the lower one called 'Khadar'. The alluvium plain is made up of sand, clay, silt and hard calcareous balls like gravel, locally called 'Kanker'.

A Semi-Desert Sandy Plain: These areas border the state of Rajasthan and include the districts of Sirsa and parts of Fatehbad, Hissar, Bhiwani and Mahendargarh district.

Aravalli Hills: This mountain range is 20 million year old, older than the Himalayan range. It is dry area with uneven, irregular landscape (www.indiatravelogue.com).

The river Yamuna flows along the Eastern boundary of the state. The ancient and some say mythical Saraswati River may flow throw Haryana but there are no traces of it evident today. The river Ghagger is a seasonal river, which flows from the outer Himalayas and transverses the district of Panchkula, Ambala and Hissar before it flows into Rajasthan and is absorbed by that arid land.

9.1.2 Background

Panipat District has significant placed in International Market for Handloom Production. Darri, Carpet Mat, Table Cover, Bed sheet, Bed Cover, Curtain etc. are export to Canada, Japan, Germany and Australia. In addition to the above Panipat city is the biggest centre of "Shoddy Yarn" in the World. Blankets prepared through Handloom and Power loom are sent to soldier. The sub division Samalkha of this district is famous for Foundry of Agriculture instruments. In this way, this district, which is continuously developing on the base of industry, has unlimited employment ness. Not only from Haryana but Businessman, Engineer, unemployed worker artist

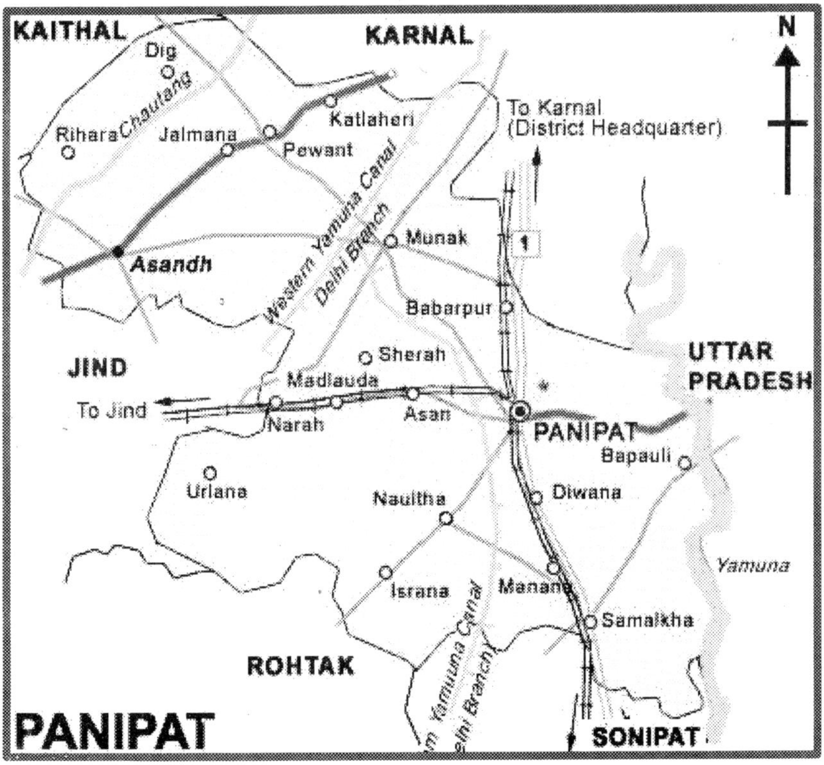

Figure 9.1: Panipat District of Haryana

***Source*: haryanaonline.com**

Weavers and labour from other state of India visits here in search of employment and settled here permanently. Panipat city (District Panipat) situated 90 KM from Delhi (National Highway No.-1) on *'Sher Shah Suri Marg'* has a significant importance in the history. Panipat city is famous in India by the name of "**City of Weaver**".

Panipat is situated on the bank of river Yamuna, it lies between 29' 09' 50" and 29' 50' 32" North latitude and 76° 31' 15" and 77° 12' 45" East longitude and its height is 255 meters above sea level. Here the three historical battles of Panipat were fought. Karnal, Sonipat, Jind, Kaithal and Uttar Pradesh bordered this district. Population of Panipat city is 261874 approximately. Panipat town is located on the national highway no.1 about 90 km toward north of Delhi has a population of about 0.27 million. Average population density of the urban area of Panipat city is 25,278 per sq. km.

Geographically, Haryana is situated between 27° 37' to 30° 35' North latitude and between 74° 28' to 77° 36' longitude on the globe. Uttar Pradesh borders Haryana on the East, Punjab on the West, Himachal Pradesh on the North, and Delhi and Rajasthan on the South direction. In the geographical conditions, Haryana is agriculture based green state of the India. The state of Haryana came in 1966, when it was curved out of Punjab. Haryana ranks as one of India's most prosperous states among all other states.

Demographically, the population of Haryana, according to the 2001 census, is 2,10,83,000, with 1,13,28,000 males and 97,55,000 females. The population density is 477 people/sq km. Hindus are about 80% of the population, Sikhs 16%, Muslims 4% and Christians 0.10% (wikipidia.org, 2006).

Topographically, Ground is flat but gently slopes towards south-east. Water table is 5 m below G.L. (Ground Level). Soil is almost sandy and alkaline in nature. The area of town is 10.8 sq. kms. Regarding the atmosphere and temperature, in summer, warmer and in winter the temp goes up to Minimum 4.4°C in December, January, However in summer the temperature goes up to 42.4°C in June (www.haryanaonline.com).

Geographical Position of Site

- ☆ Latitude- 29° 09' 50" and 29° 11' 50" N
- ☆ Longitude- 76° 31' 15" and 77° 12' 45" E
- ☆ Altitude- 255 meters above sea level.

9.1.3 Status of Industries in Area

Panipat is a famous city of handloom business in India and abroad also. Industrial scenario and status of Panipat city and salient features of the industries in the Panipat are given below (Verma and Kharat, 2000):

- ☆ Town has three major projects under public sector–IOC Refinery, NFL and Thermal Power Station.
- ☆ Biggest Centre in the Country for producing Shoddy Yarn and low priced blankets.

- ☆ Biggest Centre in the Country engaged in Export of Cotton Durries, Made-ups, Throws and Mats and larger consumer of rags for re-processing.
- ☆ Panipat Town is a very old supplier of Barrack Blankets to the Armed Forces.
- ☆ Samalkha, a smaller town near Panipat, is known for the foundry work and supply of Agriculture machinery to nearby U.P. area.
- ☆ A town has infrastructures such as Rail, Road and ICDS (Inland Container Depots) best suited to Industry and Export.

Study Area

Panipat district of Haryana was selected on the basis of existence of a large number of textile industries, those results in huge amount of effluents. Panipat city is well known for the textile industries. Binjhol village is located in the south-west of Panipat city. A large number of dye units have come up along the both side of the Jatal road in very close proximity of Binjhole village. Due to the effluent being discharge by textile industries, water used to dry down in the *Nala* itself but with the dramatic rise in the dying units, huge quantities of the effluents are transported through this *Nala* that ultimately joins the village pond.

Figure 9.2: Satellite Image Showing Industrial Area and Panipat City

A pond (12 hac), attached with a effluent drain is situated near this village and collected complete treated and non-treated effluents from the textile industries. As farmers of the area complained that the main source of the groundwater pollution due to seepage from the village pond that is being regularly fed by the effluents from the dyeing industries. Samples were collected from Binjhole village pond, textile effluents, drain and irrigated agricultural fields. Control site was selected in non-industrial area, 10 km. far from experimental sampling site.

9.1.4 Sampling Programme and Sampling Sites

Keeping in mind to assess the effect of textile industrial effluent on the quality of the groundwater and soil characteristics, the following routine sampling and analysis programme was devised:

Collection of samples	:	Monthly [Between 20th -22nd of each month]
Time of sample collection	:	Between 9.00 A.M. to 11.00 A.M.
On site analysis	:	Temperature, pH, DO and free CO_2
Analysis within 24 hours	:	COD and physico-chemical parameters
Analysis within 15 days	:	Heavy metals
Calculation of data	:	After completion of analytical work

Textile industrial effluent, Groundwater and soil samples were collected monthly from different sampling stations for the study of the status of groundwater and agricultural soils, *i.e.*

(A) Effluent Drain on Jatal Road, (EXP)
(B) Effluent Drain End with Pond, (EXP)
(C) Binjhole Village, (EXP)
(D) Agricultural fields, (EXP) and
(E) Control 10 Km Jatal Road, (C)

The samples were collected from the selected sampling sites during the month of April 2005 to March 2007 in morning hours (from 9.00 am to 11.00 am) as follows:

(A) Experimental Sampling Site

(i) Water Samples

1. Effluent from textiles outlet [EF]
2. Tube wells/Hand pumps of the area [TW/HP]
3. Surface water from pond [SW/PW]

(ii) Soil Samples

1. Effluent drain sediment [EFS]
2. Pond bottom sediment [PDS]
3. Agricultural soil [AGS]

(B) Control Sampling Site

Water and soil samples were collected from two sampling points of control, located 10 km distance in non industrial area along with Jatal Road at Panipat as follow:

1. Groundwater from tube well of 80 ft [GWC]
2. Agriculture soil [AGSC]

Parameters have studied:

(*a*) Physico-chemical parameters of Textile effluents, surface water and groundwater: *Temperature, pH, Total solids, Total suspended solids, Total dissolved solids, Electrical conductivity, Dissolved oxygen, Free-CO_2, Biochemical oxygen demand (BOD), Chemical oxygen demand (COD), Total alkalinity, Calcium (Ca^{++}), Magnesium (Mg^{++}), Potassium (K^+), Sodium (Na^+) Chloride (Cl^-)*

(*b*) Physico-chemical parameters of agriculture soils, and sediments: *Temperature, Water holding capacity, Bulk density, Soil moisture, pH, Electrical conductivity, Chloride, Potassium (K^+), Sodium (Na^+)*

(*c*) Trace heavy metals in Textile effluent, surface water, groundwater, effluent sediment soil, pond sediment soil and agriculture soil: *Cadmium (Cd), Copper (Cu), Iron (Fe), Manganese (Mn), Nickel (Ni), Lead (Pb), and Zinc (Zn)*

Chemicals and Glass Wares

The chemicals, used in the present investigation were procured by E. Merck India, S.D fine chemicals and B.D.H., India of analytical grade. All the glassware used was of corning grade, manufactured by Borosil India Ltd. All the glassware and Jeri canes were cleaned or washed with soda and chromic acid and rinsed with double distilled water 2-3 times.

Instruments

Following instruments were used during the study:

Sl.No.	*Name of Instruments*	*Manufacturers*
1.	BOD incubator	Tasco
2.	Spectrophotometer	Besto/Elico
3.	Electronic balance	Roy Electronic
4.	Conductivity meter	Tasco Chipset
5.	COD Assembly	–
6.	Atomic absorption spectrophotometer	ECIL
7.	Hot plate	Sunvic
8.	Hot air oven	Modern Scientifics
9.	Mantle heater	A.J. Enterprises
10.	pH meter	Hanna/Tasco
11.	Refrigerator	LG
12.	Distilled water assembly	–
13.	Computer system	IBM/HP

9.1.5 Sampling Methods

Grab sampling was generally applied during the sampling. A grab sample is an ordinary sample, which is taken from a particular place representing the whole water quality. This type of sample is valid only when it is certain that the water quality is not changing in a short time and effluent discharges, if any, are fairy regular. It is advisable to collect and analyze the grab samples separately at various timings, if the water quality is known to change with time. In such cases the schedule of timings shall be dependent on the frequency of discharge or change in water quality. This approach is used in studies to understand diurnal changes in pH, free CO_2, alkalinity, dissolved oxygen, etc. by collecting a 2 or 3 hour sample round the clock. In any kind of water, at least for dissolved oxygen, several grab samples spread over the whole day or even the night shall be important in limnological study, but in the case of groundwater, there is not any more diurnal changes in general water quality parameters, so a single grab sample is enough to represent the quality status of groundwater.

The sampling of water/soil from stream banks/shallow groundwater/pond/drain sediment can be easily carried out using a wide mouthed polythene bottle but a sampler has to be used if the studies are to be undertaken at various strata of water. The sampling of sediments from the bottom of natural water bodies, stabilizing ponds or effluent drains is invariably carried out using special samplers. A large number of water and sediment samplers have been developed over the year with varying degree of sophistication. Most common of them and those, which are readily available in India are Van Dron water sampler, simple laboratory made water sampler, shallow water sampler and Eckmen Dredge sediment sampler.

Eckmen Dredge sediment sampler is a most common type of sampler used for sampling the soil for physical, chemical and biological analysis. It is made up of a brass or steel box provided at the bottom with two jaws hinged together and to the box. Two hinged lids are provided at the top of the box. It has a fixed sectional area when the jaws are in open position, to sample the soil from a fixed area. The box is lowered in water with jaws in open position. When box reaches the bottom, a messenger is sent with the rope which closes the jaws with the bottom sediment enclosed in the box. The box is then hauled up with the upper lids closing automatically under the pressure of water.

The sampling was done during April 2005 to March 2007 in morning period (from 9.00 am to 11.00 am) from the selected sampling points of experimental sites as well as control site.

The samples were taken in BOD bottles and plastic Jeri cane for physical, chemical and heavy metals analysis. Following materials were used in sampling process.

(1) Sampling Bottles

300ml capacity BOD bottles were used for collecting the samples. These were washed with chromic acid and then rinse well with tap water followed by rinsing with distilled water. Then these were oven dried at 160°–180° for 3 hours.

(2) Pipettes

Pipettes were washed in same manner as in above. All the pipettes used were of borosil glass certified grade pipettes used were of 1ml capacity (micro pipettes), 5ml capacity and 10ml capacity.

(3) Reagents and Glassware

Some reagents were taken for on spot analysis and sample preservation. Glassware used in study *viz.* conical flask, beaker, burettes etc. were of Borosil glass certified grade. All the glassware were washed with chromic acid and then rinsed well with tap water and then with distilled water.

(4) Jeri Canes

Jeri cane used for carrying the samples from sampling sites to laboratories. Jeri cane made of plastic and washed well with water and then rinsed well with distilled water.

(5) Chemical Bottles

Some small chemical bottles were used for transporting some necessary chemical urgently required during the sampling for immediately analysis for selected parameters.

(6) Bag

A bag of large carrying capacity was taken during the sampling for the collection of all water, soil and sediment samples.

(7) Khurpi

A small paddle (*Khurpi*) was used for digging the soils from agricultural fields and relevant areas related to study.

(8) Polythene Bag

Poly bags were used for the collection of agricultural soils and sediment samples.

(9) Plastic Cane

Many small and big Jeri canes were used for the collection of textile industrial effluent sample, surface water and groundwater samples from different sampling spots for the study.

(10) Thermometer

Mercury thermometer was used for on spot measurement of the soil and water samples.

(11) pH Meter

A handy pen pH meter was used for on spot evaluation of the pH of surface water, groundwater, soil and sediment samples.

(12) Eckmann Dredge Sampler

This sampler was used for the collection of sediment samples from pond sediments and also effluent drain sediment.

9.1.6 Sample Collection, Preservation, Dilution and Digestion

Due to the discharging of textile effluents in to the pond directly with any adequate treatment by the dye houses, surface water may pollute (Malik *et al.*, 2006). After percolation of pollutants through the soil/sediment profile may affect the groundwater quality of the region. Effluents, surface water and groundwater samples were collected from effluent drain, pond and hand pumps/tube wells respectively. Samples collected in Borosil BOD bottles and some Jeri canes for laboratory experiments.

Some parameters were determined immediately on sampling sites, for rest parameters and heavy metals; samples were stored in refrigerator at 4°C. Heavy metals may be analyzed in the 6 months period from the preservation date.

For determination of the parameters like conductivity, total solids, pH (hydrogen ion concentration), COD, free CO_2, total alkalinity, total hardness Ca/Mg, chlorides, lead, manganese, zinc, calcium and magnesium. Samples were taken from surface water (Pond) and groundwater from Hand pumps and Tube wells by keeping and opening Jeri canes below the source of water. Caps of cans were closed tightly after filling up of cane.

For dissolved oxygen/biochemical oxygen demand, samples were collected in sterilized 300 ml capacity BOD bottles. The bottles were filled completely with sample water up to the rim and stopper was placed only avoiding any kind of air bubble inside it. DO was immediately fixed by adding 2 ml each of alkaline potassium iodide and manganese sulphate ($MnSO_4$) at sampling spot. While the sample for BOD was incubated for 5 days in BOD incubator at 20°C in the laboratory.

Water samples were acidified in the field with concentrated HNO_3 (5 ml/l of water sample, to reduce the pH of the sample, pH > 2.0) for the total metal estimation. The total metal content was determined by digesting 200 ml of sample with a mixture of concentrated HNO_3 and $HClO_4$ acid (10 ml + 2 ml) (Singh *et al.*, 2005). The digested samples were filtered through Whatman filter No. 42 and finally volume were made 10 ml with 0.1 N HNO_3 and analyzed for heavy metals using AAS (Model ECIL-4129).

In recent three decades, industrialization creates some negative impacts on environment and its all biotic and abiotic components. Industrial effluents contaminate the groundwater of the industrial region, which may further affect the agricultural soil quality due to the repeated irrigation by contaminated water tapped from groundwater resources with the help of bore wells. Affected soil samples from agriculture fields and effluent drain bed sediments were collected and analyzed for the physico-chemical parameters to assess the quality, fertility, nature of soil and effect of textile pollution on soil surface and texture.

Soil sample selection depends on the nature of analysis. Composite sampling is the best method for soil analysis. Nutritional study requires sample collected at the depth of 10-15 cm. borer samples are used for this purpose. Soil samples were normally collected in polythene bags and dispatched or transported to laboratory as early as possible. Since some parameters like pH, soil moisture, were analyzed immediately.

For rest parameters soil samples were dried below 40°C (Millar and Turk, 2002). Soil samples were collected monthly during the period April 2005 to March 2007 for analytical purpose. Samples have been collected separately from each area, which showed some difference in soil colours, texture and others parameters. During collection of samples, stony cities were avoided; sampling was done after the dry sample of soil. The surface material is removed by the help of scrubber. Approximately 500gm soil sample were collected from a depth of 15 cm for each site. These soil samples were taken and placed in a polythene bags. The stones and organic matter, like roots and pieces of leaf were removed from the samples. For the analysis of physico-chemical parameters, the 1:5 ratio soil suspensions are required. After it all the procedures of analysis are same to water analysis. Digestion of the same suspension is required for the total metal estimation same as in water analysis. Sediment and soil samples were collected in the polythene bags and transported to laboratory as early as possible. Some parameters should be determined immediately. For other parameters, the soil samples were dried and stored. For drying, temperature for soil is critical, as many constituents change with change in temperature. High temperature drying generally affects the exchangeable characteristics of clay and organic colloids.

Soon after drying, stones and other similar objects are picked up and the soil was grounded in a mortar to break up the aggregates or jumps, taking care not to break actual soil particles. The soil was passed through a 2 mm sieve. The mesh size allows all the nutritionally important factors to pass through. Brass sieve should be avoided where copper and zinc are to be estimated stainless steel or nylon sieves are preferable with smaller mesh sieve of 0.5 mm.

Total metal content in soil and sediment was determined by digesting 0.5 g of soil/sediment sample from each site with a mixture of concentrated HNO_3 and $HClO_4$ (10 ml + 2 ml). The digested samples were filtered through Whatman filter No. 42 and finally volume were made 10 ml with 0.1 N HNO_3 and analyzed for heavy metals using AAS (Model ECIL-4129).

9.1.7 Analytical Methods

The textile effluents, water and groundwater samples were analyzed by standard methods (Wetzel, 1975; Trivedi and Goel, 1984 and APHA, 1998. Soil samples were analyzed by standard methods (Trivedi and Goel, 1984; Kalra *et al.*, 1991; Saxena, 1994 and Hesse, 1994). The trace heavy metals were analyzed in the laboratory by Atomic absorption spectrophotometer *AAS 4129 model* (Singh *et al.*, 1987; APHA, 1998 and ECIL Methods Manual, 2004).

9.2 Effluent's Chemical Characteristics

9.2.1 Industrial Effluent

The untreated effluents of various textile industries can alter the physico-chemical properties of freshwater resources and increase the pollution load in environment of aquatic ecosystem. The textile effluents may affect different parts of environment in various ways. So, the impact assessment of textile effluents on physico-chemical characteristics of surface and groundwater, agriculture soil, plants and other biota must be required. A lot of researchers are engaged in bio-monitoring and evaluate the controlling strategies to check out the negative impacts on different components of environment.

Textiles industries mostly used vat and azo dyes as a constituent for dyeing and discharging the effluent directly into a common composite drain. This drainage system joined the effluent to the pond thus influencing the surface water and land quality of area. After delay of effluent in pond for a prolong time period, leaching of pollutants especially heavy metals would started and contaminate the groundwater of this particular area.

9.2.2 Historical Resume

Different workers from India and abroad have been discussed various aspects of pollution by industrial efflents in term of characteristics of water bodies, affected agricultural soils and bottom sediments from time to time. This review includes some of important contribution made in the field of industrial pollution, with references to characterization of textile industrial effluents and bottom sediment by different authors of country and abroad.

Aggarwal and Mehrotra (1952) surveyed the soil and soil water affected by effluent in some selected regions of Uttar Pradesh. Souther and Alsapaugh (1957) made some suggestion for the abatement of pollution in the textile industry e.g. process chemical substitution, closer process control and good housekeeping.

Porter (1970) highlighted the changing nature of textile processing and wastewater treatment technology according to time. Walker (1970) described the different metabolism of azo compounds used in textile dyeing unit. Nemerow (1971) described the origin of industrial water pollution, characteristics and treatment of industrial wastewater. Eckenfelder and Bornad (1971) justified the cost of waste treatment and relationship with its application for industrial waste.

Porter (1972) used the activated carbon for the treatment of textile waste. Considine (1974) described the various activities and functions of different chemicals effluents and their related internal chemical processes. Verma and Mathur (1974) studied the toxicity of industrial wastes to some organisms such as *Macrobranchium deyanum*. Widyanto (1975) conducted a survey on textiles factories and revealed that using the wastewater from textile factory a 1:1 dilution of the concentrate may stimulate the growth of water hyacinth after 10 days and suggested to utilize as a bio-agent to purify wastewater of a textile factory before reusing. Dulka and Risby (1976) stated ultra trace metals in some environmental and biological systems in the vicinity of textile industrial sector. Horing (1976) evaluated the characterization and treatment of textile dyeing wastewaters with the help of a designed model. Poots *et al.* (1976) indicated the removal of acid dye from effluent using natural absorbents.

Judlins and Hornsby (1978) carried out an observation on color removal from textile dye waste using magnesium carbonate. Hitz *et al.* (1978) stated the absorption of dyes on activated sludge. Govindan and Sunderlingam (1979) recognized the treatment of textile effluent in admixture with sewage (1:5) by the waste stabilization pond with the detention time of 8-12 days, using acclimated algae culture *Chlorella pyreoidosa, Microcystis, Aeruginosa* and *Euglena*. McKay (1979) described the color removal method from textile waste effluents.

Samy and Gananarethinam (1980) found that industrial effluents were toxic to the aquatic plants like *Eicchornia* even after dilution. Synthetic compounds were found toxic to *Spirodela polyrhiza* and *Lemna aquinoctialis*. Watler and Wint (1981) described the treatment processes of industrial effluent step by step. Wint (1981) indicated the disposal and handling problem of toxic wastes from industrial wastewater.

Chung (1983) highlighted the significance of azo-reduction in the mutagenesis and carcinogenesis of azo dyes. Ajmal and Khan (1985) analysed the effects of textile waste on physico-chemical properties of soil and seed germination. The BOD, COD and total solids, Cl, SO_4, Na, Ca and Mg concentrations in the effluents were found to be very high. Michaels and Lewis (1985) postulated the sorption and toxicity of azo and triphenyl methane dues to aquatic microbial populations.

Dayama (1987) reported that in their experimental studies on *Spinacea oleracea, Triticum aestivum, Cymopsis tetragonloba* and *Cicer arietinum* that effluent emerging from textiles industries affects the growth of plants. Zilliox (1989) determined the industrial impacts on the quality of groundwater in a large basin as a case of the Rhine aquifer in France and noticed it harmful for public consumption. Nawar and Doma (1989) studied on the removal of dyes from effluents using low-cost agricultural byproducts.

Navarro *et al.* (1993) reported the waste dumping and accumulation of industrial and domestic waste in an industrial area, and impacts of untreated textile waste water respectively. Goltenboth (1994) evaluated the impact of wastewater of textile factory in Salatiga on the freshwater aquatic ecosystem of Ledok river system at Central Java. Srinivasan and Murali (1996) carried out some studies on effect of industrial pollutants on properties of soils.

Sharma *et al.* (1999) and Sastry and Rathee (1999) reported the impact of industrial effluents on freshwater system of three villages in Rohtak district. Al-Degs, *et al.* (2000) described the effect of carbon surface chemistry on the removal of reactive dyes from textile effluent and observed a method for decolorization of wastewater of textile industry having reactive dyes with azo bond and associated chromophores.

Sheth and Patel (2001) studied on characterization, treatment and comparative cost analysis of textile processing wastewater of Vatva industrial complex. Kumar *et al.* (2001) studied on the impact of textile industry on groundwater quality of Sanagar, Jaipur and found the high amount of chemicals (e.g. sulphuric acid and acetic acid) and dyes (e.g. chrome and metal dyes) suspended solids and toxic metals in the waste which may enter in the groundwater and deteriorate its quality. Thorat and Pathade (2001) described the characterization, processes, pollution and the treatment of wastewater generated from each step of textile industry and suggested processes for the neutralization of alkaline waste and their chemical and biological treatments.

Srinivas *et al.* (2002) pointed out the groundwater pollution due to the industrial effluents in Kothur industrial area, Mahaboonagar, (A.P.). Annadurai *et al.* (2002)

used the cellulose-based wastes for adsorption of dyes from aqueous solutions, from the dye manufacturing industry, textile industry, and pulp and paper industry.

Mohanasundaram (2003) suggested the affordable and effective textile processing effluent treatment plants. Ameta *et al.* (2003) observed the prominent growth and increased sugar and protein percentage and chlorophyll content in onion grown in photo-catalytically treated effluent and described the photo-catalytic treatment of wastewater can be considered as an effective method, which will help in reusing the effluent from dye industry for irrigation purposes. Khan *et al.* (2003) harvested some *Solanum melongena* plant in a laboratory experiment using five different levels of textile waste water and observed the contamination of heavy metals in the soil of pots treated with highest ratio of distilled water and waste water.

Lee *et al.* (2004) used nitrogen for colour and COD removal by fungi in textile effluent. Bousselmi *et al.* (2004) studied textile wastewater treatment by solar catalysis from a plant in Tunisia. Krull and Dopkens (2004) recycled the dye house effluents by biological and chemical treatment in Germany. Bae *et al.* (2004) used Fenton process for textile dyeing wastewater treatment in Korea.

Yu *et al.* (2005) studied color, dye and DOC removal, and acid generation during Fenton oxidation of dyes and investigated discoloration using the synthetic dye wastewater containing various dyes. Sevimli *et al.* (2005) carried out the work on investigating the effect of some operational parameters on the decolorization of textile effluent and dye solution by ozonation. Dhar *et al.* (2005) studied the effect of acid activated sawdust on the removal of different dissolved tannery dyes (Acid dye) from aqueous solution and designed acid activated sawdust in absorbing D-Brown EGP and Lurazol Brown PM dyes from aqueous solution. Saw dust is an excellent low cost adsorbent of colored organic anions and may have significant potential as a color removal from tannery wastewater.

Aboulhassan *et al.* (2005) suggested the treatment process of textile wastewater using a natural flocculants. Bhat and Kulkarni (2005) studied on chemical oxygen demand reduction of dye industry effluent having COD in excess of 100000 mg/l and are extremely difficult to treat and pose severe pollution problems if discharged directly to treatment plants and used rice husk, saw dust and charcoal as adsorbents for the reduction of COD load of dye waste. It was found that activated charcoal is suitable adsorbent under specified condition. Also, cheaply available adsorbent such as saw dust and rice husk also show some good results.

Sheth and Desai (2005) developed the Bench Scale Completely Mixed Activated Sludge Reactor Model in the laboratory and observed the changes in various treatment parameters and terminate the experiments when reactor has reached to a steady state. Using the concept of the Monod expression by a graphical method all the bio-kinetic parameters for textile wastewater was determined.

Malik *et al.* (2006) reported the impact of textile effluents on surface water quality of Panipat industrial area. Gharaibeh *et al.* (2007) found the impact of field application of treated wastewater on hydraulic properties of vertisols.

It is necessary to reduce the levels of toxic metals from industrial effluents before discharging into surface waters. The general methods of treating wastewater-containing metals are coagulation, ion exchange, reverse osmosis and adsorption. Adsorption is a highly effective physico-chemical treatment for removing heavy metals for effluents. Due to high cost of activated carbon, efforts are being directed towards finding low cost adsorbents. Recently much interest has been shown for removal of heavy metals using a large number of low cost materials. Coal fly ash, the solid waste of power plants is one of the cheapest and non-conventional adsorbents (De, 2005).

Textile industry requires different chemical dyes in dying during wet processing and release them with the waste water discharged through industrial outlet to effluent drain. A common effluent drain contains all types of dye residuals in a composite form, which is very toxic in nature due to the presence of different synthetic dyes, which contain various toxic heavy metals. In the textile dying processes for every colour, a different metal compound is required and used for dying and ultimately washed out with the effluents of dye houses in Panipat industrial area. The common effluent drain ends up in to a pond near village Binjhole so the future of these heavy metals is not so managed and predicted. Most of the villagers think that the dye houses are the only responsible for the water quality degradation of regional groundwater system.

According to the voice of time, it is require assessing the groundwater quality of village Binjhole, industrial area and some local surroundings of dye houses. The effluents discharged from dye houses are quite important for temporal monitoring. Because the effluents store pond is highly contaminated and is a depot of heavy metals due to the presence of chemical dye portions continuously since a long period of time. Heavy metals remain in water ecosystem, but these may travel through food web at various trophic levels and environmental components as well as. Thus, metals moves pond sediments and reach in shallow water table by leaching processes and the metal contamination may disperse in a wide area of the region. Contamination of soils of close areas occurs when the effluents or polluted water comes under the contact of soil. Thus, the evaluation of textile effluents, pond water, groundwater, sediments and soils is essential to know the pollution load of heavy metals on hydrosphere and lithosphere and to determine the drinking water quality of Panipat industrial area for the assessment of its potability, suitability and evaluate some possible impacts on human health.

9.2.3 Observations

Experimental Sites

Physico-chemical Parameters of Textile Effluents

Temperature (°C)

The temperature of textile industrial effluents was recorded maximum 32.83 ± 2.65 in monsoon 2006 and minimum 25.74 ± 1.04 in winter 2005-06 ranged between 24.8 to 35.7 °C. The highest value of temperature in textile effluents was found 35.7 °C during July 2005 and lowest 24.8 °C in January 2006.

pH

The maximum pH value of textile industrial effluents were recorded 10.72 ± 0.75 in monsoon 2006 and minimum 9.65 ± 0.07 in summer 2007 ranged between 9.5 and 11.5. The highest value of pH in textile effluents was found 11.5 during July 2006 and lowest 9.5 in April 2005.

Total Solids (mg/l)

The maximum total solids in textile industrial effluents were recorded 2643.67 ± 220.73 in monsoon 2006 and minimum 2210.40 ± 39.20 in winter 2005-06 ranged between 2183 to 2780 mg/l. The highest value of total solids in textile effluents was found 2780 mg/l during August 2006 and lowest 2183 mg/l in January 2006.

Total Dissolved Solids (mg/l)

Total dissolved solids in textile industrial effluents were recorded maximum 2219.75 ± 55.18 in summer 2006 and minimum 2045.67 ± 184.03 in monsoon 2005 ranged between 1842 to 2298 mg/l. The highest value of total dissolved solids in textile effluents was found 2298 mg/l during June 2006 and lowest 1842 mg/l in September 2005.

Total Suspended Solids (mg/l)

Total suspended solids in textile industrial effluents were recorded maximum 570.67 ± 94.87 in monsoon 2006 and minimum 141.80 ± 86.18 in winter 2005-06 ranged between 49 to 680 mg/l. The highest value of total suspended solids in textile effluents was found 680 mg/l during August 2006 and lowest 49 mg/l in January 2006.

Electrical Conductivity (μmho/cm)

Maximum electric conductivity in textile industrial effluents was recorded 3.45 ±.096 in summer 2006 and minimum 3.196 ± 0.29 in monsoon 2005 ranged between 2.88 to 3.58 mho/cm. The highest value of electric conductivity in textile effluents was found 3.58 mho/cm during June 2006 and lowest 2.88 mho/cm in September 2005.

Dissolved Oxygen (mg/l)

Dissolved oxygen in textile industrial effluents was recorded maximum 3.52 ± 0.48 in winter 2006-07 and minimum 0.87 ± 0.77 in summer 2005 ranged between 0.00 to 4.5 mg/l. The highest value of dissolved oxygen in textile effluents was found 4.5 during January 2006 and lowest 0.00 mg/l in May 2005.

Free CO_2 (mg/l)

Free carbon dioxide in textile industrial effluents was recorded maximum 2.8 ± 0.30 in summer 2005 and minimum 0.38 ± 0.53 in winter 2005-06 ranged between 0.00 to 3.1 mg/l. The highest value of free carbon dioxide in textile effluents was found 3.1 mg/l during May 2005 and lowest 0.00 in January 2006.

Biochemical Oxygen Demand (mg/l)

The biochemical oxygen demand in textile industrial effluents was recorded maximum 170.0 ± 6.25 in summer 2005 and minimum 138.6 ± 16.52 in winter 2005-

06 ranged between 122.0 to 188.0 mg/l. The highest value of biochemical oxygen demand in textile effluents was found 188.0 mg/l during July 2005 and lowest 122.00 mg/l in January 2006.

Chemical Oxygen Demand (mg/l)

The chemical oxygen demand in textile industrial effluents was recorded maximum 445.0 ± 40.93 in monsoon 2005 and minimum 351.5 ± 14.85 in summer 2007 ranged between 310 to 490 mg/l. The highest value of chemical oxygen demand in textile effluents was found 490 mg/l during July 2005 and lowest in 310 mg/l January 2006.

Total Alkalinity (mg/l)

Total alkalinity in textile industrial effluents was recorded maximum 889.0 ± 47.88 in monsoon 2006 and minimum 633.60 ± 69.55 in winter 2005-06 ranged between 535 to 946 mg/l. The highest value of total alkalinity in textile effluents was found 946 mg/l during July 2005 and lowest 535 in December 2005.

Calcium (mg/l)

The concentrations of calcium in textile industrial effluents were recorded maximum 27.37 ± 6.78 in monsoon 2006 and minimum 10.58 ± 3.2 in winter 2005-06 ranged between 5.6 to 34.5 mg/l. The highest value of calcium in textile effluents was found 34.5 mg/l during July 2006 and lowest 5.6 mg/l in January 2006.

Magnesium (mg/l)

The concentrations of magnesium in textile industrial effluents were recorded maximum 16.07 ± 3.46 in summer 2005 and minimum 4.70 ± 2.12 in summer 2007 ranged between 2.4 to 18.9 mg/l. The highest value of magnesium in textile effluents was found 18.9 mg/l during July 2006 and lowest 2.4 mg/l in February 2006.

Potassium (mg/l)

The concentration of potassium in textile industrial effluents was recorded maximum 8.83 ± 0.58 in monsoon 2006 and minimum 7.40 ± 0.14 in summer 2007 ranged between 7.0 to 9.5 mg/l. The highest value of potassium in textile effluents was found 9.5 mg/l during July 2006 and lowest 7.0 mg/l in April 2005.

Sodium (mg/l)

Sodium in textile industrial effluents was recorded maximum 177.0 ± 7.21 in monsoon 2006 and minimum 145.0 ± 4.24 in summer 2007 ranged between 142.0 to 186.0 mg/l. The highest value of Sodium in textile effluents was found 186.0 mg/l during August 2005 and lowest 142.0 mg/l in March 2006.

Chloride (mg/l)

Chloride in textile industrial effluent was recorded maximum 825.67 ± 29.94 in monsoon 2006 and minimum 588.50 ± 9.19 in summer 2007 ranged between 565.0 to 860 mg/l. The highest value of Chloride in textile effluents was found 860.0 during August 2006 and lowest 565.0 mg/l in April 2005.

Physico-chemical Parameters of Drain Sediment

Temperature (°C)

Temperature of drain sediment was recorded maximum 24.93 ± 3.49 in summer 2005 and minimum 15.46 ± 3.13 in winter 2005-06 ranged between 10.5 to 28.1 °C. The highest value of temperature in drain sediment was found 28.1 °C during July 2005 and lowest 10.5 °C in January 2006.

Water Holding Capacity (%)

Water holding capacity of drain sediment was recorded maximum 31.71 ± 0.51 in summer 2005 and minimum 24.50 ± 5.11 in monsoon 2005 ranged between 20.23 to 32.25 %. The highest value of water holding capacity in drain sediment was found 32.25 % during June 2006 and lowest 20.23 % during September 2005.

Bulk Density (g/cm³)

The bulk density of drain sediment was recorded maximum 1.45 ± 0.07 in summer 2005 and minimum 1.33 ± 0.03 in winter 2005-06 ranged between 1.29 to 1.51 g/cm³. The highest value of bulk density in drain sediment was found 1.51 g/cm³ during June 2005 and lowest 1.29 g/cm³in January 2006.

Soil Moisture (%)

The soil moisture of drain sediment was recorded maximum 20.85 ± 2.25 in monsoon 2006 and minimum 13.33 ± 1.15 in summer 2005 ranged between 12.5 to 22.3 %. The highest value of soil moisture in drain sediment was found 22.3 % during August 2005 and lowest 12.5 % in April 2005.

pH

pH of drain sediment on pH scale was recorded maximum 8.32 ± 0.04 in monsoon 2006 and minimum 7.84 ± 0.12 in summer 2005 ranged between 7.7 to 8.5. The highest value of pH in drain sediment was found 8.5 during February 2006 and lowest 7.7 in June 2006.

Electrical Conductivity (μmho/cm)

Electric conductivity of drain sediment was recorded maximum 32.50 ± 0.89 in summer 2005 and minimum 27.86 ± 0.92 in winter 2005-06 ranged between 26.8 and 33.7 mho/cm. The highest value of Electric conductivity in drain sediment was found 33.7 mho/cm during June 2006 and lowest 26.8 mho/cm in January 2006.

Chloride (μg/g)

Chloride concentration in drain sediment was recorded maximum 836.67 ± 145.1 in summer 2005 and minimum 609.0 ± 33.94 in summer 2007 ranged between 580.0 to 998.0 μg/g. The highest value of chloride in drain sediment was found 998.0 μg/g during June 2005 and lowest 580.0 μg/g in January 2006.

Potassium (μg/g)

Potassium concentration in drain sediment was recorded maximum 33.50 ± 0.71 in summer 2007 and minimum 27.33 ± 1.53 in monsoon 2005 ranged between 26.0 to 34.0 μg/g. The highest value of potassium in drain sediment was found 34.0 μg/g during March 2007 and lowest 26.0 μg/g in August 2005.

Sodium (μg/g)

Sodium concentration in drain sediment was recorded maximum 587.50 ± 41.72 in summer 2007 and minimum 157.0 ± 98.85 in monsoon 2005 ranged between 95.0 to 617.0 μg/g. The highest value of sodium in drain sediment was found 617.0 μg/g during March 2007 and lowest 95.0 μg/g in September 2005.

Correlation Coefficient

Correlation between physico-chemical parameters and heavy metals of textile industrial effluent are given in tabular form for each metal. For cadmium correlation was found maximum 0.5954 and 0.6627 with temperature and free carbon dioxide respectively. Correlation for copper was found maximum 0.6126 and 0.6112 with total dissolved solids and free carbon dioxide respectively. Correlation for iron was found maximum 0.6848 and 0.7573 with total dissolved solids and free carbon dioxide respectively. Correlation for manganese was found maximum 0.3101 and 0.2820 with total dissolved solids and Electric conductivity respectively. Correlation for nickel was found maximum 0.3455 and 0.4410 with total dissolved solids and free carbon dioxide respectively. Correlation for lead was found maximum 0.7373 and 0.7303 with total dissolved solids and Electric conductivity respectively. Correlation for zinc was found maximum 0.0579 and 0.0685 with total dissolved solids and DO respectively.

Correlation between heavy metals of textile industrial effluent and heavy metals of pond water are given in tabular form for each metal. For cadmium correlation was found maximum 0.6257 and 0.5244 with copper and manganese respectively. Correlation for copper was found maximum 0.7762 and 0.7975 with nickel and lead respectively. Correlation for iron was found maximum 0.8110 and 0.8506 with nickel and lead respectively. Correlation for manganese was found maximum 0.4070 and 0.8434 with iron and zinc respectively. Correlation for nickel was found maximum 0.5772 and 0.5855 with cadmium and lead respectively. Correlation for lead was found maximum 0.6835 and 0.5946 with cadmium and nickel respectively. Correlation for zinc was found maximum 0.0683 and 0.4195 with cadmium and zinc respectively.

Correlation between physico-chemical parameters and heavy metals of effluent drain sediment are given in tabular form for each metal. For cadmium correlation was found maximum 0.7226 and 0.7258 with bulk density and electric conductivity respectively. Correlation for copper was found maximum 0.2637 and 0.3623 with temperature and bulk density respectively. Correlation for iron was found maximum 0.1399 and 0.1114 with chloride and potassium respectively. Correlation for manganese was found maximum 0.6220 and 0.7253 with sodium and potassium respectively. Correlation for nickel was found maximum 0.8752 and 0.7610 with water holding capacity and sodium respectively. Correlation for lead was found maximum 0.8233 and 0.8331 with temperature and electric conductivity respectively. Correlation for zinc was found maximum 0.7598 and 0.7570 with water holding capacity and chloride.

Correlations between heavy metals of drain sediment are given in tabular form for each metal and correlations between heavy metals of pond sediment are given in tabular form for each metal. However for both correlation values were not found highly positive and significant.

9.2.4 Discussion

With the increase in industrialization our health problems are increasing day by day. Today the pollution especially of water resources is increasing steadily due to rapid population growth, industrial proliferation, urbanization increasing living standards and wide sphere of human activities. The greatest danger to the quality of environment is posed by human activities such as poorly organized and unregulated disposal of industrial, domestic waste and crude oil spillage are the major causes of the environmental deterioration. The industrial effluent over the years has caused serious damages of the surrounding soil, groundwater and agriculture crops (Chao *et al.*, 2005).

Most of the dye houses of the Panipat region discharge their effluent directly into a common effluent drain, which carry the total of composite effluents towards the village pond at Binjhole adjoining to industrial area, ultimately has altered the water quality and biotic and nutrient dynamic of the pond ecosystem in a tremendous way and further may affect the groundwater quality. Due to post irrigation practices, the soil turns to barren or unfertile and affected agriculture productivity.

Generally, textile industry consumes substantial volume of water and chemicals in wet processing of textile materials. Wet processing of cloth or fibers dying requires huge amount of different chemical dyes and wash away them with the wastewater discharged through industrial outlet. Thus, the common effluent drain consist all types of dye residuals in a composite form. This composite effluent is very toxic in nature due to the presence of different synthetic dyes, which contain various toxic heavy metals.

Further future of these heavy metals is not so managed because the common effluent drain ends up in to a pond near village Binjhole, Industrial area and some local surroundings of dye houses. The effluents discharged from dye houses are quite important for temporal monitoring. Because the effluents store pond is highly contaminated and is a depot of heavy metals due to the presence of chemical dye portions continuously since a long period of time. Heavy metals remain in water ecosystem, but these may travel through food web at various trophic levels and environmental components as well as. Metals moves pond sediments and reach in shallow water table by leaching processes and the metal contamination may disperse in a wide area of the region. Contamination of soils of close areas occurs when the effluents or polluted water comes under the contact of soil. The regular contact of polluted water with soil makes the sodicity and alters the physico-chemical characteristics, texture and profile of soil stratum.

Thus, the quality assessment of textile effluents, pond water, groundwater, sediments and soils required to know the pollution load of heavy metals on hydrosphere and lithosphere and to determine the drinking water quality of Panipat industrial zone in term of suitability and possible impacts on human health. In the present study, water, soil and sediment samples were collected and analyzed for determination of physico-chemical characteristics and distribution of heavy metals from April 2005 to March 2007 regularly. The results are depicted in the form of tables and graphs. During the study, physico-chemical characteristics and heavy metals in textile effluents, surface (pond) water, groundwater, soils and sediments were found with some fluctuation according to seasons, place and other factors.

9.2.5 Physico-chemical Parameters of Textile Effluents

In the present investigation of water resources, physico-chemical characteristics of water directly reflect its quality for irrigation, bathing, drinking and industrial uses. Physico-chemical parameter like total dissolved solids, pH, chloride, total alkalinity, biochemical oxygen demand, chemical oxygen demand, pH are the some important parameters for assessing the quality of water for irrigation and drinking purposes.

Temperature mostly fluctuates according to climatic conditions of the region and directly depends upon seasonal air temperature. However, groundwater temperature remains comparatively lower (25.5-31.6 °C) due to the geothermal energy. The temperature of textile common effluents (25.7-32.8 °C) and pond water (25.5-32.4 °C) has fluctuated significantly due to the lentic behaviour of aquatic ecosystem. Temperature of composite effluent drops slightly while reaching in the pond (25.5-32.4 °C). Pathe *et al.* (2005) reported the temperature fluctuation trend from cluster of small cotton textile units from different sector, which follow permissible limit of B.I.S and WHO and remain always below 40°C during study. During the study period temperature of textile industrial effluent never cross the standards limits. Temperature slightly influences some parameters of water and affects the concentration of dissolved oxygen contents and can also influence the activity of bacteria and toxic chemicals in water. Textile industrial effluent may cause problems with high temperature (Groff, 1993). Temperature facilitates the oxidation process biochemical oxygen demand and chemical oxygen demand achieved maximum reduction at high temperature as compared to low temperature (Aslam *et al.*, 2004). Temperature of water depends upon the meteorological characteristics of existing environment; especially air temperature. Temperature fluctuated with air temperature with positive relation. However due to some processes in textile units, the temperature of textile effluents was slightly higher than pond water and groundwater.

In the present study, the pH of the textile effluents was recorded mostly alkaline. The pH of the composite effluents was highly alkaline, which slightly decreases in pond water system. Extreme high pH or rapid pH change can exert stresses conditions or kill aquatic life. Changes in pH can also affect aquatic system indirectly by altering other aspects of water chemistry. Low pH levels accelerate the release of metals from rocks or sediments in the water. Groff (1993) reported that textile wastewater may cause problem used as untreated effluent consist higher pH and temperature. pH has significant importance in all chemicals and biochemical reactions in an aquatic system (Basu *et al.*, 1973).

pH of textile industrial effluent was found mostly basic (9.6-10.7) due to the high salt load and high alkalinity. Pond water's pH was also alkaline (8.2-8.6) due to the directly mixing with effluent drains with pond. The pH of both, drain sediment (7.8-8.3) and pond sediments (7.9-8.4) were also noticed alkaline in nature. Similar trend is in agreement with that reported by Sial *et al.* (2006), Pathe *et al.* (2005) in textile industrial effluent, Singh *et al.* (1994) in effluent drain and Mor *et al.* (2003).

Total solids were found very high in textile industrial effluent (2210.4-2643.7 mg/l) due to the high degree of pollution. Different dyes and fibres are present in the textile waste water, which generally released dissolved solids into common effluent drain. The dissolved solids in wastewater are mainly inorganic salts and relatively unaffected by biological treatment processes and can accumulate in water recirculation system. Failure to remove them may lead to an increase in total solids content of surface water sources. The dissolved solids in wastewater may be harmful to vegetation and also preclude use in various irrigation processes. Total dissolved solids in the textile effluents were observed very high than the prescribed limits of C.P.C.B. and B.I.S values. In the pond, the values of total solids and total dissolved solids were noticed comparatively high, however, these were not found higher than textile industrial effluent. Dissolved solids vary qualitatively and quantitatively in different water depending upon the season, location and other factors. In the present study, the total dissolved solids values in effluents (2045.7-2219.7 mg/l) and pond water (1861.0-2037.5 mg/l) were not so high according to CPCB standards. Similar observations were also reported by Yusuf and Sonibare (2004), Garg and Kaushik (2006) in textile industrial effluent.

Total dissolved solids are the measure of the quantity of material dissolved in water that can pass through a filter (usually with a pore size of 0.45 micrometers). The material can include carbonate, bicarbonate, chloride, sulfate, phosphate, nitrate, calcium, magnesium, sodium, organic ions, and other ions. Similar to total suspended solids, high concentrations of total dissolved solids may also reduce water transparency, combine with toxic trace compounds and heavy metals, and lead to an increase in water temperature. Total dissolved solids are used to estimate the quality of drinking water, because it represents the amount of ions in the water. High dissolved solids concentrations can produce laxative effects and can give an unpleasant mineral taste to water. High dissolved solids concentrations in water are also unsuitable for water recycling processes and many industrial applications. The values of total dissolved solids concentrations recorded in the present study are comparable to those obtain by Pathe *et al.* (2005), Yusuf and Sonibare (2004), Garg and Kaushik (2006) in textile industrial effluent.

Total suspended solids include both organic and inorganic materials, which adversely affect the aquatic life, especially fishes and bottom fauna of surface water ecosystems. These produce carbon dioxide, hydrogen sulphide, methane gases, which are very noxious in nature. They increase the turbidity of water, reduce light penetration and impair photosynthetic activity of aquatic plants in surface water system. Total suspended solids in the effluents (141.8-570.7 mg/l) and pond water (96.8-487.7 mg/l) were found slightly high than recommended by C.P.C.B. and B.I.S. Chavan *et al.* (2005) reported the adverse impacts of total suspended solids on the surroundings environment of the industrial effluent near Sukhna river at Midc area, Aurangabad.

Because the suspended particles absorb heat from sunlight and changed dissolved oxygen levels to fall even further because warmer waters can hold less dissolved oxygen. High total suspended solids in a water body can often mean higher concentrations of bacteria, nutrients, pesticides, and metals in the water. These pollutants may attach to sediment particles on the land and be carried into water bodies with storm water. In the water, the pollutants may be released from the sediment or travel farther. The flow rate of the effluent drain is a primary factor in total suspended solids concentrations. Fast running water can carry more particles and larger-sized sediment. Heavy rains can pick up sand, silt, clay, organic particles and heavy rubbish particles from the land and carry it to surface water. A change in flow rate can also affect total suspended solids; if the speed or direction of the water current increases, particulate matter from bottom sediments may be re-suspended.

Total solids were found very high in textile industrial effluent due to the dirt release during the washing of textile materials. The ratio of total dissolved solids and total suspended solids with total solids was found quite similar during the study. Such types of trends in determining the total suspended solids load have been reported by Garg and Kaushik (2006), Yusuf and Sonibare (2004) in textile industrial effluent. Liquid wastewater from textile industries are not fit for irrigation regarding electric conductivity and total suspended solids (Bohn *et al.*, 1976, Abbas, 1991).

Conductance is a measurement of an electrical current with increasing amount and mobility of ions. These ions, which come from the breakdown of compounds, conduct electricity because they are negatively or positively charged when dissolved in water. Therefore, conductance is an indirect measure of the presence of dissolved solids such as chloride, nitrate, sulfate, phosphate, sodium, magnesium, calcium, and iron, and can be used as an indicator of water pollution.

It is not necessary that the water having high electric conductivity is not fit for irrigation. Only one parameter can't ensure the suitability of the water quality. However, the salt composition is high in the water having high Electric conductivity, but it may be beneficial for those soils having a lack or deficiency of some salts. Electric conductivity has a positive correlation with total dissolved solids in textile industrial effluent and groundwater also. Generally, there are not regulatory levels for electric conductivity. Instead, the concentration of total dissolved solids is often regulated. However, electric conductivity is an easily-obtained parameter that is a good indicator of the amount of dissolved solids in water, and thus can be used to detect contaminants in water. Total dissolved solids have a direct positive relationship with electric conductivity. If, total dissolved solids of water are high, electric conductivity will be more definitely (Mor *et al.*, 2003).

Electric conductivity was recorded very highly positive correlated to total dissolved solids due to the direct relation of total dissolved solids with electric conductivity in textile industrial effluent (3.1-3.4 mho/cm). Sial *et al.* (2006), Garg and Kaushik (2006) were made similar observations in textile industrial effluent and Singh *et al.* (1994) in drain. which support the result of present study.

The dissolved oxygen is often attributed to the fact the oxygen is dissolved more during the period of active photosynthesis. Hutchinson (1957) reported that the water has low temperature has greater capacity for holding gases. The value of dissolved oxygen in the all sampling sites was found out to be low dissolved oxygen. The DO was found nil or low in textile effluent (0.87-3.5 mg/l), however, in some months dissolved oxygen was found nil in textile industrial effluent due to the increasing rate of biodegradation of different compounds in water column. As the matter of fact that the effluents carried highly pollution load, which could not allow any flora and fauna to survive in unfavourable condition and there will be no photosynthesis process in polluted habitat. The dissolved oxygen showed an inverse relationship with temperature as reported by Das and Srivastava (1956) and Dobriyal (1985) in aquatic system.

The value of dissolved oxygen recorded in the present study are comparable to results obtained by Yusuf and Sonibare (2004), Garg and Kaushik (2006) in textile industrial effluent and Singh *et al.* (1994) in effluent drain.

Free carbon dioxide in most textile industrial effluents was fluctuated in the range of 0.38 to 2.8 mg/l. However, the dissolved oxygen contents was also not found high in textile industrial effluent (0.87-3.5 mg/l). Free carbon dioxide mainly depends upon some physico-chemical parameter like dissolved oxygen, pH, temperature, etc. (ww.holar.is). Carbon dioxide has highly positive correlations (0.6627, 0.6112, 0.7573, -0.0984, 0.4410, 0.3252, -0.0395) in textile industrial effluents with almost all heavy metals (Cd, Cu, Fe, Mn, Ni, Pb and Zn) respectively.

Biochemical oxygen demand and chemical oxygen demand are the measurement of the oxygen consuming capabilities of organic matter. Textile effluent during their process of deposition exerts biochemical oxygen demand/chemical oxygen demand, which have a catastrophic effect on the ecosystem by depleting the oxygen supply. Decay process causes the production of noxious gases as hydrogen sulphide and methane. Water with high biochemical oxygen demand/chemical oxygen demand indicates presence of decomposing organic matter and subsequent high bacterial counts that degrade its quality and potential uses (Verma and Kharat, 2000). Biochemical oxygen demands of the effluents drain (138.6-170.0 mg/l) were found high as given in standards of C.P.C.B., B.I.S. and WHO. This trend is an agreement with that reported by Aslam *et al.* (2004), Yusuf and Sonibare (2004), Sial *et al.* (2006), Pathe *et al.* (2005) in textile industrial effluent, and Singh *et al.* (1994) in drain.

Chemical oxygen demand is directly proportional to biochemical oxygen demand. Dilution of effluents for biochemical oxygen demand analysis always depends upon the value of chemical oxygen demand in a wastewater. In fact, chemical oxygen demand explains the load of pollutants and degree of pollution in effluent drain. Effluents of dye houses having a tremendous value of COD in the range of 351.5-445.0 mg/l due to the high rate of decomposition of organic material in polluted and stored water. COD shows a positive relationship with BOD and negative with DO (Khanna, 1993) and mostly remains in the ratio of approximately 1:3 ± 0.5 in the case of waste water. Sevimli *et al.* (2005) observed the increasing trends of biochemical oxygen demand and chemical oxygen demand together while performing an experiment on decolorization of textile effluent and dye solution by ozonation. Senthinathan and Azeez (1999) and Groff (1993) reported that textile wastewater may cause problem used as untreated effluent consist higher COD, pH, temperature, Phosphorous and absorbable organic halogen. COD of textile wastewater may be reduced by using some appropriate technology Bhat *et al.* (2005). Aslam *et al.* (2004), Yusuf and Sonibare (2004), Sial *et al.* (2006), Pathe *et al.* (2005) were also reported the similar values in textile industrial effluent. Waste containing high biochemical oxygen demand and chemical oxygen demand are responsible for a heavy depletion of oxygen levels in the particular sector of water body or soil (Sial *et al.*, 2006).

Alkalinity is caused by strong bases and the salts of strong alkalis and weak acids. Carbonates are added to a water system if the water passes through soil and rock that contain carbonate minerals, such as calcite ($CaCO_3$). Where limestone and sedimentary rocks and carbonate-rich soils are predominant, waters will often have high alkalinity. Where igneous rocks (such as granite) and carbonate-poor soils are predominant waters will have low alkalinity. Alkalinity is a measure of the buffering capacity of water, or the capacity of bases to neutralize acids. Waters with low alkalinity are very susceptible to changes in pH. Waters with high alkalinity are able to resist major shifts in pH. As increasing amounts of acid are added to a water body, the pH of the water decreases, and the buffering capacity of the water is consumed. Because alkalinity and pH are so closely related, changes in pH can also affect alkalinity, especially in a poorly buffered system. Above pH 8.3, alkalinity is mostly in the form of carbonate (CO_3^{2-}); below 8.3, alkalinity is present mostly as bicarbonate (HCO_3^-).

The values of alkalinity in the effluents (633.6-889.0 mg/l) were found very high. Bhat *et al.* (2005) observed the increasing trend in alkalinity of various textile effluents according to discharge points. Alkalinity not only helps regulate the pH of a water body, but also the metal content. Alkalinity has found with positive correlations with Cd (0.0237), Cu (0.809), Fe (0.8896), Mn (0.7664), Ni (0.7918), Pb (0.5841) and Zn (0.7069) Bicarbonate and carbonate ions in water can remove toxic metals (such as lead, arsenic, and cadmium) by precipitating the metals out of solution. Pathe *et al.* (2005), Garg and Kaushik (2006) have been made some observations in textile industrial effluent; which support the results of present study.

Hardness generally represents the concentration of calcium and magnesium ions, because these are the most common polyvalent cations. Other ions, such as iron and manganese, may also contribute to the hardness of water, but are generally present in much lower concentrations. Calcium, magnesium, and other polyvalent cations such as iron and manganese may be added to a natural water system as it passes through soil and rock containing large amounts of these elements in mineral deposits. Hardness mainly depends on the amount of calcium and magnesium salts or both present in the groundwater, water hardness is not health hazard but its values should remain below permissible level to restore the taste to water (WHO, 1984)

Some textile industrial processes may also produce significant amounts of calcium and manganese that are later discharged as industrial effluents. Calcium was found 10.58-27.4 mg/l in textile industrial effluent. Similar conditions were also reported by Garg and Kaushik (2006), Yusuf and Sonibare (2004) and Helena *et al.* (1999) in textile industrial effluent.

When hardness equals alkalinity, the only cations present in significant concentrations in the water are calcium and magnesium. When hardness is greater than alkalinity, the waters may contain considerable amounts of other cations.

Magnesium was found low in textile industrial effluent (4.7-16.1 mg/l). The Mg concentrations levels were comparable with those found by Yusuf and Sonibare (2004) and Helena *et al.* (1999) in textile effluents.

Potassium is one of the important element among ten chemical element required in rather large quantities fir growth of all crops. Plants growth may be limited by a deficient available supply of potassium but its high some quantity may alter the soil composition. High K in water used in irrigation may alter the soil quality (Miller and Turk, 2002). Potassium was found low in textile industrial effluent (7.4-8.8 mg/l). Similar observation were made by Pathe *et al.* (2005) and Garg and Kaushik (2006) in textile industrial effluent.

Sodium salts in the water are much more objectionable than salts of calcium and magnesium because of the tendency of sodium to cause deflocculation of the colloidal fraction of the soil and developed an undesirable structure water contain sufficient heavy metals to prove toxic to continue use by plants. As sodium chloride used in textile industry so the concentration of sodium and chloride will be high in the waste water (Aslam *et al.*, 2004). Sodium was found very high in groundwater of industrial area, because sodium should not be higher than 20 mg/l in drinking water (WHO, 2006). Sodium values were found very high in textile industrial effluent (145.0-177.0 mg/l). Helena *et al.* (1999) and Garg and Kaushik (2006) were observed the similar observations in textile industrial effluent.

Chloride is one of the most conservative constituents in wastewater, being affected very little either by vegetative growth or other biological processes, or by precipitation or anion exchange reaction. Chloride concentrations in the effluents (588.5-825.7 mg/l) were also expected to be high by the permissible limit of C.P.C.B. A work conducting on the effect of natural flocculants on textile wastewater, chloride concentration is increased in waste water used in textile industries and delayed later (Aboulhassan *et al.*, 2005).

Chloride does not have a health-based standard for drinking water. Chloride has been suggested as a standard value for drinking purposes (EPA, 1989). The Maximum Contaminant Level (MCL) of 250000 µg/L is based on poor taste chloride imparts to water. Chloride is not affected by adsorption or degradation processes and is therefore a conservative chemical in soil and groundwater. Chloride concentrations begin to increase at some depth due to dissolution reactions within the aquifer. Chloride is therefore a good indicator of human impacts in the environment (MPCA, 2001). In the waste water the concentration of chloride will be high due to the use of sodium chloride in textile industry. Chloride concentration in irrigation water should be less then 75 ppm, otherwise it may be harmful for soil structure. Textile effluents are high in toxicity not only for human beings of surroundings but also a serious threat to groundwater and surface water resources (Aslam *et al.*, 2004). The chloride concentrations levels were comparable with those found by Helena *et al.* (1999), Garg and Kaushik (2006) in textile industrial effluent.

9.2.6 Physico-chemical Parameters of Drain Sediment

Physico-chemical parameters of soil may demonstrate the pollution status in the industrial region, so, physical and chemical characteristics are important for the assessment of contamination and pollution load. Sediment characteristics are the good indicator for the pollution load in effluent drain.

The temperature of soil greatly affects the physical, biological and chemical processes occurring in soil system. Biological decomposition can come to a near standstill, thereby limiting the rate at which nutrients such as nitrogen, phosphorus, sulfur and calcium are made available. Absorption and transport of water and nutrient ions by higher plants are adversely affected by low temperature (Brady, 1995). The temperature of field soils is not subject to radical human regulation. However, two kinds of management practices have significant effects on soil temperature, those that keep some type of cover or mulch on the soil and those that reduce excess soil moisture. There is not any significant variation in the temperature of drain sediment (15.5-24.9 °C) and other soil and sediment samples. The chemical processes and activities of microorganism which convert plant nutrients into available forms are also materially influenced by temperature. Removal of excess water from soil may facilitate changes in soil temperature. Humus content, good tillage, dark color of soil are the some other factors which influence the soil temperature (Miller and Turk, 2002).

Water holding capacity is a property as to water quantity is absorbed or retained by given amount of soil (Ramani and Srivastava, 1989). Water held in the soil pores with varying degrees of tenacity depending on the amount of water present and the size of pores in soils. Depending on the soil, as much as one forth to two thirds of the moisture may remain in the soil after the plants have wilted or died due to the lack of soil water.

The phenomenon of capillarity is a common one, the classic example being the movement of water up a wick when the lower end is immersed in water. Capillary forces are at work in all moist soils. However, the rate of movement and the rise in height are less than one would expect on the basis of soil pore size. One reason is that soil pores are filled with air, which may be entrapped, showing down or preventing the movement of water by capillary. Usually the height of the rise resulting from capillarity is greater with fine textured soils if sufficient time is allowed and the pores are not too small. This is readily explained on the basis of the capillary size and the continuity of the pores. With sandy soils the adjustment is rapid but so many of the pores are non-capillary that the height of rise cannot be great (Brady, 1995). Water holding capacity was found similar in drain sediment (24.5-31.7 %) and other soil and sediment samples with much difference between soil and sediment. Yuandong *et al.* (2006) described the similar trend of water holding capacity on the basis of soil texture and chemical composition in the agricultural soil system.

Bulk density relates to the combined volumes of the solids and pore spaces, soils with a high proportion of pore space to solids have lower bulk densities than those that are more compact and have less pore space. Consequently, any factor that influences soil pore space will affect bulk density. Mainly soil texture and compactness strongly influence the bulk density of soils (Brady, 1995). The pore space of a soil is that portion of the soil volume occupied by air and water. The amount of pore space is determined by the arrangement of the solid particles. If the particles lie close together, as in stands or compact sub-soils, the total porosity is low. If they are arranged in porous aggregates, as is often the case in medium textured soils high in organic matter, the pore space per unit volume will be high. Soil aeration may influence the availability of nutrients to plants (Miller and Turk, 2002). The bulk density was found similar between drain sediment (1.33-1.45 g/cm^3) and pond sediment (1.36-1.49 g/cm^3). Bulk density was similarly described by Yuandong *et al.* (2006) and Krebs *et al.* (1999) in soil environment.

The structure of the soil influences its moisture content. A well granulated soil has more total pore space than one with poor granulation or one that has been compacted. The reduced pore space may be reflected in a lower water holding capacity. The compacted soil also has to higher proportion of small and medium sized pores, which tend to hold the water with greater tenacity than do the larger pores. Moisture content of drain sediment (13.3-20.8 %) and other soil and sediment samples were found similar during the study. Rainwater leaching have made more efficient if antecedent moisture content of the soil profile was increased by saline water irrigation just before the onset of monsoons. On a wet soil, a rainfall event is expected to displace the salts to a greater depth. Conservation and proper utilization of rainwater for leaching salts is also utmost important.

The measurement of soil pH shows the acidity and basic nature of the soil. The soil is acidic if the pH is lower, while the higher pH means that soil is basic. If the decomposition of organic matter is there in soil, it will turn the pH low, other wise some foreign substances may alter the soil nature and properties towards alkaline (Nongkynrih *et al.*, 1996). Initial soil pH is an important property of the soil because of its influence on the infiltration rate of the soil (Gupta *et al.*, 1989). There are several causes of minor fluctuation in soil pH. For instance, the movements of salts into and out of soil moisture moves up and down the profile will influence pH. Similarly, the pH of mineral soils declines during the crop-growing season as a result of the acids produced by microorganisms and by the roots of higher plants. When soil temperatures are low, an increase in pH often is noted because biotic activities during these times are considerably slower.

pH significantly influences other chemical properties as well as biological organisms. High pH of textile industrial effluent can hampers plant crop growth (Sial *et al.*, 2006). The soil pH significantly affects the availability of most of the chemical element of importance to plants and microbes. Likewise, the tendency for toxic levels of element such as iron, manganese, aluminum to be established at low pH and deficiencies of iron and manganese at high pH have been mentioned. Continuous application of effluents with high pH will render the soils unfit for further cultivation (Sial *et al.*, 2006). Soil pH was found alkaline in drain sediment (7.8-8.3) and pond sediment.

Electric conductivity is the measure of current carrying capacity, which gives a clear idea of soluble salts present in soil. Conductivity generally depends upon the dilution of suspension. However, the salt composition is high in the water having high electric conductivity, but it may be beneficial for those soils having a lack or deficiency of some salts. The electric conductivity of drain sediment was found in the range of 27.8-32.5 mho/cm with some minor fluctuations.

Chloride was found very high in effluent drain sediment and slightly low as with similar fluctuation in pond bed sediment, but in agricultural soil and soil near textile industries chloride was found comparatively low because of the high settlement of chloride in drain sediment from textile industrial effluent; while rest was reach in agricultural soil by various contacts. The chloride in drain sediment was found 609.0-836.6 μg/g with some minor fluctuations. Manchanda (1990) has also reported that pulse crops such as pea, mungbean, gram, lentil, and broadbean suffered more due to toxic accumulation of chloride, when irrigated with Cl ion then SO_4^{-2} dominant (70%) water of more salinity.

In most cases, the exchangeable potassium is the chief source of available potassium in soil (Jha and Pandey, 1984). Potassium plays many essential roles in plants. It is an activator of dozens of enzymes responsible for such plants processes as energy metabolism, starch synthesis, nitrate reduction, and sugar degradation. Potassium is extremely mobile within the plant and helps regulate the opening and closing of stomata in the leaves and the uptake of water by root cells. At any one time most of the potassium is in the primary mineral and non-exchangeable forms. To maintain the level of exchangeable and soil solution potassium high enough to encourage good crop production, chemical fertilizer are used. Potassium may deficient in alkaline soil and an excess of potassium may delay maturity of plant. In some crops it may tend to accumulate in the leaf and stem rather then in the grain (Miller and Turk, 2002). The potassium in drain sediment was found 27.3-33.5 μg/g with some minor fluctuations. Potassium has slightly positive correlation with many heavy metals *viz.* Cd (0.6852) Cu (-0.1689), Fe (0.7116), Mn (0.0611), Ni (0.2623), Pb (0.2369) and Zn (-0.6269) in agricultural soil. Korfali and Davies (2004) and Soltan (1999) have been exhibited a clear idea about the fluctuations in potassium concentrations in soil system.

Sodium in alkali soils results in a deflocculating of the colloids and hence in a breaking down of the soil structural units. This puddle condition renders the soil more or less impervious and retards entrance of irrigation and rain water impedes drainage. In heavy textured soil, the penetration of roots may be restricted by the deflocculated zone. Aeration is also much reduced, setting up aeration conditions and resulting in the formation of reduced compounds which are toxic to plants (Miller and Turk, 2002). The highly alkaline soil was due to the presence of sodium carbonate. Large quantity of adsorbed sodium repressed the availability of several nutrients especially, iron, manganese and phosphorous (Miller and Turk, 2002). The occurrence of sodium in drain sediment was found very high 157.0-587-5μg/g respectively with some minor fluctuations. Desalination of soil is usually accomplished by impounding of water at the surface of the alkaline soil. The relationship between reduction of salts and exchangeable sodium from a given depth of soil and the amount of leaching water for the sandy loam soil (Minhas and Khosla, 1986). The amount of soluble salts in soil can be reducing to safe limits for agriculture crops by leaching (Rao *et al.*, 1987).

In most experiments, usually the effects of one or more water quality parameters on the changes in physico-chemical characteristics of soils and crop productivity have been studied and evaluating the suitability of water for irrigation, however,

Table 9.2.1: Seasonal Variation of Physico-chemical Characteristics of Textile Effluents

Parameters	*Unit*	*Summer 2005*		*Monsoon 2005*		*Winter 2005-06*		*Summer 2006*		*Monsoon 2006*		*Winter 2006-07*		*Summer 2007*	
		Mean	*SD*	*Mean*	*SD*	*Mean*	*SD*	*Mean*	*SD*	*Mean*	*SD*	*Mean*	*SD*	*Mean*	*SD*
Temp.	°C	31.967	3.027	32.733	2.857	25.740	1.038	30.875	3.425	32.833	2.650	26.125	1.044	26.000	0.707
pH		9.817	0.388	10.537	0.667	10.014	0.232	9.913	0.397	10.720	0.752	10.163	0.293	9.650	0.071
TS	mg/l	2465.000	115.763	2579.667	248.902	2210.400	39.202	2479.250	109.113	2643.667	220.731	2262.750	31.245	2370.500	55.861
TSS	mg/l	281.667	33.606	534.000	122.340	141.800	86.187	259.500	66.841	570.667	94.875	165.750	83.699	184.000	43.841
TDS	mg/l	2183.333	82.513	2045.667	184.028	2068.600	93.420	2219.750	55.187	2073.000	193.915	2097.000	52.896	2186.500	12.021
EC	mho/cm	3.411	0.129	3.196	0.288	3.232	0.146	3.450	0.096	3.270	0.312	3.243	0.135	3.415	0.049
DO	mg/l	0.867	0.777	2.867	1.457	3.356	0.649	1.200	0.909	3.233	1.250	3.525	0.479	3.150	0.495
Free-CO_2	mg/l	2.800	0.300	0.900	1.559	0.380	0.531	2.500	0.716	0.733	1.270	0.425	0.492	0.750	1.061
BOD	mg/l	170.000	6.245	163.000	22.113	138.600	16.517	162.500	23.116	158.333	14.572	157.000	21.432	160.000	7.071
COD	mg/l	422.333	31.565	445.000	40.927	367.000	46.179	415.000	48.710	437.333	20.404	386.500	47.339	351.500	14.849
Total alkalinity	mg/l	836.333	52.975	865.667	70.359	633.600	69.551	813.500	77.350	889.000	47.885	642.500	73.532	715.000	14.142
Ca	mg/l	21.333	3.055	25.333	6.506	10.580	3.200	20.250	6.946	27.367	6.783	11.450	3.844	13.000	1.414
Mg	mg/l	16.067	3.465	15.200	3.119	6.580	3.353	13.275	6.734	16.067	2.676	8.950	2.431	4.700	2.121
K	mg/l	7.667	0.764	8.567	0.404	7.716	0.278	7.750	0.714	8.833	0.577	7.950	0.238	7.400	0.141
Cl	mg/l	648.333	95.144	808.667	35.921	652.200	54.843	657.250	95.503	825.667	29.939	691.750	55.030	588.500	9.192
Na	mg/l	153.000	4.359	174.000	10.817	149.600	4.219	152.750	8.302	177.000	7.211	153.750	3.500	145.000	4.243

Table 9.2.2: Seasonal Variation of Physico-chemical Characteristics of Drain Sediments

Parameters	Unit	Summer 2005		Monsoon 2005		Winter 2005-06		Summer 2006		Monsoon 2006		Winter 2006-07		Summer 2007	
		Mean	SD	Mean	SD	Mean	SD	Mean	SD	Mean	SD	Mean	SD	Mean	SD
Temp.	°C	24.933	3.485	23.433	2.259	15.460	3.131	22.838	3.772	23.767	2.250	15.700	2.988	17.600	1.980
WHC	%	31.710	0.505	24.500	5.109	25.670	2.836	31.305	0.865	24.777	5.133	24.888	2.496	29.675	0.247
Bulk density	mg/cm³	1.453	0.067	1.433	0.015	1.332	0.034	1.428	0.063	1.450	0.030	1.353	0.046	1.360	0.028
Soil moisture	%	13.333	1.154	20.723	2.409	15.298	1.163	13.713	0.831	20.850	2.252	15.963	1.436	14.500	0.707
pH		7.840	0.115	8.090	0.165	8.310	0.074	7.970	0.268	8.067	0.153	8.318	0.047	8.325	0.035
EC	mho/cm	32.500	0.889	31.233	1.250	27.860	0.918	32.050	1.529	31.267	1.286	28.100	0.829	29.150	1.344
Cl	µg/g	836.667	145.060	785.333	81.831	613.000	36.173	772.000	168.740	797.667	77.520	637.250	40.434	609.000	33.941
Na	µg/g	490.667	114.605	157.000	98.853	326.400	161.347	515.750	94.979	168.333	89.002	254.000	115.360	587.500	41.719
K	µg/g	31.000	1.000	27.333	1.528	30.800	1.304	31.750	1.258	28.000	1.000	31.000	1.155	33.500	0.707

Table 9.2.3: Seasonal Variations of Heavy Metals in Textile Effluents

Heavy Metals	Unit	Summer 2005		Monsoon 2005		Winter 2005-06		Summer 2006		Monsoon 2006		Winter 2006-07		Summer 2007	
		Mean	SD	Mean	SD	Mean	SD	Mean	SD	Mean	SD	Mean	SD	Mean	SD
Cadmium (Cd)	ppm	0.052	0.042	0.025	0.037	0.012	0.008	0.028	0.008	0.009	0.001	0.005	0.004	0.019	0.001
Copper (Cu)	ppm	0.440	0.085	0.343	0.058	0.165	0.066	0.430	0.127	0.367	0.091	0.180	0.030	0.340	0.079
Iron (Fe)	ppm	0.527	0.093	0.253	0.130	0.266	0.079	0.543	0.170	0.287	0.131	0.240	0.100	0.350	0.085
Manganese (Mn)	ppm	0.153	0.050	0.127	0.047	0.224	0.072	0.176	0.060	0.110	0.020	0.215	0.034	0.310	0.014
Nickel (Ni)	ppm	0.037	0.016	0.016	0.015	0.031	0.013	0.067	0.037	0.007	0.003	0.029	0.013	0.045	0.007
Lead (Pb)	ppm	0.500	0.207	0.250	0.085	0.422	0.133	0.475	0.111	0.330	0.028	0.408	0.158	0.485	0.092
Zinc (Zn)	ppm	0.173	0.059	0.110	0.012	0.238	0.132	0.222	0.091	0.165	0.064	0.338	0.146	0.275	0.035

Table 9.2.4: Seasonal Variations of Heavy Metals in Drain Sediments

Heavy Metals	*Unit*	*Summer 2005*		*Monsoon 2005*		*Winter 2005-06*		*Summer 2006*		*Monsoon 2006*		*Winter 2006-07*		*Summer 2007*	
		Mean	*SD*	*Mean*	*SD*	*Mean*	*SD*	*Mean*	*SD*	*Mean*	*SD*	*Mean*	*SD*	*Mean*	*SD*
Cadmium (Cd)	ppm	5.783	0.231	5.103	0.220	4.250	0.544	5.468	0.553	5.157	0.475	5.110	0.266	5.020	0.184
Copper (Cu)	ppm	49.247	4.963	45.897	6.950	46.454	6.678	54.825	7.333	47.527	10.398	49.435	7.303	45.865	5.819
Iron (Fe)	ppm	8467.667	2448.183	5656.000	1216.719	8090.000	938.127	6469.500	1179.615	6362.000	501.728	7921.250	1751.800	5813.500	185.969
Manganese (Mn)	ppm	1047.333	76.002	791.333	51.733	978.600	52.624	1105.000	107.083	699.333	124.243	1028.250	67.869	1021.000	36.770
Nickel (Ni)	ppm	75.000	3.000	58.000	3.000	60.600	5.941	74.250	4.113	58.667	6.028	58.250	8.139	68.000	4.243
Lead (Pb)	ppm	70.000	4.359	60.667	4.509	47.200	3.834	64.000	11.916	60.667	2.517	52.500	2.646	49.500	10.607
Zinc (Zn)	ppm	260.000	83.540	208.000	87.000	151.400	47.184	251.000	96.620	174.667	67.899	143.500	32.296	196.000	19.799

integration of the interactive and interdependent processes of various water quality indices with soils have required to obtain comprehensive knowledge of the whole system. It requires the development of computerized models for providing a quantitative description of the dynamic behavior of soils upon interaction with irrigation water quality and its relation with crop productivity. Modeling efforts should go a long way in making generalizations based on the experience gained under specific conditions and extrapolation of experimental findings to different locations and seasons in study area.

9.3 Impact on Surface Water

9.3.1 Surface Water

As the water, the most abundant and vital natural resource is extremely essential for survival of all living organisms, but today clean water has become a precious commodity and its quality is threatened by numerous sources of pollution. Water pollution creates physical, chemical and biological changes in the water, and further affects the water quality for a long time of period. As the heavy metals enter in the food chains of aquatic ecosystem, ultimately affect the health of higher animals of that particular ecosystem. Different heavy metals like Mercury, Lead, Chromium, and Nickel, Cadmium etc. release from various sources like agriculture, urban and industrial uses, and these factors degrade the surface water quality.

There is a main source of water in India by the rivers. In India fourteen major river systems share about 83% of the drainage basis *i.e.* Indian rivers carry about 16,45,000 million cubic meter of water annually (Rao, 1975). In India all 14 major rivers including Coocum, Ganga, Gomti, Kaveri, Damodar and Mini-Mahi have become polluted due to various anthropogenic factors especially for the development activities. The river Damodar is perhaps the most heavily polluted river. Many parts of river do not seem to have any dissolved oxygen and no wonder that they fail to support the growth of desirable aquatic fauna and flora.

The Ganga is a holy river of India. Many Indians mainly Hindus worship it like a Goddess. Ganga is also known as Bhagarithi Ganga. Ganga is one of the four mighty rivers of world with its tributaries, and it is a symbol of purity. There are more than 50 big cities situated along with 12,500 km long bank of river Ganga. According to Deming (1975) if the entire ice over of the world would keep flow for 830 years. But now a day due to the various natural and human activities including burning of fossil fuels, natural activities like volcanic eruption, deforestation etc. the earth atmosphere is warming regularly due to the increase in the Co_2 level in the atmosphere. The Himalayas are the cradle of a large number of streams and mighty rivers. These hill streams and rivers ensure all the year round availability of water for irrigating crops as well as for meeting domestic and other needs. Agriculture being the main source of livelihood, water resources generated in the Himalayas are therefore, their greatest gift to this country particularly so far the vast areas in the Indo-gangetic plains in the north. Everything originated in the water and everything is sustained by water. All life on earth depends on water. Man uses water for many purposes drinking, irrigation, fisheries, industrial purposes, transportation and recreations.

The Himalayan rivers receive 20-30% of their water from melting of snow and ice during summer and monsoon seasons. Thus a high altitude Himalayan river basin provides a natural unit within which one can examine natural weathering and agrochemical processes. However, even today the study and management of the Himalayan River is unfortunately constrained by a lock of reliable hydrological data. It is either confined to a hear source region or is based on only few samples. Adequate understanding of the Himalayan proglacial streams is extremely important for the development of a realistic program for utilizing the potential of water that exits in the form of snow and ice in this area. Several studies have been carried out in the lower part of the Ganga river system (Abbas and Subramaniam, 1984, Sarin *et al.* 1989 and Handa, 1972). But very little information is available on agrochemical and biological aspects of the Ganga headwater.

The sustainable use of river water in agriculture resources is an essential component in the future development of Asian third world countries, especially those regions bordering or connecting the Himalayas, where population growth is rapid and predicted to continue. This population pressure results in an intensification of agriculture through the adoption of multiple annual crop solution and supported by large application of inorganic and organic fertilizers and the expansion of cultivated land on to steeper will stapes and previously forested areas (Schreier *et al.* 1994) continued and excessive application of mineral and organic fertilizers to increase crop field may however, lead to detrimental effects in the form of soil and water acidification as well as downstream eutrophication. The impact on water chemistry of anthropogenic pollution from industrial, agricultural, sources, quarrying and tourists activity has concerned environmentalists and scientists for the past two decades. In consequences, the chemistry of headwater streams, lakes and lowland rivers has been monitored widely in Europe and North America in an effort to define and quantifying these anthropogenic impacts. An understanding of now anthropogenic pollutants affect water chemistry and there by the ability to predict the location and severity of potential impact can be achieved only through knowledge of hydro-chemical processes in pristine waters of similar physico-chemical characteristics (Bruns *et at.* 1991). If a sufficiently detailed knowledge has pristine, or baseline, water chemistry is available, the effects of local pollution, stemming form land use and atmospheric deposition of acidic oxides for example can be quantified.

Heavy metals are introduced into aquatic system from various anthropogenic sources. Heavy metals constitute a special group of contaminants of aquatic systems and deserve special attention. Since natural degradation processes do not remove metals, they may become enriched in sediments over time. Metal contamination of sediments is an issue of growing concerns worldwide (NRC, 1989). Both natural processes and anthropogenic activities are responsible for introducing metals in to the aquatic system (Nriagu, 1989). Many contaminants discharged into surface waters rapidly become associated with the particulate matter and incorporated in sediments. Metals in aquatic systems become part of the water-sediment system and their distribution is controlled by a dynamic set of physical-chemical interactions and equilibria, largely governed by pH and type of legends and chelating agents, oxidation state of the mineral components and the redox conditions of the system. Metal contaminated sediments may release heavy metals back to the overlying water column and, thus, pose risk to aquatic life and ecosystems. Due to their particle reactivity, heavy metals tend to accumulate in sediment as a result may persist in the environment long after their primary sources have been removed (Forstner and Wittman, 1981).

Textile effluent pollution may also alter the characteristics of sediment and soil of industrial area directly or indirectly. Composite effluents from textile industries and dye houses of Panipat industrial area normally discharged openly into a common effluent drain without any adequate treatment and commences in a large pond near Binjhole village near to industrial area, which may change the quality of bottom sediments of drain and pond sediment quality and also the physico-chemical characteristics.

The sediments existing as the bottom of the water column play a major role in the pollution scheme of an aquatic system by heavy metals (Forstner, 1985). They reflect the current quality of the water system and can be used in detecting the presence of contaminants that do not remain soluble after discharge into surface water. As a result of complex physical, chemical and biological processes a major fraction of heavy metals (contributed naturally as well as through various anthropogenic activities) is found to be associated with bottom sediments (Baruah *et al.*, 1996). Bed sediments in surface water systems thus act both as a sink and source of metals. Metal accumulation in sediments provides a record of the spatial and temporal history of pollution (Martin and Whitfield, 1983). Hence, sediment monitoring can provide important information on various pollution events.

Beside rivers, large ponds and lakes are the important surface water resiouces of ecological and socio-economical values. But due to the increasing rate of industrialization almost ponds are going polluted day by day. In the present work, textile industrial effluent drained out into a common effluent drain in Panipat industrial area, which flows alongwith industrial region and ultimately joins a large pond (approx. 12 hac) near Binjhole village.

9.3.2 Historical Resume

Different workers from India and abroad have been discussed various aspects of water pollution in term of characteristics of water bodies time to time. This review includes some of important contribution made in the field of industrial pollution, with references to physical, chemical and biological parameters of surface water by different authors of country and abroad.

Hyene (1970) observed the biology of polluted water of a water body near industrial area in New York. Katz (1975) highlighted the effect of heavy metals on some environmental components and biotic organisms of aquatic environment in New York.

Dulka and Risby (1976) stated ultra trace metals in some environmental and biological systems in the vicinity of textile industrial sector. Samy and Gananarethinam (1980) found that industrial effluents were toxic to the aquatic plants like *Eicchornia* even after dilution. Synthetic compounds were found toxic to *Spirodela polyrhiza* and *Lemna aquinoctialis*. Wint (1981) indicated the disposal and handling problem of toxic wastes from industrial wastewater.

Martin and Cougherty (1982) stated the basic monitoring techniques for detection of heavy metals pollution through the biological agents. Ireland (1983) described the heavy metals uptake and their distribution in tissues of organisms. Numberg (1984) studied on the volumetric approach in trace metal chemistry of natural waters and atmospheric precipitation. Nriagu and Pacyna (1988) carried out a study on the quantitative assessment of worldwide contamination of air, water and soil with trace metals.

Goltenboth (1994) evaluated the impact of wastewater of textile factory in Salatiga on the freshwater aquatic ecosystem of Ledok river system at Central Java. Singh *et al.* (1994) highlighted the degradation of water and soil quality of Parwanoo area with respect to heavy metals. Khurshid and Shabeer (1997) observed the degradation of water quality due to heavy metal pollution.

Sharma *et al.* (1999) and Sastry and Rathee (1999) reported the impact of industrial effluents on freshwater system of three villages in Rohtak district. Pujari and Sinha (1999) studied on the water and soil quality of some villages of Attabira area irrigated by bargarg main canal originated from Hirakund reservoir of Orissa.

Chao *et al.* (2005) reported the heavy metal contaminated site in Taiwan and described the status and distribution of heavy metals in environment. Reduce the levels of toxic metals from industrial effluents is necessary before discharging into surface waters. The general methods of treating wastewater-containing metals are coagulation, ion exchange, reverse osmosis and adsorption. Adsorption is a highly effective physico-chemical treatment for removing heavy metals for effluents. Due to high cost of activated carbon, efforts are being directed towards finding low cost adsorbents. Recently much interest has been shown for removal of heavy metals using a large number of low cost materials. Coal fly ash, the solid waste of power plants is one of the cheapest and non-conventional adsorbents (De, 2005).

Saed *et al.* (2005) prepared a novel adsorbent from sugarcane bagasse for removing dye from water and adsorption process was carried out in a batch process with different concentrations of the dye concentrations of the dye solution, different adsorbent doses, adsorbent with different particle size at different pH values and contact times. Kumar *et al.* (2005) described the status of water resources of India and highlighted the hydrological cycle, monsoon and precipitation, surface and groundwater resources, water requirements in domestic use, irrigation, hydroelectric power, industrial requirement and groundwater management in India.

Malik *et al.* (2006) reported the impact of textile effluents on surface water quality of Panipat industrial area. Lokeshwari and Chandrappa (2006) evaluated the impact of heavy metals contamination of a Lake on soil and cultivated vegetation near Bangalore and found the presence of some heavy metals in rice and vegetables, beyond the limit of Indian Standards and calculated metal transfer factors from soil to vegetation are found significant for Zn, Cu, Pb and Cd. Hedge *et al.* (2006) revealed the provenance of heavy minerals with special reference to ilmenite of the Honnevar beach in central west coast of India and observed some trace heavy elements like Co, Cr, V and Ni in the sandy soil of the beach.

Trevors and Saier (2007) described the regulation of pollution in various environmental components *viz.* water, air and soil.

9.3.3 Observations

Physico-chemical Parameters of Pond Water

Temperature (°C)

Temperature of pond water was recorded maximum 32.4 ± 2.5 in monsoon 2006 and minimum 25.3 ± 1.2 in winter 2005-06 ranged between 24.0 to 35.2 °C. The highest value of temperature in pond water was found 35.2 °C during July 2005 and lowest 24.0 °C in January 2006.

pH

The maximum pH value of pond water was recorded 8.63 ± 0.15 in summer 2005 and minimum 8.17 ± 0.12 in monsoon 2005 ranged between 8.1 and 8.8 on pH scale. The highest value of pH in pond water was found 8.8 during May 2005 and lowest 8.1 in September 2006.

Total Solids (mg/l)

The maximum total solids in pond water were recorded 2365.67 ± 104.18 in monsoon 2006 and minimum 2033.20 ± 30.38 in winter 2005-06 ranged between 2012.0 to 2476.0 mg/l. The highest value of total solids in pond water was found 2476 mg/l July 2006 during and lowest 2012 mg/l in January 2006.

otal Dissolved Solids (mg/l)

Total dissolved solids in pond water were recorded maximum 2037.50 ± 44.46 in summer 2006 and minimum 1861.00 ± 102.62 in monsoon 2005 ranged between 1776.0 to 2093.0 mg/l. The highest value of total dissolved solids in pond water was found 2093.0 mg/l during June 2006 and lowest 1776.0 mg/l in September 2005.

Total Suspended Solids (mg/l)

Total suspended solids in pond water were recorded maximum 487.67 ± 23.0 in monsoon 2006 and minimum 96.80 ± 76.81 in winter 2005-06 ranged between 20.0 to 525.0 mg/l. The highest value of total suspended solids in pond water was found 525.0 mg/l during August 2005 and lowest 20.0 mg/l in January 2006.

Electrical Conductivity (µmho/cm)

Maximum electric conductivity in pond water was recorded 3.18 ± 0.07 in summer 2006 and minimum 2.91 ± 0.16 in monsoon 2005 ranged between 2.78 and 3.27 mho/cm. The highest value of electric conductivity in pond water was found 3.27 mho/cm during June, 2006 and lowest 2.78 mho/cm in September 2005.

Dissolved Oxygen (mg/l)

Dissolved oxygen in pond water was recorded maximum 3.43 ± 0.81 in monsoon 2005 and minimum 1.23 ± 0.25 in summer 2005 ranged between 0.9 to 4.2 mg/l. The highest value of dissolved oxygen in pond water was found 4.2 mg/l during January 2006 and lowest 0.9 mg/l in June 2006.

Free CO_2 (mg/l)

Free carbon dioxide in pond water was recorded maximum 2.77 ± 0.25 in summer 2005 and minimum 0.50 ± 0.46 in winter 2005-06 ranged between 0.00 to 3.1 mg/l. The highest value of free carbon dioxide in pond water was found 3.1 mg/l during June, 2006 and lowest 0.00 mg/l in August 2005.

Biochemical Oxygen Demand (mg/l)

The biochemical oxygen demand in pond water was recorded maximum 136.0 ± 4.58 in summer 2005 and minimum 99.0 ± 4.24 in summer 2007 ranged between 90.0 to 161.0 mg/l. The highest value of biochemical oxygen demand in pond water was found 161.0 mg/l during July 2006 and lowest 90.0 mg/l in January 2006.

Chemical Oxygen Demand (mg/l)

The chemical oxygen demand in pond water was recorded maximum 359.67 ± 19.65 in summer 2005 and minimum 274.50 ± 4.95 in summer 2007 ranged between 252.0 to 405.0 mg/l. The highest value of chemical oxygen demand in pond water was found 405.0 mg/l during July 2006 and lowest 252.0 mg/l in January 2006.

Total Alkalinity (mg/l)

Total alkalinity in pond water was recorded maximum 732.33 ± 50.21 in monsoon 2006 and minimum 563.40 ± 45.11 in winter 2005-06 ranged between 505.0 to 785.0 mg/l. The highest value of total alkalinity in pond water was found 785.0 mg/l during July 2006 and lowest 505.0 mg/l in December 2005.

Calcium (mg/l)

The concentration of calcium in pond water was recorded maximum 236.7 ± 51.3 in monsoon 2006 and minimum 104.0 ± 11.4 in winter 2005-06 ranged between 80.0 to 280.0 mg/l. The highest value of calcium in pond water was found 280.0 mg/l during July 2005 and lowest 80.0 mg/l in December 2006.

Magnesium (mg/l)

The concentration of magnesium in pond water was recorded maximum 141.7 ± 41.0 in summer 2005 and minimum 42.5 ± 16.3 in summer 2007 ranged between 25.0 to 178.0 mg/l. The highest value of magnesium in pond water was found 178.0 mg/l during July 2005 and lowest 25.0 mg/l in February 2006.

Potassium (mg/l)

The concentration of potassium in pond water was recorded maximum 8.43 ± 0.21 in monsoon 2006 and minimum 7.3 ± 0.85 in summer 2005 ranged between 6.5 to 8.6 mg/l. The highest value of potassium in pond water was found 8.6 mg/l during July 2006 and lowest 6.5 mg/l in April 2005.

Sodium (mg/l)

Sodium in pond water was recorded maximum 158.67 ± 8.62 in monsoon 2006 and minimum 128.5 ± 8.62 in summer 2007 ranged between 120.0 to 168.0 mg/l. The highest value of Sodium in pond water was found 168.0 mg/l during August 2006 and lowest 120.0 mg/l in March 2006.

Chloride (mg/l)

Chloride in pond water was recorded maximum 770.67 ± 21.13 in monsoon 2006 and minimum 576.50 ± 17.68 in summer 2007 ranged between 512.0 to 793.0 mg/l. The highest value of Chloride in pond water was found 793.0 mg/l during August 2006 and lowest 512.0 mg/l in April 2005.

Textile effluent pollution may also alter the characteristics of sediment and soil of industrial area directly or indirectly. Composite effluents from textile industries and dye houses of Panipat industrial area normally discharged openly into a common effluent drain without any adequate treatment and commences in a large pond near Binjhole village near to industrial area, which may change the quality of bottom sediments of pond sediment quality and also the physico-chemical characteristics. The sediments existing as the bottom of the water column play a major role in the pollution scheme of an aquatic system by heavy metals (Forstner, 1985). They reflect the current quality of the water system and can be used in detecting the presence of contaminants that do not remain soluble after discharge into surface water. As a result of complex physical, chemical and biological processes a major fraction of heavy metals (contributed naturally as well as through various anthropogenic activities) is found to be associated with bottom sediments (Baruah *et al.*, 1996). Bed sediments in surface water systems thus act both as a sink and source of metals. Metal accumulation in sediments provides a record of the spatial and temporal history of pollution (Martin and Whitfield, 1983). Hence, sediment monitoring can provide important information on various pollution events.

Physico-chemical Parameters of Pond Sediment

Temperature (°C)

Temperature of pond sediment was recorded maximum 24.83 ± 3.48 in summer 2005 and minimum 15.35 ± 3.19 in winter 2005-06 ranged between 10.25 to 28.0 °C. The highest value of temperature in pond sediment was found 28.0 °C during June 2005 and lowest 10.25 °C in January 2006.

Water Holding Capacity (%)

Water holding capacity of pond sediment was recorded maximum 36.36 ± 0.77 in summer 2005 and minimum 29.52 ± 4.99 in monsoon 2005 ranged between 25.33 to 37.75 %. The highest value of water holding capacity in pond sediment was found 37.75 % during June 2006 and lowest 25.33 % in September 2005.

Bulk Density (g/cm³)

The bulk density of pond sediment was recorded maximum 1.49 ± 0.05 in monsoon 2006 and minimum 1.36 ± 0.03 in winter 2005-06 ranged between 1.32 to 1.58 g/cm^3. The highest value of bulk density in pond sediment was found 1.58 g/cm^3 during June 2006 and lowest 1.32 g/cm^3 in January 2006.

Soil Moisture (%)

The soil moisture of pond sediment was recorded maximum 20.94 ± 2.37 in monsoon 2006 and minimum 13.54 ± 1.14 in summer 2005 ranged between 12.8 to 22.5 %. The highest value of soil moisture in pond sediment was found 22.5 % during August 2005 and lowest 12.8 % in April 2005.

pH

pH of pond sediment on pH scale was recorded maximum 8.37 ± 0.08 in winter 2005-06 and minimum 7.92 ± 0.09 summer 2005 ranged between 7.82 to 8.45 on pH scale. The highest value of pH in pond sediment was found 8.45 during February 2006and lowest 7.82 in May 2005.

Electrical Conductivity (µmho/cm)

Electric conductivity of pond sediment was recorded maximum 31.93 ± 0.81 in summer 2005 and minimum 27.30 ± 0.91 in winter 2005-06 ranged between 26.3 and 33.0 mho/cm. The highest value of Electric conductivity in pond sediment was found 33.0 mho/cm during June 2006 and lowest 26.3 mho/cm in January 2006.

Chloride (µg/g)

Chloride concentration in pond sediment was recorded maximum 827.0 ± 147.55 in summer 2005 and minimum 588.50 ± 10.61 summer 2007 ranged between 561.0 to 991.0 µg/g. The highest value of chloride in pond sediment was found 991.0 µg/g during June 2005 and lowest 561.0 µg/g in January 2007.

Potassium (µg/g)

Potassium concentration in pond sediment was recorded maximum 33.50 ± 0.71 in summer 2007 and minimum 28.33 ± 1.53 monsoon 2005 ranged between 27.0 to 34.0 µg/g. The highest value of potassium in pond sediment was found 34.0 µg/g during March 2007 and lowest 27.0 µg/g in August 2005.

Sodium (µg/g)

Sodium concentration in pond sediment was recorded maximum 556.00 ± 32.53 in summer 2007 and minimum 143.67 ± 93.0 in monsoon 2005 ranged between 87.0 and 589.0 µg/g. The highest value of sodium in pond sediment was found 589.0 µg/g during April 2005 and lowest 87.0 µg/g in September 2005.

Correlation between heavy metals of pond water and heavy metals of groundwater are given in tabular form. For cadmium correlation was found maximum 0.7155 and 0.7618 with manganese and lead respectively. Correlation for copper was found maximum 0.9116 and 0.8906 with copper and manganese respectively. Correlation for iron was found maximum 0.9580 and 0.9422 with iron and zinc respectively Correlation for manganese was found maximum 0.8076 and 0.7998 with nickel and lead respectively. Correlation for nickel was found maximum 0.9223 and 0.9085 with nickel and zinc respectively. Correlation for lead was found maximum 0.9387 and 0.8863 with iron and lead respectively. Correlation for zinc was found maximum 0.6681 and 0.5405 with cadmium and zinc respectively.

Correlation between heavy metals of pond sediment and heavy metals of effluent drain sediment are given in tabular form for each metal. For cadmium correlation was found maximum 0.9493 and 0.7144 with cadmium and lead respectively. Correlation for copper was found maximum 0.3647 and 0.9273 with cadmium and copper respectively. Correlation for iron was found maximum 0.9466 and 0.1694 with iron and manganese respectively. Correlation for manganese was found maximum 0.9223 and 0.5129 with manganese and nickel respectively. Correlation for nickel was found maximum 0.8060 and 0.9359 with nickel and zinc respectively.

Correlation for lead was found maximum 0.6434 and 0.9388 with cadmium and lead respectively. Correlation for zinc was found maximum 0.7559 and 0.9563 with nickel and zinc respectively.

Correlation between physico-chemical parameters and heavy metals of pond sediment are given in tabular form each metal. For cadmium correlation was found maximum 0.6199 and 0.6032 with electric conductivity and chloride respectively. Correlation for copper was found maximum 0.3937 and 0.3652 with temperature and electric conductivity respectively. Correlation for manganese was found maximum 0.6170 and 0.7442 with sodium and potassium respectively. Correlation for nickel was found maximum 0.8307 and 0.6717 with water holding capacity and chloride respectively. Correlation for lead was found maximum 0.7460 and 0.7158 with temperature and chloride respectively. Correlation for zinc was found maximum 0.8126 and 0.7137 with water holding capacity and chloride respectively.

9.3.4 Discussion

Dye houses of the Panipat region discharge their effluent directly into a common effluent drain, which carry the total of composite effluents towards the village pond at Binjhole adjoining to industrial area, ultimately has altered the water quality and biotic and nutrient dynamic of the pond ecosystem in a tremendous way and further may affect the groundwater quality. Due to post irrigation practices, the soil turns to barren or unfertile and affected agriculture productivity. Further future of these heavy metals is not so managed because the common effluent drain ends up in to a pond near village Binjhole, Industrial area and some local surroundings of dye houses. The effluents discharged from dye houses are quite important for temporal monitoring. Because the effluents store pond is highly contaminated and is a depot of heavy metals due to the presence of chemical dye portions continuously since a long period of time. Heavy metals remain in water ecosystem, but these may travel through food web at various trophic levels and environmental components as well as. Metals moves pond sediments and reach in shallow water table by leaching processes and the metal contamination may disperse in a wide area of the region. Contamination of soils of close areas occurs when the effluents or polluted water comes under the contact of soil. The regular contact of polluted water with soil makes the sodicity and alters the physico-chemical characteristics, texture and profile of soil stratum.

The quality assessment of pond water required to know the alteration in physico-chemical characteristics and pollution load of heavy metals on hydrosphere and lithosphere and to determined the drinking water quality of Panipat industrial zone in term of suitability and possible impacts on human health. The results are depicted in the form of tables and graphs. During the study, physico-chemical characteristics and heavy metals in surface (pond) water were found with some fluctuation according to seasons, place and other factors.

9.3.5 Physico-chemical Parameters of Pond Water

In the present investigation of water resources, physico-chemical characteristics of water directly reflect its quality for irrigation, bathing, drinking and industrial uses. Physico-chemical parameter like total dissolved solids, pH, chloride, total alkalinity, biochemical oxygen demand, chemical oxygen demand, pH are the some important parameters for assessing the quality of water for irrigation and drinking purposes.

Temperature mostly fluctuates according to climatic conditions of the region and directly depends upon seasonal air temperature. The temperature of pond water (25.5-32.4 °C) has fluctuated significantly due to the lentic behaviour of aquatic ecosystem. Temperature of composite effluent drops slightly while reaching in the pond (25.5-32.4 °C). Pathe *et al.* (2005) reported the temperature fluctuation trend from cluster of small cotton textile units from different sector, which follow permissible limit of B.I.S and WHO and remain always below 40°C during study. During the study period temperature of textile industrial effluent never cross the standards limits. Temperature slightly influences some parameters of water and affects the concentration of dissolved oxygen contents and can also influence the activity of bacteria and toxic chemicals in water. Textile industrial effluent may cause problems with high temperature (Groff, 1993). Temperature facilitates the oxidation process biochemical oxygen demand and chemical oxygen demand achieved maximum reduction at high temperature as compared to low temperature (Aslam *et al.*, 2004). Temperature of water depends upon the meteorological characteristics of existing environment; especially air temperature. Temperature fluctuated with air temperature with positive relation. However due to some processes in textile units, the temperature of textile effluents was slightly higher than pond water and groundwater. In drain sediments, temperature has positive relation with lead (0.8233), Zn (0.673), Cd (0.6827); while temperature has not any significant correlation with heavy metal in pond sediment'.

Extreme high pH or rapid pH change can exert stresses conditions or kill aquatic life. Changes in pH can also affect aquatic system indirectly by altering other aspects of water chemistry. Low pH levels accelerate the release of metals from rocks or sediments in the water. Groff (1993) reported that textile wastewater may cause problem used as untreated effluent consist higher pH and temperature. pH has significant importance in all chemicals and biochemical reactions in an aquatic system (Basu *et al.*, 1973). Pond water's pH was also alkaline (8.2-8.6) due to the directly mixing with effluent drains with pond. The pH of both, drain sediment (7.8-8.3) and pond sediments (7.9-8.4) were also noticed alkaline in nature.

The total solids in pond surface water were fluctuated in the range of 2033.2 to 2365.7 mg/l. Similar alterations in surface water quality of the pond were observed by Malik *et al.* (2006). The dissolved solids in wastewater are mainly inorganic salts and relatively unaffected by biological treatment processes and can accumulate in water recirculation system. Failure to remove them may lead to an increase in total solids content of surface water sources. The dissolved solids in wastewater may be harmful to vegetation and also preclude use in various irrigation processes. In the pond, the values of total solids and total dissolved solids were noticed comparatively high, however, these were not found higher than textile industrial effluent. Dissolved solids vary qualitatively and quantitatively in different water depending upon the season, location and other factors. In the present study, the total dissolved solids values in pond water (1861.0-2037.5 mg/l) were not so high according to CPCB standards.

Total dissolved solids are the measure of the quantity of material dissolved in water that can pass through a filter (usually with a pore size of 0.45 micrometers). The material can include carbonate, bicarbonate, chloride, sulfate, phosphate, nitrate, calcium, magnesium, sodium, organic ions, and other ions. Similar to total suspended solids, high concentrations of total dissolved solids may also reduce water transparency, combine with toxic trace compounds and heavy metals, and lead to an increase in water temperature. Total dissolved solids are used to estimate the quality of drinking water, because it represents the amount of ions in the water. High dissolved solids concentrations can produce laxative effects and can give an unpleasant mineral taste to water. High dissolved solids concentrations in water are also unsuitable for water recycling processes and many industrial applications.

Total suspended solids include both organic and inorganic materials, which adversely affect the aquatic life, especially fishes and bottom fauna of surface water ecosystems. These produce carbon dioxide, hydrogen sulfide, methane gases, which are very noxious in nature. They increase the turbidity of water, reduce light penetration and impair photosynthetic activity of aquatic plants in surface water system. Total suspended solids in the pond water (96.8-487.7 mg/l) were found slightly high than recommended by C.P.C.B. and B.I.S.

Because the suspended particles absorb heat from sunlight and changed dissolved oxygen levels to fall, because even further warmer waters can hold less dissolved oxygen. High total suspended solids in a water body can often mean higher concentrations of bacteria, nutrients, pesticides, and metals in the water. These pollutants may attach to sediment particles on the land and be carried into water bodies with storm water. In the water, the pollutants may be released from the sediment or travel farther. Fast running water can carry more particles and larger-sized sediment. Heavy rains can pick up sand, silt, clay, organic particles and heavy rubbish particles from the land and carry it to surface water. A change in flow rate can also affect total suspended solids; if the speed or direction of the water current increases, particulate matter from bottom sediments may be re-suspended.

In pond water, total solids were slightly low due to the settlement of heavy particles on bottom sediment. The ratio of total dissolved solids and total suspended solids with total solids was found quite similar during the study.

Conductance is a measurement of an electrical current with increasing amount and mobility of ions. These ions, which come from the breakdown of compounds, conduct electricity because they are negatively or positively charged when dissolved in water. Therefore, conductance is an indirect measure of the presence of dissolved solids such as chloride, nitrate, sulfate, phosphate, sodium, magnesium, calcium, and iron, and can be used as an indicator of water pollution.

It is not necessary that the water having high electric conductivity is not fit for irrigation. Only one parameter can't ensure the suitability of the water quality. However, the salt composition is high in the water having high Electric conductivity, but it may be beneficial for those soils having a lack or deficiency of some salts.

Generally, there are not regulatory levels for electric conductivity. Instead, the concentration of total dissolved solids is often regulated. However, electric conductivity is an easily-obtained parameter that is a good indicator of the amount of dissolved solids in water, and thus can be used to detect contaminants in water. Total dissolved solids have a direct positive relationship with electric conductivity. If, total dissolved solids of water are high, electric conductivity will be more definitely (Mor *et al.*, 2003). Electric conductivity was recorded very highly positive correlated to total dissolved solids due to the direct relation of total dissolved solids with electric conductivity in pond water (2.9-3.2 mho/cm). The dissolved oxygen in water is often attributed to the fact the oxygen is dissolved more during the period of active photosynthesis. Hutchinson (1957) reported that the water has low temperature has greater capacity for holding gases. The value of dissolved oxygen in the all sampling sites was found out to be low dissolved oxygen. The DO was found low in pond water (1.2-3.4 mg/l), however, in some months dissolved oxygen was found very low in pond water due to the increasing rate of biodegradation of different compounds in water column. As the matter of fact that the effluents carried highly pollution load, which could not allow any flora and fauna to survive in unfavourable condition and there will be no photosynthesis process in polluted habitat. The value of dissolved oxygen was recorded even less values (2.56±0.21 mg/l) in the summer month. This trend was stated by Khanna *et al.* (1992) and Joshi (1996) in surface water system. The dissolved oxygen showed an inverse relationship with temperature as reported by Das and Srivastava (1956) and Dobriyal (1985) in aquatic system.

Biochemical oxygen demand and chemical oxygen demand are the measurement of the oxygen consuming capabilities of organic matter. Textile effluent during their process of deposition exerts biochemical oxygen demand/chemical oxygen demand, which have a catastrophic effect on the ecosystem by depleting the oxygen supply. Decay process causes the production of noxious gases as hydrogen sulfide and methane. Water with high biochemical oxygen demand/chemical oxygen demand indicates presence of decomposing organic matter and subsequent high bacteria counts that degrade its quality and potential uses (Verma and Kharat, 2000). Biochemical oxygen demands of the pond water (99.0-136.0 mg/l) were found high as given in standards of C.P.C.B., B.I.S. and WHO.

Chemical oxygen demand is directly proportional to biochemical oxygen demand. In fact, chemical oxygen demand explains the load of pollutants and degree of pollution in aquatic system. COD was observed 274.5-359.7 mg/l in pond water due to the high rate of decomposition of organic material in polluted and stored water. COD shows a positive relationship with BOD and negative with DO (Khanna, 1993) and mostly remains in the ratio of approximately 1:3 ± 0.5 in the case of waste water. Water containing high biochemical oxygen demand and chemical oxygen demand are responsible for a heavy depletion of oxygen levels in the particular sector of water body or soil (Sial *et al.*, 2006).

Water alkalinity is caused by strong bases and the salts of strong alkalis and weak acids. Carbonates are added to a water system if the water passes through soil and rock that contain carbonate minerals, such as calcite ($CaCO_3$). Where limestone and sedimentary rocks and carbonate-rich soils are predominant, waters will often have high alkalinity. Where igneous rocks (such as granite) and carbonate-poor soils are predominant waters will have low alkalinity. Alkalinity is a measure of the buffering capacity of water, or the capacity of bases to neutralize acids. Waters with low alkalinity are very susceptible to changes in pH. Waters with high alkalinity are able to resist major shifts in pH. As increasing amounts of acid are added to a water body, the pH of the water decreases, and the buffering capacity of the water is consumed. Because alkalinity and pH are so closely related, changes in pH can also affect alkalinity, especially in a poorly buffered system. Above pH 8.3, alkalinity is mostly in the form of carbonate (CO_3^{2-}); below 8.3, alkalinity is present mostly as bicarbonate (HCO_3^-).

The values of alkalinity in the pond water (563.4-732.3 mg/l) were found very high. Alkalinity not only helps regulate the pH of a water body, but also the metal content. Alkalinity has found with positive correlations with Cd (0.0237), Cu (0.809), Fe (0.8896), Mn (0.7664), Ni (0.7918), Pb (0.5841) and Zn (0.7069) Bicarbonate and carbonate ions in water can remove toxic metals (such as lead, arsenic, and cadmium) by precipitating the metals out of solution.

Hardness represents the concentration of calcium and magnesium ions, because these are the most common polyvalent cations. Other ions, such as iron and manganese, may also contribute to the hardness of water, but are generally present in much lower concentrations. Calcium, magnesium, and other polyvalent cations such as iron and manganese may be added to a natural water system as it passes through soil and rock containing large amounts of these elements in mineral deposits. Hardness mainly depends on the amount of calcium and magnesium salts or both present in the groundwater, water hardness is not health hazard but its values should remain below permissible level to restore the taste to water (WHO, 1984)

Some textile industrial processes may also produce significant amounts of calcium and manganese that are later discharged as industrial wastewater. Calcium was found 10.4-23.6 mg/l in pond water. When hardness equals alkalinity, the only cations present in significant concentrations in the water are calcium and magnesium. When hardness is greater than alkalinity, the waters may contain considerable amounts of other cations. Magnesium was found low in pond water (4.2-14.1 mg/l). Potassium is one of the important element among ten chemical element required in rather large quantities fir growth of all crops. Plants growth may be limited by a deficient available supply of potassium but its high some quantity may alter the soil composition. High K in water used in irrigation may alter the soil quality (Miller and Turk, 2002). Potassium was found low in pond water (7.3-8.4 mg/l).

Sodium salts in the water are much more objectionable than salts of calcium and magnesium because of the tendency of sodium to cause deflocculation of the colloidal fraction of the soil and developed an undesirable structure water contain sufficient heavy metals to prove toxic to continue use by plants. As sodium chloride used in textile industry so the concentration of sodium and chloride will be high in the waste water (Aslam *et al.*, 2004). Sodium was found very high in groundwater of industrial area, because sodium should not be higher than 20 mg/l in drinking water (WHO, 2006). Sodium values were found very high in pond water (128.5-158.7 mg/l).

Chloride is one of the most conservative constituents in wastewater, being affected very little either by vegetative growth or other biological processes, or by precipitation or anion exchange reaction. Chloride concentrations in pond water (576.5-770.7 mg/l) were also expected to be high by the permissible limit of C.P.C.B. Chloride does not have a health-based standard for drinking water. Chloride has been suggested as a standard value for drinking purposes (EPA, 1989). The Maximum Contaminant Level (MCL) of 250000 µg/L is based on poor taste chloride imparts to water. Chloride is not affected by adsorption or degradation processes and is therefore a conservative chemical in soil and groundwater. Chloride concentrations begin to increase at some depth due to dissolution reactions within the aquifer. Chloride is therefore a good indicator of human impacts in the environment (MPCA, 2001). Chloride concentration in irrigation water should be less than 75 ppm, otherwise it may be harmful for soil structure. Textile effluents are high in toxicity not only for human beings of surroundings but also a serious threat to groundwater and surface water resources (Aslam *et al.*, 2004).

9.3.6 Physico-chemical Parameters of Pond Sediment

Physico-chemical characteristics of soil may demonstrate the pollution status in the industrial region, so, physical and chemical characteristics are important for the assessment of contamination and pollution load. Sediment characteristics are the good indicator for the pollution load in pond bottom. The temperature of soil greatly affects the physical, biological and chemical processes occurring in soil system. Biological decomposition can come to a near standstill, thereby limiting the rate at which nutrients such as nitrogen, phosphorus, sulphur and calcium are made available. Absorption and transport of water and nutrient ions by higher plants are adversely affected by low temperature (Brady, 1995). The temperature of field soils is not subject to radical human regulation. However, two kinds of management practices have significant effects on soil temperature, those that keep some type of cover or mulch on the soil and those that reduce excess soil moisture. There is not any significant variation in the temperature of drain sediment (15.5-24.9 °C) and pond sediment (15.3-24.8 °C) and also between agricultural soil (17.4-27.8 °C) and control soil (17.5-27.8 °C). The chemical processes and activities of microorganism which convert plant nutrients into available forms are also materially influenced by temperature. Removal of excess water from soil may facilitate changes in soil temperature. Humus content, good tillage, dark color of soil are the some other factors which influence the soil temperature (Miller and Turk, 2002).

Water holding capacity is a property as to water quantity is absorbed or retained by given amount of soil (Ramani and Srivastava, 1989). Water held in the soil pores with varying degrees of tenacity depending on the amount of water present and the size of pores in soils. Depending on the soil, as much as one forth to two thirds of the moisture may remain in the soil after the plants have wilted or died due to the lack of soil water. The phenomenon of capillarity is a common one, the classic example being the movement of water up a wick when the lower end is immersed in water. Capillary forces are at work in all moist soils. However, the rate of movement and the rise in height are less than one would expect on the basis of soil pore size. One reason is that soil pores are filled with air, which may be entrapped, showing down or preventing the movement of water by capillary. Usually the height of the rise resulting from capillarity is greater with fine textured soils if sufficient time is allowed and the pores are not too small. This is readily explained on the basis of the capillary size and the continuity of the pores. With sandy soils the adjustment is rapid but so many of the pores are non-capillary that the height of rise cannot be great (Brady, 1995). Water holding capacity was found similar in drain sediment (24.5-31.7 %) and pond sediment (29.5-36.3 %) and also between agricultural soil (36.1-43.7 %) and control soil (36.8-44.2 %) with much difference between soil and sediment. Yuandong *et al.* (2006) described the similar trend of water holding capacity on the basis of soil texture and chemical composition in the agricultural soil system. The pore space of a soil is that portion of the soil volume occupied by air and water. The amount of pore space is determined by the arrangement of the solid particles. If the particles lie close together, as in stands or compact sub-soils, the total porosity is low. If they are arranged in porous aggregates, as is often the case in medium textured soils high in organic matter, the pore space per unit volume will be high. Soil aeration may influence the availability of nutrients to plants (Miller and Turk, 2002). Bulk density relates to the combined volumes of the solids and pore spaces, soils with a high proportion of pore space to solids have lower bulk densities than those that are more compact and have less pore space. Consequently, any factor that influences soil pore space will affect bulk density. Mainly soil texture and compactness strongly influence the bulk density of soils (Brady, 1995). The bulk density was found similar between drain sediment (1.33-1.45 g/cm^3) and pond sediment (1.36-1.49 g/cm^3) and exhibited same between agricultural soil (1.15-1.24 g/cm^3) and control soil (1.10-1.22 g/cm^3) Bulk density was similarly described by Yuandong *et al.* (2006) and Krebs *et al.* (1999) in soil environment.

The soil structure influences its moisture content. A well granulated soil has more total pore space than one with poor granulation or one that has been compacted. The reduced pore space may be reflected in a lower water holding capacity. The compacted soil also has to higher proportion of small and medium sized pores, which tend to hold the water with greater tenacity than do the larger pores. Moisture content of drain sediment (13.3-20.8 %) and pond sediment (13.5-20.9 %), agricultural soil (3.5-10.7 %) and control soil (3.7-11.06 %) were found similar during the study. Rainwater leaching have made more efficient if antecedent moisture content of the soil profile was increased by saline water irrigation just before the onset of monsoons. On a wet soil, a rainfall event is expected to displace the salts to a greater depth. Conservation and proper utilization of rainwater for leaching salts is also utmost important.

The soil pH shows the acidity and basic nature of the soil. The soil is acidic if the pH is lower, while the higher pH means that soil is basic. The pH value was observed slightly high (7.11-7.63) in agriculture land, which shows that agriculture land is going to alkaline in nature which confirms that agriculture land again disturbed by its proper pH values whereas due to the decay of organic matter has produced the acidic properties of soil. If the decomposition of organic matter is there in soil, it will turn the pH low, other wise some foreign substances may alter the soil nature and properties towards alkaline (Nongkynrih *et al.*, 1996). Initial soil pH is an important property of the soil because of its influence on the infiltration rate of the soil (Gupta *et al.*, 1989). There are several causes of minor fluctuation in soil pH. For instance, the movements of salts into and out of soil moisture moves up and down the profile will influence pH. Similarly, the pH of mineral soils declines during the crop-growing season as a result of the acids produced by microorganisms and by the roots of higher plants. When soil temperatures are low, an increase in pH often is noted because biotic activities during these times are considerably slower. Soil pH significantly influences other soil chemical properties as well as biological organisms. High pH of textile industrial effluent can hampers plant crop growth (Sial *et al.*, 2006). The soil pH significantly affects the availability of most of the chemical element of importance to plants and microbes. Likewise, the tendency for toxic levels of element such as iron, manganese, aluminum to be established at low pH and deficiencies of iron and manganese at high pH have been mentioned. Continuous application of effluents with high pH will render the soils unfit for further cultivation (Sial *et al.*, 2006). Soil pH was found alkaline in drain sediment (7.8-8.3) and pond sediment (7.9-8.37), and slightly alkaline in agricultural soil (7.1-7.6) and control soil (7.2-7.4). Similar trend of pH fluctuation have been described by Kasem and Singh (1999) in agricultural soil environment.

Electric conductivity is the measure of current carrying capacity, which gives a clear idea of soluble salts present in soil. Conductivity generally depends upon the dilution of suspension. However, the salt composition is high in the water having high electric conductivity, but it may be beneficial for those soils having a lack or deficiency of some salts. The electric conductivity of drain sediment, pond sediment, agricultural soil and control soil was found in the range of 27.8-32.5, 27.3-31.9, 24.1-27.7 and 23.0-23.7 mho/cm respectively with some minor fluctuations. Electric conductivity has positive correlation with all heavy metals *viz.* Cd (0.3965) Cu (0.9454), Fe (0.4198), Mn (0.9076), Ni (0.8286), Pb (0.8596) and Zn (0.7586) in agricultural soil.

Chloride was found very high in effluent drain sediment and slightly low as with similar fluctuation in pond bed sediment, but in agricultural soil and soil near textile industries chloride was found comparatively low because of the high settlement of chloride in drain sediment from textile industrial effluent; while rest was reach in agricultural soil by various contacts. The chloride in drain sediment, pond sediment, agricultural soil and control soil was found 609.0-836.6, 588.5-827.0, 499.5-734.3 and 313.8-529.3 μg/g respectively with some minor fluctuations. Chloride has positive correlation with all heavy metals *viz.* Cd (0.3654) Cu (0.8479), Fe (0.3249), Mn (0.7254), Ni (0.6603), Pb (0.6972) and Zn (0.7744) in agricultural soil environment. Manchanda (1990) has also reported that pulse crops such as pea, mungbean, gram, lentil, and broadbean suffered more due to toxic accumulation of chloride, when irrigated with Cl ion then SO_4^{-2} dominant (70%) water of more salinity.

The exchangeable potassium is the chief source of available potassium in soil, in most cases (Jha and Pandey, 1984). Potassium plays many essential roles in plants. It is an activator of dozens of enzymes responsible for such plants processes as energy metabolism, starch synthesis, nitrate reduction, and sugar degradation. Potassium is extremely mobile within the plant and helps regulate the opening and closing of

Table 9.3.1: Seasonal Variation of Physico-chemical Characteristics of Pond Water

Parameters	Unit	Summer 2005		Monsoon 2005		Winter 2005-06		Summer 2006		Monsoon 2006		Winter 2006-07		Summer 2007	
		Mean	*SD*	*Mean*	*SD*	*Mean*	*SD*	*Mean*	*SD*	*Mean*	*SD*	*Mean*	*SD*	*Mean*	*SD*
Temperature	°C	31.733	3.035	32.133	3.002	25.300	1.204	30.050	3.730	32.400	2.506	25.625	0.854	25.500	0.707
pH		8.633	0.153	8.167	0.115	8.360	0.114	8.550	0.129	8.233	0.153	8.450	0.129	8.500	0.000
TS	mg/l	2251.333	73.009	2308.667	109.792	2033.200	30.376	2255.000	103.418	2365.667	104.175	2102.250	36.854	2155.500	6.364
TSS	mg/l	230.333	32.868	447.667	67.002	96.800	76.810	217.500	60.688	487.667	23.007	158.750	96.555	141.500	37.477
TDS	mg/l	2021.000	40.951	1861.000	102.621	1936.400	73.040	2037.500	44.463	1878.000	91.831	1943.500	81.127	2014.000	31.113
EC	mho/cm	3.158	0.064	2.908	0.160	3.026	0.114	3.184	0.069	2.934	0.143	3.037	0.127	3.147	0.049
DO	mg/l	1.233	0.252	3.433	0.814	3.360	0.513	1.600	0.707	3.067	0.751	3.250	0.526	3.000	0.283
Free-CO_2	mg/l	2.767	0.252	0.833	1.443	0.500	0.458	2.250	0.794	0.700	1.212	0.650	0.443	0.800	0.141
BOD	mg/l	136.000	4.583	129.000	23.302	106.800	16.423	125.250	19.687	134.333	23.438	117.250	17.095	99.000	4.243
COD	mg/l	359.667	19.655	335.000	52.431	282.600	28.387	333.000	45.233	346.667	51.404	298.250	24.918	274.500	4.950
Total alkalinity	mg/l	696.667	56.607	725.000	46.872	563.400	45.114	696.500	52.399	732.333	50.213	571.250	51.370	647.500	36.062
Ca	mg/l	180.000	30.000	216.667	65.064	104.000	11.402	172.500	51.235	236.667	51.316	115.000	28.868	110.000	14.142
Mg	mg/l	141.667	41.016	140.000	34.699	61.000	31.297	114.500	62.804	157.000	20.298	78.500	25.891	42.500	16.263
K	mg/l	7.300	0.854	8.200	0.265	7.540	0.207	7.500	0.668	8.433	0.208	7.675	0.206	7.350	0.071
Cl	mg/l	609.333	105.235	762.667	33.262	633.200	58.538	610.250	91.482	770.667	21.127	664.250	57.570	576.500	17.678
Na	mg/l	137.667	2.517	152.333	11.676	130.600	4.879	134.500	11.387	158.667	8.622	137.750	6.076	128.500	2.121

Table 9.3.2: Seasonal Variation of Physico-chemical Characteristics of Pond Sediments

Parameters	Unit	Summer 2005		Monsoon 2005		Winter 2005-06		Summer 2006		Monsoon 2006		Winter 2006-07		Summer 2007	
		Mean	*SD*	*Mean*	*SD*	*Mean*	*SD*	*Mean*	*SD*	*Mean*	*SD*	*Mean*	*SD*	*Mean*	*SD*
Temperature	°C	24.833	3.485	23.317	2.251	15.350	3.185	23.450	3.903	23.733	2.359	15.775	2.777	17.150	2.333
WHC	%	36.360	0.777	29.517	4.998	30.544	2.767	36.275	1.253	30.367	4.849	29.958	2.349	34.425	1.011
Bulk density	mg/cm^3	1.483	0.071	1.460	0.046	1.366	0.034	1.463	0.085	1.493	0.051	1.373	0.040	1.385	0.007
Soil moisture	%	13.543	1.135	20.900	2.433	15.456	1.097	13.965	0.731	20.943	2.376	16.150	1.666	14.740	0.099
pH		7.923	0.093	8.167	0.153	8.370	0.077	8.063	0.180	8.100	0.100	8.350	0.058	8.350	0.071
EC	mho/cm	31.933	0.808	30.833	1.350	27.300	0.914	31.450	1.605	31.233	1.250	27.500	0.963	28.650	1.626
Cl	µg/g	827.000	147.553	775.333	81.513	603.000	34.792	761.500	171.148	798.333	71.459	608.000	46.890	588.500	10.607
Na	µg/g	472.000	115.052	143.667	93.002	310.200	160.243	495.250	93.053	151.000	73.750	267.500	126.234	556.000	32.527
K	µg/g	32.000	1.000	28.333	1.528	31.400	1.342	32.750	0.500	28.667	1.528	31.500	1.291	33.500	0.707

Table 9.3.3: Seasonal Variations of Heavy Metals in Pond Water

Heavy Metals	*Unit*	*Summer 2005*		*Monsoon 2005*		*Winter 2005-06*		*Summer 2006*		*Monsoon 2006*		*Winter 2006-07*		*Summer 2007*	
		Mean	*SD*	*Mean*	*SD*	*Mean*	*SD*	*Mean*	*SD*	*Mean*	*SD*	*Mean*	*SD*	*Mean*	*SD*
Cadmium (Cd)	ppm	0.009	0.001	0.001	0.002	0.004	0.002	0.012	0.006	0.002	0.003	0.004	0.002	0.007	0.001
Copper (Cu)	ppm	0.427	0.045	0.397	0.136	0.252	0.084	0.423	0.053	0.403	0.150	0.245	0.070	0.370	0.014
Iron (Fe)	ppm	9.700	3.035	4.233	1.450	4.820	2.961	9.450	1.529	4.567	1.501	3.850	2.111	8.750	0.636
Manganese (Mn)	ppm	0.530	0.061	0.463	0.070	0.172	0.062	0.490	0.122	0.470	0.056	0.170	0.059	0.295	0.035
Nickel (Ni)	ppm	0.127	0.025	0.073	0.033	0.054	0.045	0.130	0.014	0.082	0.022	0.047	0.038	0.115	0.007
Lead (Pb)	ppm	1.800	0.557	0.610	0.412	0.504	0.364	1.725	0.287	0.727	0.448	0.503	0.346	1.165	0.332
Zinc (Zn)	ppm	0.156	0.031	0.110	0.020	0.158	0.066	0.165	0.017	0.113	0.012	0.183	0.025	0.195	0.007

Table 9.3.4: Seasonal Variations of Heavy Metals in Pond Sediments

Heavy Metals	*Unit*	*Summer 2005*		*Monsoon 2005*		*Winter 2005-06*		*Summer 2006*		*Monsoon 2006*		*Winter 2006-07*		*Summer 2007*	
		Mean	*SD*	*Mean*	*SD*	*Mean*	*SD*	*Mean*	*SD*	*Mean*	*SD*	*Mean*	*SD*	*Mean*	*SD*
Cadmium (Cd)	ppm	5.717	0.451	4.780	0.455	4.054	0.595	5.410	0.677	4.993	0.359	5.073	0.153	4.795	0.120
Copper (Cu)	ppm	51.520	5.098	43.880	6.877	43.834	7.332	52.463	6.505	43.477	12.357	44.450	13.422	38.645	9.228
Iron (Fe)	ppm	5640.333	2179.050	4312.667	463.092	6013.400	856.579	4356.500	998.172	4157.667	403.026	5844.000	1878.244	3803.500	113.844
Manganese (Mn)	ppm	942.000	48.135	724.000	56.471	836.400	38.708	928.000	56.291	605.000	161.707	883.500	27.791	927.500	4.950
Nickel (Ni)	ppm	63.667	8.083	52.333	9.074	52.800	3.768	63.750	11.117	54.333	7.024	49.000	5.944	56.500	2.121
Lead (Pb)	ppm	69.000	6.245	55.333	9.292	44.000	5.385	62.000	13.491	57.333	6.028	49.250	3.403	44.500	10.607
Zinc (Zn)	ppm	240.000	92.601	142.333	59.341	123.200	42.032	207.250	86.496	153.667	62.963	116.250	32.755	166.500	12.021

stomata in the leaves and the uptake of water by root cells. At any one time most of the potassium is in the primary mineral and non-exchangeable forms. To maintain the level of exchangeable and soil solution potassium high enough to encourage good crop production, chemical fertilizer are used. Potassium may deficient in alkaline soil and an excess of potassium may delay maturity of plant. In some crops it may tend to accumulate in the leaf and stem rather than in the grain (Miller and Turk, 2002). The potassium in drain sediment, pond sediment, agricultural soil and control soil was found almost in uniform pattern 27.3-33.5, 28.3-33.5, 31.0-36.5 and 30.3-34.5 µg/g respectively with some minor fluctuations. Potassium has slightly positive correlation with many heavy metals *viz.* Cd (0.6852) Cu (-0.1689), Fe (0.7116), Mn (0.0611), Ni (0.2623), Pb (0.2369) and Zn (-0.6269) in agricultural soil. Korfali and Davies (2004) and Soltan (1999) have been exhibited a clear idea about the fluctuations in potassium concentrations in soil system.

Sodium in alkali soils results in a deflocculation of the colloids and hence in a breaking down of the soil structural units. This puddle condition renders the soil more or less impervious and retards entrance of irrigation and rain water impedes drainage. In heavy textured soil, the penetration of roots may be restricted by the deflocculated zone. Aeration is also much reduced, setting up aeration conditions and resulting in the formation of reduced compounds which are toxic to plants (Miller and Turk, 2002). The highly alkaline soil was due to the presence of sodium carbonate. Large quantity of adsorbed sodium repressed the availability of several nutrients especially, iron, manganese and phosphorous (Miller and Turk, 2002).

The occurrence of sodium in pond sediment was found very high 143.6-556.0 µg/g with some minor fluctuations. Desalination of soil is usually accomplished by impounding of water at the surface of the alkaline soil. The relationship in between reduction of salts and exchangeable sodium from a given depth of soil and the amount of leaching water for the sandy loam soil (Minhas and Khosla, 1986). The amount of soluble salts in soil can be reduce to safe limits for agriculture crops by leaching (Rao *et al.*, 1987).

Usually the effects of one or more water quality parameters on the changes in physico-chemical characteristics of soils and crop productivity have been studied and evaluating the suitability of water for irrigation in most experiments, however, integration of the interactive and interdependent processes of various water quality indices with soils have required to obtain comprehensive knowledge of the whole system. It requires the development of computerized models for providing a quantitative description of the dynamic behavior of soils upon interaction with irrigation water quality and its relation with crop productivity. Modeling efforts should go a long way in making generalizations based on the experience gained under specific conditions and extrapolation of experimental findings to different locations and seasons in study area.

9.4 Impact on Groundwater

9.4.1 Groundwater

Clean groundwater is needed for more than drinking purposes. Agriculture depends highly on groundwater for irrigation; as a large number of groundwater pumps were used for crop irrigation in India. Poor or contaminated groundwater could jeopardize crops and threaten the health of livestock. Groundwater is connected to surface water in the hydrological cycle, and some aquifers actually feed area springs and rivers. Sometimes contamination occurs naturally by mixing the sallow aquifers with other contaminated sources of water table. Saline water from deeper aquifers may reach aquifers that provide water for human beings, livestock and others agricultural activities. Some groundwater may have naturally high levels of nitrates, metals, iron, sulfate, or chloride, all of which provides an odd odor, color, or taste in water. Groundwater contamination has become a major problem in recent decades due to exploring industrialization. Groundwater, as a wide resource for irrigation in most part of country, may contaminate the soil quality by repeated irrigation of agricultural fields. Bed quality of groundwater used in irrigation may alter the characteristics of agriculture soils of the area.

Groundwater is used for industries, domestic supply and agriculture irrigation in most part of the world as it is a replenishable resource and has inherent advantage over surface water. There has been a tremendous increase in the demand of freshwater due to growth in population, advanced agriculture practices and industrial usages (Bachmat, 1994). In the last two decades, the rapid growth of industrialization and urbanization has created negative impacts on the environment. Due to industrial, municipal and agricultural wastes containing pesticides, insecticides, fertilizers residues and heavy metals with water; groundwater has been polluted by leaching process of pollutants present in effluents (Sastry and Rathee, 1999). In Haryana, about 90% of the population of rural areas utilizes groundwater for drinking, washing and other daily uses. But groundwater in Haryana is very saline and large variation in salinity can be observed over a short distance. Water table is also very high. Therefore, scarcity of drinking water is very big problem faced by population of this state. Panipat district of Haryana is well known for the textile industries. A large number of small-scale industries mainly textile printing and textile dying have been established in Panipat city. These industries discharge their effluent openly into pond or other water bodies. The seepage of effluents posed serious threat to the groundwater resources (Groff, 1993). So, groundwater must be managed and protected carefully for the most beneficial use in the future.

In the present study, the impact of textile effluents was found on pond environment and polluted pond may alter the ecological parameters of surroundings, so, groundwater may be polluted. This contaminated groundwater used in irrigation purposes may harmful for soils of agriculture fields and ultimately effects on productivity of agriculture crop plants, and soil macrobiotic community.

Different workers from India and abroad have been discussed various aspects of water pollution in term of characteristics of water bodies, affected agricultural soils and bottom sediments from time to time. This review includes some of important contribution made in the field of industrial pollution, with references to physical, chemical and biological parameters of groundwater, surface water, characterization of textile industrial effluents, contaminated agricultural irrigated soil and bottom sediment soils by different authors of country and abroad.

9.4.2 Historical Resume

Eaton (1950) described the significance of carbonates in waters mostly used for irrigation purposes in agriculture. Gardner (1957) suggested some steady state solutions of the unsaturated moisture flow equation with application to evaporation from a water table. Kanwar (1961) assessed the quality of irrigation water as an index of suitability for irrigation purposes. Seeber (1962) highlighted the cation hydrological facies of groundwater in the English town Formation in New Jersey. Darra *et al.* (1964) evaluated the water quality of irrigation water used in Rajasthan. Hoston (1965) stated that water quality index is a rating of water quality parameters by a single numerical expression reflecting the composite influence of water quality parameters (physical, chemical and bacteriological) significant for a specific beneficial use.

Saksena *et al.* (1966) evaluated the quality of groundwaters for irrigation in Ahor developmental block, Jalore. Singh and Bhumbla (1968) analyzed the effect of quality of irrigation water on soil properties. Singh *et al.* (1969) reported the salinity problem in high water table areas of north India.

Singh and Sharma (1971) studied on the effects of saline irrigation waters on physico-chemical properties of some soils of Rajasthan. Sharma and Parihar (1973) evaluated the effect of depth and salinity of groundwater on evaporation and soil salinization. Sharma *et al.* (1975) presented the status of groundwaters quality of Jind district, Haryana with special reference to the chemical composition of waters used in irrigation in agricultural sector. Sharma *et al.* (1976) described the status of groundwaters quality of Karnal district of Haryana with special reference to the chemical composition of waters used in irrigation in agricultural sector. Singh *et al.* (1977) highlighted the salinity and sodium hazards of underground irrigation waters of Bhatinda district of Punjab state. Shivakumar *et al.* (1977) made a geo-graphical approach for toxic trace element pollution in groundwater around Patancheru and Bollaram Industrial area, A.P., India. Sharma (1978) studied on the testing of a model for prediction sodium hazards of irrigation waters.

Todd (1980) described the groundwater movement; groundwater properties and hydrogeology for explain the behaviour of groundwater pollution. Vates (1986) made a study on septic tank density and groundwater contamination by different composite effluents of textile industries. Rhoades (1987) studied on the use of saline water for irrigation. Nriagu and Pacyna (1988) carried out a study on the quantitative assessment of worldwide contamination of air, water and soil with trace metals. Zilliox (1989) determined the industrial impacts on the quality of groundwater in a large basin as a case of the Rhine aquifer in France and noticed it harmful for public consumption. Narayan and Suresh (1989) evaluated the chemical quality of groundwater of Mangalore city in state Karnataka.

Minhas and Gupta (1992) indicated the effects of wastewater irrigation in agriculture soils and found sodicity due to the poor water quality. Karle *et al.* (1992) studied groundwater quality in Pravaranagar area of Ahmednagar district and Kumar *et al.* (1992) studied the relationship between Fluoride, total hardness and total alkalinity in the groundwater of Bharmar District (Rajsthan). PPCB (1993) released a report on groundwater quality of Ludhiana city, Punjab based on the quality of the tube wells and hand pumps in shallow waters.

Kataria *et al.* (1995) studied organic contamination in Bore well waters of BHEL area of Bhopal and give a baseline data for further study on same problem. Sharma *et al.* (1995) assessed the quality of groundwater in municipal and fringe areas near Gwalior. Singh *et al.* (1996) carried out a hydrological analysis on groundwater samples collected from 19 open wells in different parts of Varanasi city. Sharma and Patel (1996) determined copper in water of Raipur with the help of spectrophotometer. Kataria (1996) analysed the BOD and COD contents in bore well water of Bhopal (M.P.). Prasad and Chandra (1997) studied well water quality status of Hyderabad and Khurshid and Shabeer (1997) observed water quality degradation due to heavy metal pollution. Garg *et al.* (1998) observed the fluoride concentrations in undergroundwater of Hissar, Haryana. Mohan *et al.* (1998) observed heavy metals (Fe, Pb, Ca and Zn) in the groundwater of Naini industrial area; Dist. Allahabad, U.P. Kashem and Singh (1999) had also found the decreasing concentration of Cu, Mn, Pb and Zn in groundwater with increasing distance from disposal point. Stetzenbach *et al.* (1999) evaluated the heavy metals in groundwater and used multivariate statistical analysis. Dutta (1999) highlighted the groundwater situation in Delhi. Rao and Rao (1999) identified the path lines of pollutants migration in groundwater of the Visakhpatanam urban area of south India using computer models. Particles path lines in the groundwater indicated a predominant northeast and southwest migration of groundwater pollution in the area.

Tyagi and Budhi (2000) postulated the degradation of groundwater quality due to heavy metals in industrial area of India. Reddy and Linn (2000) used catalysts against nitrate pollution in groundwater and observed it significantly suitable for abatement of groundwater pollution. Kumar *et al.* (2001) studied on the impact of textile industry on groundwater quality of Sanagar, Jaipur and found the high amount of chemicals (e.g. sulphuric acid and acetic acid) and dyes (e.g. chrome and metal dyes) suspended solids and toxic metals in the waste which may enter in the groundwater and deteriorate its quality. Aurangabadkar *et al.* (2001) studied on groundwater quality at Chennai. Srinivas *et al.* (2002) pointed out the groundwater pollution due to the industrial effluents in Kothur industrial area, Mahaboonagar, (A.P.). Siddiqui and Pathania (2002) made some studies on heavy metals in surface and groundwater of Jalandhar and Ludhiana districts of Punjab state. Vishwanath and Ananthmurthy (2002) assessed the groundwater quality around a solid waste dumping site and concluded that groundwater contains high electric conductivity; TDS, hardness and fluorides but the nitrates and chlorides were with in the permissible limits of potable drinking water standards. Yadav *et al.* (2002) highlighted the post irrigation impact of domestic sewage effluent on composition of soils, crops and groundwater in Kurukshetra district. Mohan and Sharma (2002) and Yadav *et al.* (2003) determined the groundwater quality of different places of Rajasthan. Reshma and Prakasham (2003) studied the potability of Dug wells in Kerala. Royee and Prakasham (2003) analysed the water characteristics of dug and tube wells of Kollam municipality in Tamilnadu. Yadav and Lata (2003) indicated the heavy metal pollution in groundwater in Bahadurgarh block of districts Jhajjar, Haryana. Mishra and Sahoo (2003) evaluated the groundwater quality in and around Deogarh. Mor *et al.* (2003) assessed the quality of groundwater of Jind city in Haryana state. Malik *et al.* (2004) evaluated the accumulation of heavy metals in crop plants through irrigation of contaminated groundwater in Panipat region and emphasized on bioremediation processes for combat groundwater pollution. Mahesha and Prasad (2004) elaborated the physico-chemical characteristics of bore well water in Arsikara taluk, Hassan.

Reduction of the levels of toxic metals from industrial effluents is necessary before discharging into surface waters. The general methods of treating wastewater-containing metals are coagulation, ion exchange, reverse osmosis and adsorption. Adsorption is a highly effective physico-chemical treatment for removing heavy metals for effluents. Due to high cost of activated carbon, efforts are being directed towards finding low cost adsorbents. Recently much interest has been shown for removal of heavy metals using a large number of low cost materials. Coal fly ash, the solid waste of power plants is one of the cheapest and non-conventional adsorbents (De, 2005).

Dwivedi *et al.* (2005) indicated the contamination of groundwater due to the artificial groundwater recharging in Gengetic plain area. Kumar *et al.* (2005) described the status of water resources of India and highlighted the hydrological cycle, monsoon and precipitation, surface and groundwater resources, water requirements in domestic use, irrigation, hydroelectric power, industrial requirement and groundwater management in India. Dutta (2005) highlighted the ethics of groundwater for its sustainability and the vulnerability and depletion of groundwater due to rapid growth of population, urbanization, industrialization and competition for economic development and also stated the groundwater contamination, concepts of groundwater management, strategies for the groundwater protection and suggested use of contaminated groundwater. Palanivelu *et al.* (2006) evidenced the poor groundwater quality in areas like Kottivakkam beach, Kuppam Oorurokot, Kuppam. Singh (2006) indicated the contamination of groundwater of Ganges-Brahmaputra river basin in north east India and found the groundwater unfit for direct human consumption and noticed the rice and vegetable fields irrigated by groundwater received a large amount of arsenic through shallow tube wells in the affected areas of north 24 *Parganas* and Murshidabad, West Bangal.

Malik *et al.* (2007) assessed the migration of heavy metals in the groundwater regime of Panipat industrial area on the behalf of different spatial variations the heavy metals were found in maximum quantities at point source of pollution. Rizk *et al.* (2007) identified the sources of dissolved solids and water in Wadi Al Bih aquifer, Ras Al Khaimah Emirate in United Arab Emirates. Vijith and Satheesh (2007) completed the Geographical Information System (GIS) based assessment of spatiotemporal characteristics of groundwater quality of upland sub-watersheds of Meenachil River, parts of Western Ghats, Kottayam District of Kerala, India. Obiri (2007) determined the heavy metals in water from boreholes in Dumasi in the Wassa West District of Western Region of Republic of Ghana. Fransson (2007) studied on to verify the methods for estimating transmissivity distributions along boreholes. Mico *et al.* (2007) described the comparison of two digestion methods for the analysis of heavy metals by flame atomic absorption spectroscopy.

9.4.3 Observations

Experimental Site

Physico-chemical Parameters of Groundwater

Temperature (°C)

Temperature of groundwater was recorded maximum 31.63 ± 2.5 in monsoon 2006 and minimum 25.5 ± 0.71 in summer 2007 ranged between 25.0 to 34.5 °C. The highest value of temperature in groundwater was found 34.5 °C during July 2005 and lowest 25.0 °C in February 2007.

pH

The maximum pH value of groundwater was recorded 7.7 ± 0.1 in summer 2005 and minimum 7.43 ± 0.06 in monsoon 2005 ranged between 7.3 to 7.8 on pH scale. The highest value of pH in groundwater was found 7.8 during June 2006 and lowest 7.3 in October 2005.

Total Solids (mg/l)

The maximum total solids in groundwater were recorded 1464.67 ± 191.20 in summer 2005 and minimum 782.75 ± 121.72 in winter 2006-07 ranged between 641.0 to 1688.0 mg/l. The highest value of total solids in groundwater was found 1688 mg/l during June 2006 and lowest 641.0 mg/l in November 2005.

Total Dissolved Solids (mg/l)

Total dissolved solids in groundwater were recorded maximum 1331.67 ± 169.74 in summer 2005 and minimum 710.25 ± 110.09 in winter 2006-07 ranged between 612.0 to 1537.0 mg/l. The highest value of total dissolved solids in groundwater was found 1537.0 mg/l during June 2006 and lowest 612.0 mg/l in December 2005.

Total Suspended Solids (mg/l)

Total suspended solids in groundwater were recorded maximum 133.0 ± 21.52 in summer 2005 and minimum 72.50 ± 11.73 in winter 2006-07 ranged between 62.0 to 155.0 mg/l. The highest value of total suspended solids in groundwater was found 155.0 mg/l during June 2005 and lowest 62.0 mg/l in November 2006.

Electrical Conductivity (μmho/cm)

Maximum electric conductivity in groundwater was recorded 2.08 ± 0.265 in summer 2005 and minimum 1.11 ± 0.17 in winter 2006-07 ranged between 0.90 and 2.40 mho/cm. The highest value of electric conductivity in groundwater was found 2.40 during June 2006 and lowest 0.90 in November 2005.

Dissolved Oxygen (mg/l)

Dissolved oxygen in groundwater was recorded maximum 4.0 ± 0.45 in monsoon 2006 and minimum 2.57 ± 0.21 in summer 2005 ranged between 2.4 to 4.8 mg/l. The highest value of dissolved oxygen in groundwater was found 4.8 mg/l during January 2006 and lowest 2.4 mg/l in April 2005.

Free CO_2 (mg/l)

Free carbon dioxide in groundwater was recorded maximum 0.93 ± 0.15 in summer 2005 and minimum 0.10 ± 0.20 in winter 2006-07 ranged between 0.00 to 1.1

mg/l. The highest value of free carbon dioxide in groundwater was found 1.1 mg/l during April 2005 and lowest 0.0 mg/l in August 2005.

Biochemical Oxygen Demand (mg/l)

The biochemical oxygen demand in groundwater was recorded maximum 35.67 ± 8.15 in summer 2005 and minimum 11.00 ± 2.82 in summer 2007 ranged between 5.0 to 57.0 mg/l. The highest value of biochemical oxygen demand in groundwater was found 57.0 mg/l during July 2005 and lowest 5.0 mg/l in January 2006.

Chemical Oxygen Demand (mg/l)

The chemical oxygen demand in groundwater was recorded maximum 93.00 ± 16.52 in summer 2005 and minimum 27.50 ± 7.78 in summer 2007 ranged between 12.0 to 130.0 mg/l. The highest value of chemical oxygen demand in groundwater was found 130.0 mg/l during July 2006 and lowest 12.0 mg/l in January 2006.

Total Alkalinity (mg/l)

Total alkalinity in groundwater was recorded maximum 596.67 ± 48.91 in monsoon 2006 and minimum 493.60 ± 31.1in winter 2005-06 ranged between 448.0 to 653.0 mg/l. The highest value of total alkalinity in groundwater was found 653.0 mg/l during July 2006 and lowest 448.0 mg/l in November 2005.

Calcium (mg/l)

The concentration of calcium in groundwater was recorded maximum 143.3 ± 47.3 in monsoon 2006 and minimum 46.0 ± 16.7 in winter 2005-06 ranged between 20.0 to 180.0 mg/l. The highest value of calcium in groundwater was found 180.0 mg/l during July 2005 and lowest 20.0 mg/l in December 2005.

Magnesium (mg/l)

The concentration of magnesium in groundwater was recorded maximum 97.7 ± 35.2 in monsoon 2006 and minimum 14.02 ± 22.0 in summer 2007 ranged between 15.0 to 141.0 mg/l. The highest value of magnesium in groundwater was found 141.0 mg/l during June 2006 and lowest 15.0 mg/l in January 2006.

Potassium (mg/l)

The concentration of potassium in groundwater was recorded maximum 6.10 ± 0.10 in monsoon 2005 and minimum 4.90 ± 0.14 in summer 2007 ranged between 4.8 to 6.2 mg/l. The highest value of potassium in groundwater was found 6.2 mg/l during August 2006 and lowest 4.8 mg/l in April 2005.

Sodium (mg/l)

Sodium in groundwater was recorded maximum 97.67 ± 11.24 in monsoon 2006 and minimum 51.00 ± 13.45 in winter 2005-06 ranged between 36.0 to 110.0 mg/l. The highest value of Sodium in groundwater was found 110.0 mg/l during July 2006 and lowest 36.0 mg/l in December 2005.

Chloride (mg/l)

Chloride in groundwater was recorded maximum 151.33 ± 17.95 in monsoon 2006 and minimum 47.50 ± 3.54 in summer 2007 ranged between 24.0 to 172.0 mg/l. The highest value of Chloride in groundwater was found 172.0 mg/l during July 2005 and lowest 24.0 mg/l in January 2006.

Control Site

Physico-chemical Parameters of Groundwater

Temperature (°C)

Temperature of groundwater on control site was recorded maximum 30.60 ± 2.15 in monsoon 2005 and minimum 26.64 ± 0.47 in winter 2005-06 ranged between 26.0 to 32.8 °C. The highest value of temperature in groundwater was found 32.8 °C during July 2005 and lowest 26.0 °C in November 2005.

pH

The maximum pH value of groundwater on control site was recorded 7.45 ± 0.07 in summer 2007 and minimum 7.13 ± 0.058 in summer 2005 ranged between 7.1 and 7.6 on pH scale. The highest value of pH in groundwater was found 7.6 during January 2007 and lowest 7.1 in September 2005.

Total Solids (mg/l)

The maximum total solids in groundwater on control site were recorded 780.50 ± 110.30 in winter 2006-07 and minimum 446.75 ± 76.16 in summer 2006 ranged between 363.0 to 907.0 mg/l. The highest value of total solids in groundwater was found 907.0 mg/l during November 2005 and lowest 363.0 mg/l in April 2005.

Total Dissolved Solids (mg/l)

Total dissolved solids in groundwater on control site were recorded maximum 709.50 ± 100.14 in winter 2006-07 and minimum 404.50 ± 69.02 in summer 2006 ranged between 328.0 to 822.0 mg/l. The highest value of total dissolved solids in groundwater was found 822.0 mg/l during November 2005 and lowest 328.0 mg/l in April 2005.

Total Suspended Solids (mg/l)

Total suspended solids in groundwater on control site were recorded maximum 71.00 ± 10.17 in winter 2006-07 and minimum 42.25 ± 7.18 in summer 2006 ranged between 35.0 to 85.0 mg/l. The highest value of total suspended solids in groundwater was found 85.0 mg/l during November 2005 and lowest 35.0 mg/l in April 2006.

Electrical Conductivity (mho/cm)

Maximum electric conductivity in groundwater on control site was recorded 1.11 ± 0.16 in winter 2006-07 and minimum 0.632 ± 0.11 in summer 2006 ranged between 0.513 and 1.284 mho/cm. The highest value of electric conductivity in groundwater was found 1.284 mho/cm during November 2005, and lowest 0.513 mho/cm in April 2005.

Dissolved Oxygen (mg/l)

Dissolved oxygen in groundwater on control site was recorded maximum 3.57 ± 0.50 in monsoon 2005 and minimum 2.37 ± 0.51 in summer 2005 ranged between 1.8 to 4.1 mg/l. The highest value of dissolved oxygen in groundwater was found 4.1 mg/l during September 2005 and lowest 1.8 mg/l in April 2005.

Free CO_2 (mg/l)

Free carbon dioxide in groundwater on control site was recorded maximum 0.93 ± 0.15 in summer 2005 and minimum 0.17 ± 0.29 in monsoon 2005 ranged between

0.00 to 1.1 mg/l. The highest value of free carbon dioxide in groundwater was found 1.1 mg/l during April 2005 and lowest 0.00 mg/l in October 2005.

Biochemical Oxygen Demand (mg/l)

The biochemical oxygen demand in groundwater on control site was recorded maximum 15.67 ± 6.11 in monsoon 2006 and minimum 6.60 ± 5.69 in winter 2005-06 ranged between 0.00 to 22.0 mg/l. The highest value of biochemical oxygen demand in groundwater was found 22.0 mg/l during July 2005 and lowest 0.00 mg/l in January 2006.

Chemical Oxygen Demand (mg/l)

The chemical oxygen demand in groundwater on control site was recorded maximum 40.67 ± 15.04 in monsoon 2006 and minimum 16.00 ± 13.17 in winter 2005-06 ranged between 0.00 to 57.00 mg/l. The highest value of chemical oxygen demand in groundwater was found 57.0 mg/l during July 2005 and lowest 0.00 mg/l in January 2006.

Total Alkalinity (mg/l)

Total alkalinity in groundwater on control site was recorded maximum 303.00 ± 22.91 in summer 2005 and minimum 216.40 ± 41.62 in winter 2005-06 ranged between 156.0 to 331.0 mg/l. The highest value of total alkalinity in groundwater was found 331.0 mg/l during May 2006 and lowest 156.0 mg/l in October 2005.

Calcium (mg/l)

The concentration of calcium in groundwater on control site was recorded maximum 110.0 ± 10.0 in monsoon 2005 and minimum 40.0 ± 14.1 in summer 2005 ranged between 30.0 to 120.0 mg/l. The highest value of calcium in groundwater was found 120.0 mg/l during August 2005 and lowest 30.0 mg/l in February 2007.

Magnesium (mg/l)

The concentration of magnesium in groundwater on control site was recorded maximum 101.0 ± 23.3 in monsoon 2006 and minimum 21.0 ± 4.2 in summer 2007 ranged between 15.0 to 127.0 mg/l. The highest value of magnesium in groundwater was found 127.0 mg/l during July 2006 and lowest 15.0 mg/l in February 2006.

Potassium (mg/l)

The concentration of potassium in groundwater on control site was recorded maximum 5.80 ± 0.10 in monsoon 2005 and minimum 4.65 ± 0.21 in summer 2007 ranged between 4.4 to 5.9 mg/l. The highest value of potassium in groundwater was found 5.9 during August 2005 and lowest 4.4 in April 2005.

Sodium (mg/l)

Sodium in groundwater on control site was recorded maximum 58.33 ± 10.26 in monsoon 2005 and minimum 18.50 ± 3.54 in summer 2007 ranged between 9.0 to 67.0 mg/l. The highest value of Sodium in groundwater was found 67.0 mg/l during July 2005 and lowest 9.0 mg/l in December 2005.

Chloride (mg/l)

Chloride in groundwater on control site was recorded maximum 13.00 ± 3.78 in monsoon 2005 and minimum 4.90 ± 1.11 in summer 2006 ranged between 3.9 to 21.0

mg/l. The highest value of Chloride in groundwater was found 21.0 mg/l during October 2005 and lowest 3.9 mg/l in April 2005.

Correlation Coefficient

Correlations between the heavy metals of groundwater of 40 ft depth are given in tabular form for each metal. Correlation between lead and manganese was found 0.9365, 0.8564 for nickel and lead, 0.8227 for nickel and zinc. Correlation value for iron and zinc was found 0.9363. Correlations between the heavy metals of groundwater of 80 ft depth are given in tabular form for each metal. For manganese correlation was 0.9446, 0.9195 and 0.9207 for nickel, lead and zinc respectively. For copper correlation was found 0.9623, 0.9548, 0.8559 and 0.9000 for manganese, nickel, lead and zinc respectively. Correlations between the heavy metals of deep groundwater of more than 120 ft depth are given in tabular form for each metal. Correlation for copper was found maximum 0.8289, 0.9427, 0.9122, 0.5557 and 0.9509 with iron, manganese, nickel, lead and zinc respectively. Correlation for iron was found 0.9104, 0.7884, 0.8446 and 0.8660 with manganese, nickel, lead and zinc respectively. Correlation for nickel was found 0.5299 and 0.8346 with lead and zinc respectively.

Correlation between heavy metals of groundwater and heavy metals of agricultural soil are given in tabular form for each metal. For cadmium correlation was found maximum 0.7611 and 0.6466 with cadmium and lead respectively. Correlation for copper was found maximum 0.9733 and 0.9121 with iron and nickel respectively. Correlation for iron was found maximum 0.8074 and 0.8628 with manganese and lead respectively. Correlation for manganese was found maximum 0.9279 and 0.9548 with nickel and zinc respectively. Correlation for nickel was found maximum 0.9458 and 0.9475 with manganese and nickel respectively. Correlation for lead was found maximum 0.9482 and 0.9664 with copper and manganese respectively. Correlation for zinc was found maximum 0.8065 and 0.5301 with iron and nickel respectively.

9.4.4 Discussion

With the increase in industrialization our health problems are increasing day by day. Today the pollution especially of water resources is increasing steadily due to rapid population growth, industrial proliferation, urbanization increasing living standards and wide sphere of human activities. The greatest danger to the quality of environment is posed by human activities such as poorly organized and unregulated disposal of industrial, domestic waste and crude oil spillage are the major causes of the environmental deterioration. The industrial effluent over the years has caused serious damages of the surrounding soil, groundwater and agriculture crops (Chao *et al.*, 2005). Most of the dye houses of the Panipat region discharge their effluent directly into a common effluent drain, which carry the total of composite effluents towards the village pond at Binjhole adjoining to industrial area, ultimately has altered the water quality and biotic and nutrient dynamic of the pond ecosystem in a tremendous way and further may affect the groundwater quality. Due to post irrigation practices, the soil turns to barren or unfertile and affected agriculture productivity.

Generally, textile industry consumes substantial volume of water and chemicals in wet processing of textile materials. Wet processing of cloth or fibers dying requires huge amount of different chemical dyes and wash away them with the wastewater discharged through industrial outlet. Thus, the common effluent drain consist all types of dye residuals in a composite form. This composite effluent is very toxic in nature due to the presence of different synthetic dyes, which contain various toxic heavy metals. Further future of these heavy metals is not so managed because the common effluent drain ends up in to a pond near village Binjhole, Industrial area and some local surroundings of dye houses. The effluents discharged from dye houses are quite important for temporal monitoring. Because the effluents store pond is highly contaminated and is a depot of heavy metals due to the presence of chemical dye portions continuously since a long period of time. Heavy metals remain in water ecosystem, but these may travel through food web at various trophic levels and environmental components as well as. Metals moves pond sediments and reach in shallow water table by leaching processes and the metal contamination may disperse in a wide area of the region. Contamination of soils of close areas occurs when the effluents or polluted water comes under the contact of soil. The regular contact of polluted water with soil makes the sodic and alters the physico-chemical characteristics, texture and profile of soil stratum.

Thus, the quality assessment of groundwater required to know the pollution load of heavy metals on hydrosphere and lithosphere and to determine the drinking water quality of Panipat industrial zone in term of suitability and possible impacts on human health. In the present study, water samples were collected and analyzed for determination of physico-chemical characteristics and distribution of heavy metals from April 2005 to March 2007 regularly. The results are depicted in the form of tables and graphs.

9.4.5 Physico-chemical Parameters of Groundwater

In the present investigation of water resources, physico-chemical characteristics of water directly reflect its quality for irrigation, bathing, drinking and industrial uses. Physico-chemical parameter like total dissolved solids, pH, chloride, total alkalinity, biochemical oxygen demand, chemical oxygen demand, pH are the some important parameters for assessing the quality of water for irrigation and drinking purposes.

The distribution of groundwater is not uniform in a region due to the unequal utilization and exploitation rate of groundwater. In certain areas there are quite a large number of tube wells whereas in other areas there are practically no tube wells. Water consumption from groundwater is negligible in some areas due to the less exploitation of groundwater resources. So, for proper monitoring of water quality random sampling is the best option for analyzing the physico-chemical parameter of water.

Temperature mostly fluctuates according to climatic conditions of the region and directly depends upon seasonal air temperature. However, groundwater temperature remains comparatively lower (25.5-31.6 °C) due to the geothermal energy. The temperature of textile common effluents (25.7-32.8 °C) and pond water (25.5-32.4 °C) has fluctuated significantly due to the lentic behaviour of aquatic ecosystem. Temperature of composite effluent drops slightly while reaching in the pond (25.5-

32.4 °C). Pathe *et al.* (2005) reported the temperature fluctuation trend from cluster of small cotton textile units from different sector, which follow permissible limit of B.I.S and WHO and remain always below 40°C during study. During the study period temperature of textile industrial effluent never cross the standards limits. Temperature slightly influences some parameters of water and affects the concentration of dissolved oxygen contents and can also influence the activity of bacteria and toxic chemicals in water. Textile industrial effluent may cause problems with high temperature (Groff, 1993). Temperature facilitates the oxidation process biochemical oxygen demand and chemical oxygen demand achieved maximum reduction at high temperature as compared to low temperature (Aslam *et al.*, 2004). Temperature of water depends upon the meteorological characteristics of existing environment; especially air temperature. Temperature fluctuated with air temperature with positive relation. However due to some processes in textile units, the temperature of textile effluents was slightly higher than pond water and groundwater. With the increasing of depth of water table temperature often decreases, but increased in winter season due to the geo-thermal energy. Temperature of agricultural soil fluctuated in the range of (17.4-27.8 °C), and comparatively low than the temperature of drain sediment (15.5-24.9 °C) and pond sediment (15.3-24.8 °C) in almost all seasons. Temperature has positive correlation with iron (0.9188) Mn (0.6670), Ni (0.7044), Cu (0.6860) in groundwater sample, while in soil and sediment having negative relation. In drain sediments, temperature has positive relation with lead (0.8233), Zn (0.673), Cd (0.6827); while temperature has not any significant correlation with heavy metal in pond sediment'. Similar observations were made by Mahesh and Prasad (2004), Mustafa *et al.* (1998) in groundwater samples.

In the present study, the pH of the textile effluents was recorded mostly alkaline. The pH of the composite effluents was highly alkaline, which slightly decreases in pond water system. Extreme high pH or rapid pH change can exert stresses conditions or kill aquatic life. Changes in pH can also affect aquatic system indirectly by altering other aspects of water chemistry. Low pH levels accelerate the release of metals from rocks or sediments in the water. Groff (1993) reported that textile wastewater may cause problem used as untreated effluent consist higher pH and temperature. pH has significant importance in all chemicals and biochemical reactions in an aquatic system (Basu *et al.*, 1973).

pH of textile industrial effluent was found mostly basic (9.6-10.7) due to the high salt load and high alkalinity. Pond water's pH was also alkaline (8.2-8.6) due to the directly mixing with effluent drains with pond. The pH of both, drain sediment (7.8-8.3) and pond sediments (7.9-8.4) were also noticed alkaline in nature. The pH of groundwater was found slightly alkaline (7.4-7.7) and decreasing alkalinity with increasing depth. The pH of deep groundwater and agricultural soil was found slightly alkaline (7.1-7.6) respectively and very near to 7 (neutral) during present study. Similar trend is in agreement with that reported by Sial *et al.* (2006), Pathe *et al.* (2005) in textile industrial effluent, Singh *et al.* (1994) in effluent drain and Mor *et al.* (2003), Yadav and Lata (2003) in groundwater.

Total solids were found very high in textile industrial effluent (2210.4-2643.7 mg/l) due to the high degree of pollution. Different dyes and fibers are present in the textile waste water, which generally released dissolved solids into common effluent drain. The total solids in pond surface water were fluctuated in the range of 2033.2 to 2365.7 mg/l. Similar alterations in surface water quality of the pond were observed by Malik *et al.* (2006). The dissolved solids in wastewater are mainly inorganic salts and relatively unaffected by biological treatment processes and can accumulate in water recirculation system. Failure to remove them may lead to an increase in total solids content of surface water sources. The dissolved solids in wastewater may be harmful to vegetation and also preclude use in various irrigation processes. Total dissolved solids in the textile effluents were observed very high than the prescribed limits of C.P.C.B. and B.I.S values. In the pond, the values of total solids and total dissolved solids were noticed comparatively high, however, these were not found higher than textile industrial effluent. Dissolved solids vary qualitatively and quantitatively in different water depending upon the season, location and other factors. In the present study, the total dissolved solids values in effluents (2045.7-2219.7 mg/l) and pond water (1861.0-2037.5 mg/l) were not so high according to CPCB standards. Similar observations were also reported by Yusuf and Sonibare (2004), Garg and Kaushik (2006) in textile industrial effluent and Mor *et al.* (2003), Mustafa *et al.* (2003) in groundwater.

Total dissolved solids are the measure of the quantity of material dissolved in water that can pass through a filter (usually with a pore size of 0.45 micrometers). The material can include carbonate, bicarbonate, chloride, sulfate, phosphate, nitrate, calcium, magnesium, sodium, organic ions, and other ions. Similar to total suspended solids, high concentrations of total dissolved solids may also reduce water transparency, combine with toxic trace compounds and heavy metals, and lead to an increase in water temperature. Total dissolved solids are used to estimate the quality of drinking water, because it represents the amount of ions in the water. High dissolved solids concentrations can produce laxative effects and can give an unpleasant mineral taste to water. High dissolved solids concentrations in water are also unsuitable for water recycling processes and many industrial applications. The values of total dissolved solids concentrations recorded in the present study are comparable to those obtain by Pathe *et al.* (2005), Yusuf and Sonibare (2004), Garg and Kaushik (2006) in textile industrial effluent and Mustafa *et al.* (2003), Mor *et al.* (2003) and Sastry and Rathee (1999) in groundwater.

Total suspended solids include both organic and inorganic materials, which adversely affect the aquatic life, especially fishes and bottom fauna of surface water ecosystems. These produce carbon dioxide, hydrogen sulfide, methane gases, which are very noxious in nature. They increase the turbidity of water, reduce light penetration and impair photosynthetic activity of aquatic plants in surface water system. Total suspended solids in the effluents (141.8-570.7 mg/l) and pond water (96.8-487.7 mg/l) were found slightly high than recommended by C.P.C.B. and B.I.S. Chavan *et al.* (2005) reported the adverse impacts of total suspended solids on the surroundings environment of the industrial effluent near Sukhna river at Midc area, Aurangabad.

High total suspended solids in a water body can often mean higher concentrations of bacteria, nutrients, pesticides, and metals in the water. These pollutants may attach to sediment particles on the land and be carried into water bodies with storm water. In the water, the pollutants may be released from the sediment or travel farther. The flow rate of the effluent drain is a primary factor in total suspended solids concentrations. Fast running water can carry more particles and larger-sized sediment. Heavy rains can pick up sand, silt, clay, organic particles and heavy rubbish particles from the land and carry it to surface water. A change in flow rate can also affect total suspended solids; if the speed or direction of the water current increases, particulate matter from bottom sediments may be re-suspended.

Total solids were found very high in textile industrial effluent due to the dirt release during the washing of textile materials. In pond water, total solids were slightly low due to the settlement of heavy particles on bottom sediment. In shallow groundwater, total solids were found slightly higher than those of in deep groundwater. Similarly, total dissolved solids and total suspended solids were also correlated to groundwater of various depth. The ratio of total dissolved solids and total suspended solids with total solids was found quite similar during the study. Such types of trends in determining the total suspended solids load have been reported by Garg and Kaushik (2006), Yusuf and Sonibare (2004) in textile industrial effluent and Mor *et al.* (2003), Mustafa *et al.* (2003) in groundwater. Liquid wastewater from textile industries are not fit for irrigation regarding electric conductivity and total suspended solids (Bohn *et al.*, 1976, Abbas, 1991).

Conductance is a measurement of an electrical current with increasing amount and mobility of ions. These ions, which come from the breakdown of compounds, conduct electricity because they are negatively or positively charged when dissolved in water. Therefore, conductance is an indirect measure of the presence of dissolved solids such as chloride, nitrate, sulfate, phosphate, sodium, magnesium, calcium, and iron, and can be used as an indicator of water pollution.

It is not necessary that the water having high electric conductivity is not fit for irrigation. Only one parameter can't ensure the suitability of the water quality. However, the salt composition is high in the water having high Electric conductivity, but it may be beneficial for those soils having a lack or deficiency of some salts. Electric conductivity has a positive correlation with total dissolved solids in textile industrial effluent and groundwater also. Generally, there are not regulatory levels for electric conductivity. Instead, the concentration of total dissolved solids is often regulated. However, electric conductivity is an easily-obtained parameter that is a good indicator of the amount of dissolved solids in water, and thus can be used to detect contaminants in water. Total dissolved solids have a direct positive relationship with electric conductivity. If, total dissolved solids of water are high, electric conductivity will be more definitely (Mor *et al.*, 2003).

Electric conductivity was recorded very highly positive correlated to total dissolved solids due to the direct relation of total dissolved solids with electric conductivity in textile industrial effluent (3.1-3.4 mho/cm), pond water (2.9-3.2 mho/cm) and groundwater (1.1-2.0 mho/cm), while minimum at control site (0.63-1.1 mho/cm). Fluctuation in electric conductivity chiefly depends upon the quantity of ions in groundwater in various seasons. Electric conductivity has highly positive relation with Manganese (0.8544), nickel (0.8021) and lead (0.8340) in groundwater samples, while positive relations with almost all metals in agricultural soil. Sial *et al.* (2006), Garg and Kaushik (2006) were made similar observations in textile industrial effluent, Singh *et al.* (1994) in drain, Mahesh and Prasad (2004), Mor *et al.* (2003), Mustafa *et al.* (2003) in groundwater; which support the result of present study.

The dissolved oxygen in water is often attributed to the fact the oxygen is dissolved more during the period of active photosynthesis. Hutchinson (1957) reported that the water has low temperature has greater capacity for holding gases. The value of dissolved oxygen in the all sampling sites was found out to be low dissolved oxygen. The DO was found low in textile effluent (0.87-3.5 mg/l) and pond water (1.2-3.4 mg/l), however, in some months dissolved oxygen was found nil in textile industrial effluent and very low in pond water due to the increasing rate of biodegradation of different compounds in water column. As the matter of fact that the effluents carried highly pollution load, which could not allow any flora and fauna to survive in unfavourable condition and there will be no photosynthesis process in polluted habitat. The value of dissolved oxygen was recorded even less values (2.56±0.21 mg/l) in the summer month. This trend was stated by Khanna *et al.* (1992) and Joshi (1996) in surface water system. The dissolved oxygen showed an inverse relationship with temperature as reported by Das and Srivastava (1956) and Dobriyal (1985) in aquatic system.

Groundwater usually has low concentrations of dissolved oxygen, but it is also often colder than stream water. Oxygen is more easily dissolved into water at low altitudes than at high altitudes, because of higher atmospheric pressure. Oxygen is more easily dissolved into water with low levels of dissolved or suspended solids. Very low dissolved oxygen concentrations in water can result in mobilization of trace metals. DO have mostly negative correlation (-0.4459, -0.4396, -0.6278, -0.6314, -0.4856, -0.6519, -0.4412) in groundwater and (-0.6152, -0.5741, -0.8010, 0.1536, -0.4807, -0.2132, 0.0685) in textile industrial effluent with almost heavy metals (Cd, Cu, Fe, Mn, Ni, Pb and Zn) respectively. The value of dissolved oxygen recorded in the present study are comparable to results obtained by Yusuf and Sonibare (2004), Garg and Kaushik (2006) in textile industrial effluent, Singh *et al.* (1994) in effluent drain, Mahesh and Prasad (2004) and Mustafa *et al.* (2003) in groundwater.

Free carbon dioxide in most textile industrial effluents was fluctuated in the range of 0.38 to 2.8 mg/l. However, the dissolved oxygen contents was also not found high in textile industrial effluent (0.87-3.5 mg/l) and pond water (2.57-4.00 mg/l) and remain low (2.5-4.0 mg/l) in groundwater samples. Free carbon dioxide mainly depends upon some physico-chemical parameter like dissolved oxygen, pH, temperature, etc. (www.holar.is). Carbon dioxide has highly positive correlations (0.4060, 0.5115, 0.6729, 0.6306, 0.5276, 0.6839 and 0.5164) in groundwater and also (0.6627, 0.6112, 0.7573, -0.0984, 0.4410, 0.3252, -0.0395) in textile industrial effluents with almost all heavy metals (Cd, Cu, Fe, Mn, Ni, Pb and Zn) respectively.

Biochemical oxygen demand and chemical oxygen demand are the measurement of the oxygen consuming capabilities of organic matter. Textile effluent during their process of deposition exerts biochemical oxygen demand/chemical oxygen demand, which have a catastrophic effect on the ecosystem by depleting the oxygen supply. Decay process causes the production of noxious gases as hydrogen sulfide and methane. Water with high biochemical oxygen demand/chemical oxygen demand indicates presence of decomposing organic matter and subsequent high bacteria counts that degrade its quality and potential uses (Verma and Kharat, 2000). Biochemical oxygen demands of the effluents drain (138.6-170.0 mg/l) and pond water (99.0-136.0 mg/l) were found high as given in standards of C.P.C.B., B.I.S. and WHO. However, in groundwater of different depth biochemical oxygen demand was found to be low or sometimes nil. This trend is an agreement with that reported by Aslam *et al.* (2004), Yusuf and Sonibare (2004), Sial *et al.* (2006), Pathe *et al.* (2005) in textile industrial effluent, Singh *et al.* (1994) in drain and Mahesh and Prasad (2004), Mustafa *et al.* (2003) in groundwater.

Chemical oxygen demand is directly proportional to biochemical oxygen demand. Dilution of effluents for biochemical oxygen demand analysis always depends upon the value of chemical oxygen demand in a wastewater. In fact, chemical oxygen demand explains the load of pollutants and degree of pollution in effluent drain. Effluents of dye houses having a tremendous value of COD in the range of 351.5-445.0 mg/l, while it was observed 274.5-359.7 mg/l in pond water due to the high rate of decomposition of organic material in polluted and stored water. COD shows a positive relationship with BOD and negative with DO (Khanna, 1993) and mostly remains in the ratio of approximately 1:3 ± 0.5 in the case of waste water. Sevimli *et al.* (2005) observed the increasing trends of biochemical oxygen demand and chemical oxygen demand together while performing an experiment on decolorization of textile effluent and dye solution by ozonation. Senthinathan and Azeez (1999) and Groff (1993) reported that textile wastewater may cause problem used as untreated effluent consist higher COD, pH, temperature, Phosphorous and absorbable organic halogen. COD of textile wastewater may be reduced by using some appropriate technology Bhat *et al.* (2005). Aslam *et al.* (2004), Yusuf and Sonibare (2004), Sial *et al.* (2006), Pathe *et al.* (2005) were also reported the similar values in textile industrial effluent, and Mahesh and Prasad (2004), Mustafa *et al.* (2003) in groundwater. Waste containing high biochemical oxygen demand and chemical oxygen demand are responsible for a heavy depletion of oxygen levels in the particular sector of water body or soil (Sial *et al.*, 2006).

Water alkalinity is caused by strong bases and the salts of strong alkalis and weak acids. Carbonates are added to a water system if the water passes through soil and rock that contain carbonate minerals, such as calcite ($CaCO_3$). Where limestone and sedimentary rocks and carbonate-rich soils are predominant, waters will often have high alkalinity. Where igneous rocks (such as granite) and carbonate-poor soils are predominant waters will have low alkalinity. Alkalinity is a measure of the buffering capacity of water, or the capacity of bases to neutralize acids. Waters with low alkalinity are very susceptible to changes in pH. Waters with high alkalinity are able to resist major shifts in pH. As increasing amounts of acid are added to a water body, the pH of the water decreases, and the buffering capacity of the water is consumed. Because alkalinity and pH are so closely related, changes in pH can also affect alkalinity, especially in a poorly buffered system. Above pH 8.3, alkalinity is mostly in the form of carbonate (CO_3^{2-}); below 8.3, alkalinity is present mostly as bicarbonate (HCO_3^-).

The values of alkalinity in the effluents (633.6-889.0 mg/l) and in the pond water (563.4-732.3 mg/l) were found very high, while in the groundwater of various depths it was quite low according to depths as it was found 493.6-596.7 in 40 ft, 261.6-337.3 in 80 ft and 181.5-263.3 in 120 ft water samples. Bhat *et al.* (2005) observed the increasing trend in alkalinity of various textile effluents according to discharge points. Alkalinity not only helps regulate the pH of a water body, but also the metal content. Alkalinity has found with positive correlations with Cd (0.0237), Cu (0.809), Fe (0.8896), Mn (0.7664), Ni (0.7918), Pb (0.5841) and Zn (0.7069) Bicarbonate and carbonate ions in water can remove toxic metals (such as lead, arsenic, and cadmium) by precipitating the metals out of solution. Pathe *et al.* (2005), Garg and Kaushik (2006) have been made some observations in textile industrial effluent and Sastry and Rathee (1999), Mahesh and Prasad (2004), Mor *et al.* (2003), Yadav and Lata (2003) in groundwater; which support the results of present study. In irrigated area, a major portion receives water through exploitation of groundwater aquifers. The quality of groundwater is poor on account of excessive salt contents, high sodium or high toxic elements. The interactions of these parametric factors of water quality with soils influence their physico-chemical properties (Minhas and Gupta, 1992).

Hardness generally represents the concentration of calcium and magnesium ions, because these are the most common polyvalent cations. Other ions, such as iron and manganese, may also contribute to the hardness of water, but are generally present in much lower concentrations. Calcium, magnesium, and other polyvalent cations such as iron and manganese may be added to a natural water system as it passes through soil and rock containing large amounts of these elements in mineral deposits. Hardness mainly depends on the amount of calcium and magnesium salts or both present in the groundwater, water hardness is not health hazard but its values should remain below permissible level to restore the taste to water (WHO, 1984)

Some textile industrial processes may also produce significant amounts of calcium and manganese that are later discharged as industrial effluents. Calcium was found 10.58-27.4 mg/l in textile industrial effluent, 10.4-23.6 mg/l in pond water, 4.6-14.3 mg/l in groundwater of 40 ft and 3.4-11.7 mg/l in groundwater of 120 ft depth. Similar conditions were also reported by Garg and Kaushik (2006), Yusuf and Sonibare (2004) and Helena *et al.* (1999) in textile industrial effluent, Mustafa *et al.* (1998), Senthilnathan and Azeez (1999), Mor *et al.* (2003) and Yadav and Lata (2003) in groundwater.

When hardness equals alkalinity, the only cations present in significant concentrations in the water are calcium and magnesium. When hardness is greater than alkalinity, the waters may contain considerable amounts of other cations. Magnesium was found low in textile industrial effluent (4.7-16.1 mg/l), pond water (4.2-14.1 mg/l), groundwater of 40 ft (2.2-9.7 mg/l) and minimum in groundwater of 120 ft depth (1.9-9.2 mg/l). The Mg concentrations levels were comparable with those found by Yusuf and Sonibare (2004) and Helena *et al.* (1999) in textile effluents, Garg *et al.* (1998), Mor *et al.* (2003), Yadav and Lata (2003), Senthilnathan and Azeez (1999) and Mustafa *et al.* (1998) in groundwater.

Potassium is one of the important element among ten chemical element required in rather large quantities fir growth of all crops. Plants growth may be limited by a deficient available supply of potassium but its high some quantity may alter the soil composition. High K in water used in irrigation may alter the soil quality (Miller and Turk, 2002). Potassium was found low in textile industrial effluent (7.4-8.8 mg/l), pond water (7.3-8.4 mg/l), groundwater of 40 ft (4.9-6.1 mg/l) and groundwater at 120 ft (4.3-5.7 mg/l). Similar observation were made by Pathe *et al.* (2005) and Garg and Kaushik (2006) in textile industrial effluent, Das and Sahoo (2003), Mor *et al.* (2003), Yadav and Lata (2003) and Senthilnathan and Azeez (1999) in groundwater.

Sodium salts in the water are much more objectionable than salts of calcium and magnesium because of the tendency of sodium to cause deflocculation of the colloidal fraction of the soil and developed an undesirable structure water contain sufficient heavy metals to prove toxic to continue use by plants. As sodium chloride used in textile industry so the concentration of sodium and chloride will be high in the waste water (Aslam *et al.*, 2004). Sodium was found very high in groundwater of industrial area, because sodium should not be higher than 20 mg/l in drinking water (WHO, 2006). Sodium values were found very high in textile industrial effluent (145.0-177.0 mg/l), pond water (128.5-158.7 mg/l), groundwater of 40 ft (51.0-97.7 mg/l) and groundwater at 120 ft (8.7-37.0 mg/l). Helena *et al.* (1999) and Garg and Kaushik (2006) in textile industrial effluent and Das and Sahoo (2003), Mor *et al.* (2003), Mahesh and Prasad (2004) and Senthilnathan and Azeez (1999) in groundwater were observed the similar observations.

Chloride is one of the most conservative constituents in wastewater, being affected very little either by vegetative growth or other biological processes, or by precipitation or anion exchange reaction. Chloride concentrations in the effluents (588.5-825.7 mg/l) and pond water (576.5-770.7 mg/l) were also expected to be high by the permissible limit of C.P.C.B., while the occurrence of chloride have reported in GW40 (47.5-151.3 mg/l), GW80 (4.7-19.6 mg/l) and GW120 (4.7-13.7 mg/l) in very low concentrations. A work conducting on the effect of natural flocculants on textile wastewater, chloride concentration is increased in waste water used in textile industries and delayed later (Aboulhassan *et al.*, 2005).

Chloride does not have a health-based standard for drinking water. Chloride has been suggested as a standard value for drinking purposes (EPA, 1989). The Maximum Contaminant Level (MCL) of 250000 μg/L is based on poor taste chloride imparts to water. Chloride is not affected by adsorption or degradation processes and is therefore a conservative chemical in soil and groundwater. Chloride concentrations begin to increase at some depth due to dissolution reactions within the aquifer. Chloride is therefore a good indicator of human impacts in the environment (MPCA, 2001). In the waste water the concentration of chloride will be high due to the use of sodium chloride in textile industry. Chloride concentration in irrigation water should be less than 75 ppm, otherwise it may be harmful for soil structure. Textile effluents are high in toxicity not only for human beings of surroundings but also a

Table 9.4.1: Seasonal Variation of Physico-chemical Characteristics of Groundwater at 40 ft Depth from Hand Pump in Village Binjhole

Parameters	Unit	Summer 2005		Monsoon 2005		Winter 2005-06		Summer 2006		Monsoon 2006		Winter 2006-07		Summer 2007	
		Mean	SD	Mean	SD	Mean	SD	Mean	SD	Mean	SD	Mean	SD	Mean	SD
Temperature	°C	31.433	2.183	31.500	2.784	25.600	0.652	29.325	3.031	31.633	2.503	26.200	0.572	25.500	0.707
pH		7.700	0.100	7.433	0.058	7.460	0.114	7.700	0.082	7.500	0.100	7.475	0.096	7.550	0.071
TS	mg/l	1464.667	191.197	1229.000	154.088	797.200	165.915	1393.000	310.321	1280.667	166.572	782.750	121.722	1057.000	45.255
TSS	mg/l	133.000	21.517	120.667	16.921	79.000	14.816	125.500	27.887	118.333	13.503	72.500	11.733	95.000	4.243
TDS	mg/l	1331.667	169.742	1108.333	137.508	718.200	151.136	1267.500	283.580	1162.333	153.070	710.250	110.089	962.000	41.012
EC	mho/cm	2.081	0.265	1.732	0.215	1.122	0.236	1.980	0.443	1.816	0.239	1.110	0.172	1.503	0.064
DO	mg/l	2.567	0.208	3.967	0.681	3.800	0.604	2.925	0.206	4.000	0.436	3.950	0.420	3.650	0.212
Free-CO_2	mg/l	0.933	0.153	0.167	0.289	0.220	0.303	0.700	0.183	0.167	0.289	0.100	0.200	0.250	0.354
BOD	mg/l	35.667	8.145	31.333	23.159	14.400	11.149	27.750	12.580	35.333	18.610	20.750	10.689	11.000	2.828
COD	mg/l	93.000	16.523	75.000	48.775	37.000	30.725	71.750	33.540	88.000	42.509	54.750	31.020	27.500	7.778
Total alkalinity	mg/l	557.667	59.744	584.667	23.714	493.600	31.061	579.500	38.631	596.667	48.911	502.500	22.128	564.500	28.991
Ca	mg/l	106.667	15.275	136.667	51.316	46.000	16.733	102.500	40.311	143.333	47.258	52.500	12.583	65.000	7.071
Mg	mg/l	92.667	25.423	88.000	32.604	32.400	16.227	82.500	59.360	97.667	35.233	39.000	14.024	22.000	4.243
K	mg/l	5.267	0.569	6.100	0.100	5.280	0.319	5.300	0.560	6.033	0.208	5.475	0.250	4.900	0.141
Cl	mg/l	104.333	34.269	145.000	33.151	72.200	35.252	66.838	62.522	151.333	17.954	83.750	39.778	47.500	3.536
Na	mg/l	88.333	4.163	95.000	11.790	51.000	13.454	75.500	24.365	97.667	11.240	59.000	12.780	51.500	4.950

Table 9.4.2: Seasonal Variation of Physico-chemical Characteristics of Hroundwater at 80 ft Depth from Tube Well and Deep Hand Pump

Parameters	Unit	Summer 2005		Monsoon 2005		Winter 2005-06		Summer 2006		Monsoon 2006		Winter 2006-07		Summer 2007	
		Mean	SD	Mean	SD	Mean	SD	Mean	SD	Mean	SD	Mean	SD	Mean	SD
Temperature	°C	30.833	2.021	31.100	2.651	26.340	0.422	29.250	2.327	31.333	2.255	26.550	0.666	26.900	0.141
pH		7.333	0.153	7.233	0.153	7.860	0.195	7.500	0.082	7.300	0.100	7.900	0.283	7.750	0.071
TS	mg/l	615.333	104.902	944.667	85.149	788.200	308.086	580.500	118.329	950.333	68.223	852.000	252.052	476.500	61.518
TSS	mg/l	59.333	7.371	85.000	11.790	75.000	31.217	52.000	9.695	87.333	5.686	80.000	25.100	45.000	4.243
TDS	mg/l	556.000	97.535	859.667	74.842	713.200	277.196	528.500	108.911	863.000	62.554	772.000	226.995	431.500	57.276
EC	mho/cm	0.869	0.152	1.343	0.117	1.114	0.433	0.826	0.170	1.348	0.098	1.206	0.355	0.674	0.089
DO	mg/l	2.633	0.513	3.900	0.361	4.000	0.381	2.850	0.351	3.900	0.265	3.950	0.300	3.950	0.636
Free CO_2	mg/l	0.900	0.100	0.167	0.289	0.100	0.224	0.700	0.183	0.167	0.289	0.100	0.200	0.250	0.354
BOD	mg/l	24.000	7.000	23.333	19.296	10.200	7.294	19.000	6.733	26.667	9.074	12.500	7.594	8.500	2.121
COD	mg/l	62.000	8.718	52.667	41.053	26.600	17.601	48.000	16.793	68.667	21.197	33.750	22.051	20.500	3.536
Total alkalinity	mg/l	337.333	50.063	296.000	27.785	261.600	5.225	327.750	47.183	303.000	34.117	262.000	10.985	283.500	7.778
Ca	mg/l	96.667	15.275	136.667	23.094	44.000	23.022	87.500	33.040	136.667	15.275	55.000	26.458	50.000	14.142
Mg	mg/l	82.333	22.368	89.000	28.160	29.400	14.622	71.500	40.739	97.333	23.159	38.000	16.145	23.000	2.828
K	mg/l	4.933	0.513	5.967	0.153	5.180	0.277	5.050	0.580	5.967	0.115	5.400	0.216	4.900	0.141
Cl	mg/l	4.700	0.954	18.333	6.028	12.940	11.812	5.025	1.459	19.667	8.083	15.125	11.229	4.800	0.424
Na	mg/l	57.333	5.508	62.333	11.240	24.800	10.592	46.500	20.486	69.333	12.503	31.250	10.210	23.000	2.828

Table 9.4.3: Seasonal Variation of Physico-chemical Characteristics of Groundwater (more than 120 ft depth) of Tube Well

Parameters	*Unit*	*Summer 2005*		*Monsoon 2005*		*Winter 2005-06*		*Summer 2006*		*Monsoon 2006*		*Winter 2006-07*		*Summer 2007*	
		Mean	*SD*	*Mean*	*SD*	*Mean*	*SD*	*Mean*	*SD*	*Mean*	*SD*	*Mean*	*SD*	*Mean*	*SD*
Temperature	°C	30.267	2.040	31.167	2.350	26.880	0.526	28.950	2.027	31.000	2.000	26.500	0.408	27.000	0.000
pH		7.167	0.058	7.167	0.115	7.620	0.179	7.300	0.082	7.200	0.100	7.600	0.183	7.500	0.000
TS	mg/l	285.667	38.004	494.333	70.002	620.800	201.268	290.500	38.144	505.667	71.038	687.250	139.801	370.000	98.995
TSS	mg/l	27.000	4.000	47.000	5.000	57.800	18.913	27.250	3.403	47.333	7.095	63.500	13.026	35.000	9.899
TDS	mg/l	258.667	34.005	447.333	65.003	563.000	182.391	263.250	34.760	458.333	64.010	623.750	126.790	335.000	89.095
EC	mho/cm	0.404	0.053	0.699	0.102	0.880	0.285	0.411	0.054	0.716	0.100	0.975	0.198	0.523	0.139
DO	mg/l	2.767	0.252	4.167	0.351	4.040	0.321	3.200	0.356	4.133	0.115	4.125	0.299	3.700	0.707
Free CO_2	mg/l	0.800	0.100	0.000	0.000	0.100	0.224	0.675	0.206	0.000	0.000	0.000	0.000	0.250	0.354
BOD	mg/l	14.000	5.292	12.000	14.422	3.600	5.128	10.500	7.937	16.333	8.505	6.250	7.228	2.000	2.828
COD	mg/l	38.000	14.799	28.000	33.422	8.400	11.845	25.750	18.464	42.333	23.798	17.250	20.123	4.500	6.364
Total alkalinity	mg/l	263.333	31.070	207.667	17.786	184.000	8.337	252.000	23.409	211.333	13.503	181.500	8.062	221.000	22.627
Ca	mg/l	80.000	20.000	116.667	15.275	34.000	11.402	75.000	35.119	116.667	15.275	50.000	21.602	40.000	14.142
Mg	mg/l	74.000	24.021	83.333	24.440	27.200	12.814	59.000	39.875	92.000	30.050	35.500	14.731	19.500	2.121
K	mg/l	4.633	0.513	5.700	0.200	4.960	0.305	4.550	0.480	5.467	0.252	5.150	0.332	4.350	0.212
Cl	mg/l	4.833	0.551	12.167	4.368	7.740	2.830	4.775	0.629	13.733	4.941	9.850	3.576	5.000	0.141
Na	mg/l	26.667	8.386	37.000	13.454	10.420	3.582	21.625	12.605	36.000	8.185	11.450	5.318	8.700	0.849

Table 9.4.4: Seasonal Variation of Physico-chemical Characteristics of Groundwater of 80 ft Depth at Control Site (C)

Parameters	Unit	Summer 2005		Monsoon 2005		Winter 2005-06		Summer 2006		Monsoon 2006		Winter 2006-07		Summer 2007	
		Mean	SD	Mean	SD	Mean	SD	Mean	SD	Mean	SD	Mean	SD	Mean	SD
Temperature	°C	30.500	1.179	30.600	2.152	26.640	0.472	29.250	1.555	30.233	2.159	26.825	0.236	27.250	0.354
pH		7.133	0.058	7.133	0.058	7.420	0.164	7.250	0.129	7.200	0.100	7.425	0.171	7.450	0.071
TS	mg/l	451.333	87.512	630.000	50.269	726.600	151.085	446.750	76.164	651.000	50.507	780.500	110.301	485.500	103.945
TSS	mg/l	42.333	7.506	57.667	4.509	68.200	13.627	42.250	7.182	60.000	4.583	71.000	10.165	46.000	7.071
TDS	mg/l	409.000	80.019	572.333	45.764	658.400	137.467	404.500	69.019	591.000	46.033	709.500	100.142	439.500	96.874
EC	mho/cm	0.639	0.125	0.894	0.072	1.029	0.215	0.632	0.108	0.923	0.072	1.109	0.156	0.687	0.151
DO	mg/l	2.367	0.513	3.567	0.503	3.340	0.391	2.500	0.356	3.467	0.462	3.300	0.245	2.950	0.212
Free CO_2	mg/l	0.933	0.153	0.167	0.289	0.260	0.358	0.775	0.126	0.333	0.289	0.275	0.320	0.700	0.141
BOD	mg/l	15.000	3.000	13.667	7.371	6.600	5.683	13.250	4.787	15.667	6.110	7.500	5.802	8.500	0.707
COD	mg/l	38.000	7.000	35.667	18.903	16.000	13.172	33.250	12.816	40.667	15.044	18.000	13.880	21.500	4.950
Total alkalinity	mg/l	303.000	22.913	233.667	30.089	216.400	41.621	296.000	31.602	249.000	31.193	216.500	35.828	273.500	6.364
Ca	mg/l	86.667	15.275	110.000	10.000	42.000	8.367	80.000	31.623	106.667	5.774	55.000	17.321	40.000	14.142
Mg	mg/l	78.333	17.502	88.000	18.682	29.800	15.401	65.250	42.414	101.000	23.302	40.000	16.693	21.000	4.243
K	mg/l	4.833	0.666	5.800	0.100	5.060	0.404	4.925	0.506	5.733	0.058	5.250	0.311	4.650	0.212
Cl	mg/l	5.200	1.758	13.000	3.775	10.960	6.886	4.900	1.111	12.200	3.897	12.925	5.518	5.050	0.778
Na	mg/l	52.667	6.807	58.333	10.263	22.600	9.343	40.750	23.472	58.000	7.000	24.500	10.247	18.500	3.536

Table 9.4.5: Mean Values (±SD) of Physico-chemical Characteristics of Groundwater at Control and Experiment Sites

Parameters	Unit	2005-06				2006-07			
		Control Site	SD	Experimental sites	SD	Control Site	SD	Experimental sites	SD
Temperature	°C	28.583	2.323	28.661	0.134	28.500	1.942	28.583	2.630
pH		7.267	0.178	7.483	0.095	7.325	0.166	7.525	0.214
TS	mg/l	606.000	165.808	774.806	309.575	619.833	159.929	794.444	248.689
TSS	mg/l	56.583	15.163	73.528	30.262	57.250	13.877	72.778	22.893
TDS	mg/l	549.417	150.672	701.278	279.320	562.583	146.087	721.667	225.916
EC	mho/cm	0.858	0.235	1.096	0.436	0.879	0.228	1.128	0.353
DO	mg/l	3.083	0.644	3.583	0.118	3.083	0.497	3.692	0.581
Free-CO_2	mg/l	0.450	0.423	0.347	0.063	0.483	0.319	0.280	0.348
BOD	mg/l	10.583	6.244	15.944	7.682	11.583	5.869	17.861	10.414
COD	mg/l	26.667	15.848	39.917	19.398	29.250	15.149	45.917	26.573
Total alkalinity	mg/l	245.583	47.149	348.167	171.459	257.417	44.933	355.389	41.818
Ca	mg/l	70.833	31.467	77.500	9.610	74.167	31.176	84.433	41.800
Mg	mg/l	55.750	32.311	56.306	4.257	62.083	37.609	62.033	39.100
K	mg/l	5.142	0.571	5.231	0.226	5.225	0.465	5.306	0.479
Cl	mg/l	9.458	5.692	39.889	52.379	9.492	5.134	37.604	22.806
Na	mg/l	38.083	20.120	44.544	24.806	38.417	19.228	46.755	18.636

serious threat to groundwater and surface water resources (Aslam *et al.*, 2004). The chloride concentrations levels were comparable with those found by Helena *et al.* (1999), Garg and Kaushik (2006) in textile industrial effluent, Senthilnathan and Azeez (1999), Yadav and Lata (2003), Mor *et al.* (2003), Mahesh and Prasad (2004), in groundwater.

9.5 Heavy Metals Route

9.5.1 General

The toxic heavy metals entering the ecosystem may lead to geo-accumulation, bioaccumulation and biomagnifications. Heavy metals like Fe, Cu, Zn, Ni and other trace elements are important for proper functioning of biological systems and their deficiency or excess could lead to a number of disorders. Food chain contamination by heavy metals has become a burning issue in recent years because of their potential accumulation in biosystems through contaminated water, soil and air. Therefore, a better understanding of heavy metal sources, their accumulation in the soil and the effect of their presence in water and soil on plant systems seem to be particularly important issues of present-day research on risk assessments (Lokeshwari and Chandrappa, 2006).

Metals that are naturally introduced into the waterbody come primarily from such sources as rock weathering, soil erosion, or the dissolution of water-soluble salts. Naturally occurring metals move through aquatic environments independently of human activities, usually without any detrimental effects. Humans consume metallic elements through both water and food. Some metals such as sodium, potassium, magnesium, calcium, and iron are found in living tissue and are essential to human life-biological anomalies arise when they are depleted or removed. Probably less well known is that currently no less than six other heavy metals including molybdenum, manganese, cobalt, copper, and zinc, have been linked to human growth, development, achievement, and reproduction (Vahrenkamp, 1979; Friberg *et al.*, 1979). Even these metals, however, can become toxic or aesthetically undesirable when their concentrations are too great. Several heavy metals, like cadmium, lead, and mercury, are highly toxic at relatively low concentrations, can accumulate in body tissues over long periods of time, and are nonessential for human health.

9.5.2 Historical Resume

Different researchers from India and abroad have been discussed various aspects of heavy metals pollution of water and soil in term of characteristics of water bodies, affected agricultural soils and bottom sediments from time to time. This review includes some of important contribution made in the field of industrial pollution, with references to heavy metals parameters of groundwater, surface water, characterization of textile industrial effluents, contaminated agricultural irrigated soil and bottom sediment soils by different authors of country and abroad.

Aggarwal and Mehrotra (1952) surveyed the soil and soil water affected by effluent in some selected regions of Uttar Pradesh. Richards (1954) evaluated the quality of saline and alkali soils and gave a technique for the improvement of these sick soil systems in the agricultural sector for good performance of agriculture productivity. Kanwar (1961) assessed the quality of irrigation water as an index of suitability for irrigation purposes. Darra *et al.* (1964) evaluated the water quality of irrigation water used in Rajasthan. Saksena *et al.* (1966) evaluated the quality of groundwaters for irrigation in Ahor developmental block, Jalore. Bhakuni and Bopardikar (1967) stated the method of recovery Zinc from the spinning bath waste of Viscos reyon factory by using ion exchange method and found it significant useful in metal removal process.

Williums (1972) described the characteristics and various properties of Metals. Katz (1975) highlighted the effect of heavy metals on some environmental components and biotic organisms of aquatic environment in New York. Dowedy and Larson (1975) reported the availability of some metals in various vegetable crops in a polluted region in the vicinity of an industrial area. Dulka and Risby (1976) stated ultra trace metals in some environmental and biological systems in the vicinity of textile industrial sector. Shivakumar *et al.* (1977) made a geo-graphical approach for toxic trace element pollution in groundwater around Patancheru and Bollaram Industrial area, A.P., India.

Martin and Cougherty (1982) stated the basic monitoring techniques for detection of heavy metals pollution through the biological agents. Ireland (1983) described the heavy metals uptake and their distribution in tissues of organisms. Numberg (1984) studied on the volumetric approach in trace metal chemistry of natural waters and atmospheric precipitation. Nriagu and Pacyna (1988) carried out a study on the quantitative assessment of worldwide contamination of air, water and soil with trace metals. Mishra *et al.* (1990) reported the occurrence of heavy metals in crop plants of Sanagar more than the permissible limits presence of which may cause the adverse effect on the plant/human health and may cause high mortality of fish population in affected aquatic environment.

Singh *et al.* (1994) highlighted the degradation of water and soil quality of Parwanoo area with respect to heavy metals. Sharma and Patel (1996) determined copper in water of Raipur with the help of spectrophotometer. Prasad and Chandra (1997) studied well water quality status of Hyderabad and Khurshid and Shabeer (1997) observed water quality degradation due to heavy metal pollution. Mohan *et al.* (1998) observed heavy metals (Fe, Pb, Ca and Zn) in the groundwater of Naini industrial area; Dist. Allahabad, U.P. Kashem and Singh (1999) had also found the decreasing concentration of Cu, Mn, Pb and Zn with increasing distance from disposal point. Stetzenbach *et al.* (1999) evaluated the heavy metals in groundwater and used multivariate statistical analysis.

Tyagi and Budhi (2000) postulated the degradation of groundwater quality due to heavy metals in industrial area of India. Kumar *et al.* (2001) studied on the impact of textile industry on groundwater quality of Sanagar, Jaipur and found the high amount of chemicals (e.g. sulphuric acid and acetic acid) and dyes (e.g. chrome and metal dyes) suspended solids and toxic metals in the waste which may enter in the groundwater and deteriorate its quality. Siddiqui and Pathania (2002) made some studies on heavy metals in surface and groundwater of Jalandhar and Ludhiana districts of Punjab state. Shrivastava *et al.* (2003) collected soil samples from surface of the soil from different agriculture fields in the Khandesh region and Tapi River sediment samples were also collected from five different stations which were 7-8 km away from each other and detected the concentrations of heavy metals have been determined by ICP-AES. Khan *et al.* (2003) harvested some *Solanum melongena* plant in a laboratory experiment using five different levels of textile waste water and observed the contamination of heavy metals as 1.417 mg/g of Zn, 1.003 mg/g of Cu, 0.378 mg/g of Ni, 0.378 mg/g of Cd, 0.773 mg/g of Cr, 1.139 mg/g of Pb and 0.427 mg/g of Co in the soil of pots treated with highest ratio of distilled water and waste water. Yadav and Sumanlata (2003) indicated the heavy metal pollution in groundwater in Bahadurgarh block of districts Jhajjar, Haryana. Malik *et al.* (2004) evaluated the accumulation of heavy metals in crop plants through irrigation of contaminated groundwater in Panipat region and emphasized on bioremediation processes for combat groundwater pollution. Chao *et al.* (2005) reported the heavy metal contaminated site in Taiwan and described the status and distribution of heavy metals in environment. It is necessary to reduce the levels of toxic metals from industrial effluents before discharging into surface waters. The general methods of treating wastewater-containing metals are coagulation, ion exchange, reverse osmosis and adsorption. Adsorption is a highly effective physico-chemical treatment for removing heavy metals for effluents. Due to high cost of activated carbon, efforts are being directed towards finding low cost adsorbents. Recently much interest has been shown for removal of heavy metals using a large number of low cost materials. Coal fly ash, the solid waste of power plants is one of the cheapest and non-conventional adsorbents (De, 2005).

Zheng *et al.* (2006) assessed the heavy metals pollution of agricultural soil in Guanzhong district of China. Lokeshwari and Chandrappa (2006) evaluated the impact of heavy metals contamination of a Lake on soil and cultivated vegetation near Bangalore and found the presence of some heavy metals in rice and vegetables, beyond the limit of Indian Standards and calculated metal transfer factors from soil to vegetation are found significant for Zn, Cu, Pb and Cd. Hedge *et al.* (2006) revealed the provenance of heavy minerals with special reference to ilmenite of the Honnevar beach in central west coast of India and observed some trace heavy elements like Co, Cr, V and Ni in the sandy soil of the beach. Singh (2006) indicated the contamination of groundwater of Ganges-Brahmaputra river basin in north east India and found the groundwater unfit for direct human consumption and noticed the rice and vegetable fields irrigated by groundwater received a large amount of arsenic through shallow tube wells in the affected areas of north 24 *Parganas* and Murshidabad, West Bangal. Malik *et al.* (2007) assessed the migration of heavy metals in the groundwater regime of Panipat industrial area on the behalf of different spatial variations the heavy metals were found in maximum quantities at point source of pollution. Malik and Bharti (2007) studied on soil quality of irrigated agricultural fields in a textile industrial area of Panipat city.

Va´zquez, *et al.* (2007) monitored the heavy metal pollution in San Antonio Bay, Rio Negro, Argentina. Obiri (2007) determined the heavy metals in water from boreholes in Dumasi in the Wassa West District of Western Region of Republic of

Ghana. Huang *et al.* (2007) indicated the speciation and mobility of heavy metals in mud in coastal reclamation areas in Shenzhen in China. Walker *et al.* (2007) identified the influence of heavy metals and mineral nutrient supply on *Bituminaria bituminosa*.

Golia *et al.* (2007) measured the accumulation of metals on tobacco leaves (primings) grown in an agricultural area in relation to soil. Mico *et al.* (2007) described the comparison of two digestion methods for the analysis of heavy metals by flame atomic absorption spectroscopy. Padmavathiamma and Li (2007) explained the phytoremediation technology through the hyper-accumulation metals in plants and different aspects of phytoremediation technology and the biological mechanisms underlying phytoremediation.

9.5.3 Metal Analysis

Collected, preserved, diluted water samples were prepared for the evaluation of metal concentrations with the help of AAS 4129. In the case of soil samples, a suspension (1:5) should be prepared in the distilled water; rest processes are like surface water and groundwater samples.

Metals enter in the surface, groundwater and soil/sediments through the disposing of toxic textile effluents of dye houses. For every metal a standard was required and concentration may be detected by AAS. Diluted and completely digested samples were required for metal detection by AAS 4129. Metal elements were determined with the help of Atomic absorption spectrophotometer (Model AAS 4129). Alan Walsh first developed the technique of atomic absorption spectrophotometry in 1955, and since then it has emerged as a powerful tool in quantitative analysis of more than 70 metals. The major advantages of the method are that it is free from any kind of interferences and very small concentrations are possible to be measured (De, 2002). The AAS is based on the principle that atoms of elements, which normally remain in ground state under flame condition, absorb energy when subjected to radiation of specific wavelength. The absorption of radiation is proportional to the concentration of atoms of the element. The absorption of radiation by the atoms is independent of the wavelength of absorption and temperature of the atoms. These to feature provide AAS a distinct advantage over flame spectroscopy.

Copper (Cu)

Copper in the natural waters also results in higher concentration due to pollution. It is used with sulphate as a pesticides and also separately as an algicide. Although, it passes as such through the body but there is evidence of accumulation of trace quantities in liver. The limits of it in the standards are not due to its toxic effects but are due to its taste producing capacity. Preparation of 1000 Cu (µg/ml) standard: Dissolve 1 gm of Cu in 50 ml of 6N of HNO_3 and dilute to 1 L to give 1000 µg/ml Cu.

Cadmium (Cd)

Cadmium is fairy dense silver white malleable and most toxic metal, which melts at 320.9°C. Cadmium is used for dye and paint pigment production, batteries, ceramic industries, wooden industries and plastic production. The Cd found in a sample of Ca is likely in a inorganic form and may be relatively less toxic to plants and animals, while same amount of Cd when present in zinc or phosphates may be highly toxic to plants and animals, especially when there is calcium deficiency in soil or livestock rations. Preparation of 1000 Cd (µg/ml) standard: Dissolve 1 gm of Cd Metal in 20 ml of 5N HCl containing 0.5 ml of concentrated HNO_3 and dilute to 1 L to give 1000 µg/ml Cd.

Iron (Fe)

Iron is one of the most abundant elements of the rocks and soil, ranking fourth by weight. All kinds of waters including groundwater have appreciable quantities of iron. Iron has more solubility at acidic pH, therefore large quantities of iron are leached out from the soils by acidic waters. In the alkaline medium iron remain comparatively low in soluble phase. Preparation of 1000 Fe (µg/ml) standard, dissolve 1.000 g of iron wire in 50 ml of (1+1) HNO_3 and dilute to 1 liter with de-ionized water to give 1000 µg/ml Fe.

Manganese (Mn)

Although it is not a toxic metal, Mn imparts objectionable and tenacious stains to laundry plumbing fixtures and clothing. It occurs in domestic waste water, industrial effluents, acid mine drainage and receiving strums and therby enters water bodies. Mn is relatively non-toxic to animals, but toxic to plants at higher levels. Preparation of 1000 Mn (µg/ml) standard: Dissolve 1 gm of Mn in 50 ml of 6N of HNO_3 and dilute to 1 L to give 1000 µg/ml Mn.

Nickel (Ni)

At high concentrations, nickel has toxic properties. Aquatic organisms have varying sensitivities to nickel salts depending on the water's pH, hardness, alkalinity and type of nickel compound under consideration. Nickel as a metal is a carcinogen. Preparation of 1000 Ni (µg/ml) standard: Dissolve 1 gm of Ni metal in 50 ml of 6N of HNO_3 and dilute to 1 L to give 1000 µg/ml Ni.

Lead (Pb)

It is a dense soft metal and is quite resistant to corrosion. It has melting point of 327°C. Major source of lead is PbS (Galena). Lead is used for pipes, solders, electrodes, batteries, newsprint, and pigments in paints. Lead is also used in insecticides, beverages, ointments and synthetic dyes. The chemical form of lead determines its solubility in water and biological fluids, the extent of its fixation on soil and type of chemical reactions occurring in atmospheric, aquatic as well as soil environment. Preparation of 1000 Pb (µg/ml) standard: Dissolve 1 gm of Pb metal in 20 ml of 6N of HNO_3 and dilute to 1 L to give 1000 µg/ml Pb.

Zinc (Zn)

Zinc is present in high concentrations in the wastes from pharmaceuticals, paint, galvanizing, cosmetics, dyes and pigments, etc., and their discharge increases its concentration in appreciable amounts in the waters. Zinc is very essential micronutrient in human beings and only at very high concentration it may cause some toxic effects. Zinc salts produce an undesirable taste to the water and causes water to appear milky and on boiling, a greasy surface scum may also form in the water (Mani *et al.*, 2005). Preparation of 1000 Zn (µg/ml) standard: Dissolve 1 gm of Zn metal in 40 ml of 5N HCl and dilute to 1 L to give 1000 µg/ml Zn.

Standards and Calibration

Whenever, possible metals and metals oxides are to be preferred in the preparation of standards. This enables the analyst to dissolve them that samples and standards will contain identical elements and hence minimizes any chemical or physical interference effects. Only concentrated standards (above 1000 µg/ml) should be held in storage. Working standards should be diluted from standards stock solutions only when needed. At low concentrations (less than 10 µg/ml) solutions have been found to deteriorate quite quickly because of the absorption on the walls of the container. Similar standard addition solutions can be prepared containing all of the required elements. This will avoid multiple splitting of the sample for individual elements and reduce the amount of time spent in preparing standards.

Before weighting, standards materials should be treated to ensure that they are in a standard state.

- ☆ Metals: Wash with acetone and ether to remove any oil layers. Remove any oxide coating by abrasion with emery cloth or by acid pickling and drying.
- ☆ Oxides: Dry at 110 °C for two hours. If necessary, heat to evaluated temperatures to remove bound water.

Compounds: Equilibration at constant water content, or drying at 110 °C for two hours to remove any water.

Standards of known concentrations were prepared and evaluated the concentration of metal in water/soil digested sample. Every metal has some specific properties and atomic weight, so for every metal different condition of standard and calibration was applied for every metal (ECIL methods manual, 2004).

Standard Conditions for Cadmium (Cd)

Stock Standard solution

Cadmium 1000 µg/ml. Dissolve 1.000 g of cadmium metal in a minimum volume of (1+1) HCl. Dilute to 1 liter with 1% (V/V) HCl.

Operating Parameters

Instruments: ECIL AAS

Wave length: 228.8 nm

Slit setting: 0.5 nm

Light source: Hollow cathode lamp

Flame type: Air-acetylene flame oxidizing (lean, blue)

Sensitivity

For the standard conditions, the sensitivity is about 0.02 µg/ml Cd for 1% absorption. A standard containing 1.5 µg/ml Cd will typically give an absorbance reading of about 0.33 absorbance units (about 53% absorption).

Linear Working Range

For the standard conditions, the working range for Cd is linear up to concentrations of approximately 1.5 µg/ml in aqueous solution.

Other Analytical Lines

Wave Length	Slit	Relative Sensitivity
22.5 nm	0.5 nm	1
326.1 nm	0.5 nm	410

Standard Conditions for Copper (Cu)

Stock Standard Solution

Copper, 1000 µg/ml. Dissolve 1.000 g of copper metal in a minimum volume of (1+1) HNO_3. Dilute to 1 liter with 1% (V/V) HNO_3.

Operating Parameters

Instruments: ECIL AAS

Wave length: 324.7 nm

Slit setting: 0.5 nm

Light source: Hollow cathode lamp

Flame type: Air-acetylene flame oxidizing (lean, blue)

Sensitivity

The sensitivity is about 0.04 µg/ml Cu for 1% absorption. A standard containing 2 µg/ml Cu will typically give an absorbance reading of about 0.22 absorbance units (39% absorption).

Linear Working Range

For the standard conditions, the working range for Cu is linear upto concentrations of approximately 3 µg/ml in aqueous solution.

Other Analytical Lines

Wave Length	Slit	Relative Sensitivity
324.7 nm	0.5 nm	1
222.6 nm	0.2 nm	38
244.2 nm	1.0 nm	280

Lamps

With multi element lamps containing nickel or iron, a 0.2 nm spectral slit width should be used with the copper 324.7 nm line.

Standard Conditions for Manganese (Mn)

Stock Standard Solution

Manganese, 1000 µg/ml. Dissolve 1.000 g of manganese metal in a minimum volume of (1+1+ HNO_3). Dilute to 1 liter with 1% (V/V) HCl.

Operating Parameters

Instruments: ECIL AAS

Wave length: 279.5 nm

Slit setting: 0.2 nm

Light source: Hollow cathode lamp

Flame type: Air-acetylene flame oxidizing (lean, blue)

Sensitivity

For the standard conditions, the sensitivity is about 0.04 µg/ml Mn for 1% absorption. A standard containing 1 µg/ml Mn will typically give an absorbance reading of about 0.11 absorbance units (about 40% absorption).

Linear Working Range

For the standard conditions, the working range for Mn is linear upto concentrations of approximately 2 µg/ml in aqueous solution.

Other Analytical Lines:

Wave Length	*Slit*	*Relative Sensitivity*
279.5 nm	0.2 nm	1.0
403.1 nm	0.2 nm	12.5
321.7 nm	0.2 nm	2750.0

Standard Conditions for Nickel (Ni)

Stock Standard Solution

Nickel, 1000 µg/ml. Dissolve 1.000 g of nickel metal in a minimum volume of (1+1) HNO_3. Dilute to 1 liter with 1% (V/V) HNO_3.

Operating Parameters

Instruments: ECIL AAS

Wave length: 232.0 nm

Slit setting: 0.2 nm

Light source: Hollow cathode lamp

Operating current: 3.5 mA

Flame type: Air-acetylene flame oxidizing (lean, blue)

Sensitivity

The sensitivity is about 0.10 µg/ml Ni for 1% absorption. Standard containing 2.5 µg/ml Ni will typically give an absorbance reading of about 0.11 absorbance units (23% absorption).

Linear Working Range

For the standard conditions, the working range for Ni is linear upto concentrations of approximately 3 µg/ml in aqueous solution.

Other Analytical Lines

Wave Length	*Slit*	*Relative Sensitivity*
232.0 nm	0.2 nm	1.0
352.5 nm	0.5 nm	5.1
351.5 nm	0.5 nm	11.0
362.5 nm	0.5 nm	540.0

Lamps

With multi-element lamps containing iron, interference may occur when using the 232.0 nm nickel line if nickel is being determined in an iron matrix. A secondary nickel line (352.4 or 341.5 nm) should be used.

Standard Conditions for Lead (Pb)

Stock Standard Solution

Lead, 1000 µg/ml. Dissolve 1.598 g of lead nitrate Pb $(NO_3)_2$ 1 liter of 1% (V/V) HNO_3.

Operating Parameters

Instruments: ECIL AAS

Wave length: 217.0 nm

Slit setting: 1.0 nm

Light source: Hollow cathode lamp

Operating current: 5 mA

Flame type: Air-acetylene flame oxidizing (lean, blue)

Sensitivity

The sensitivity is about 0.25 µg/ml Pb for 1% absorption. Standard containing 6 µg/ml Pb will typically give an absorbance reading of about 0.10 absorbance units (about 34% absorption).

Linear Working Range

For the standard conditions, the working range for Pb is linear upto concentrations of approximately 8 µg/ml in aqueous solution.

Other Analytical Lines

Wave Length	*Slit*	*Relative Sensitivity*
217.0 nm	1.0 nm	1.0
283.3 nm	0.5 nm	2.0
261.4 nm	0.5 nm	6.0
205.3 nm	0.5 nm	340.0

Lamps

With multi-element lamps containing copper, the Cu 216.5 resonance line may interfere with lead determinations at the lead 217.0 nm line. The lead 283.3 nm line should be used instead.

Flame Emission

The most sensitive emission wavelength for lead is at 405.8 nm. A nitrous oxide, acetylene flame is recommended. Lead can also be determined at the 368.4, 283.3 and 261.4 nm wavelengths, but with reduced sensitivity. An air acetylene flame may also be used with reduced sensitivity.

Standard Conditions for Zinc (Zn)

Stock Standard Solution

Zinc, 1000 µg/ml. Dissolve 0.500 g of zinc metal in a minimum volume of (1/1) HCl and dilute to 1 liter with 1% (V/V) HCl.

Operating Parameters

Instruments: ECIL AAS

Wave length: 213.9 nm

Slit setting: 1.0 nm

Light source: Hollow cathode lamp

Operating current: 5 mA

Flame type: Air-acetylene flame oxidizing (lean, blue)

Sensitivity

For the standard conditions, the sensitivity is about 0.012 µg/ml Zn for 1% absorption. A standard containing 0.5 µg/ml Zn will typically give an absorbance reading of about 0.18 absorbance units (about 25% absorption).

Linear Working Range

For the standard conditions, the working range for Zn is linear upto concentrations of approximately 1.0 µg/ml in aqueous solution.

Other Analytical Lines

Wave Length	*Slit*	*Relative Sensitivity*
213.9 nm	1.0 nm	1.0
307.6 nm	1.0 nm	8400.0

Standard Conditions for Iron (Fe)

Stock Standard Solution

Iron, 1000 µg/ml. Dissolve 1.000 g of iron wire in 50 ml of (1+1) HNO_3. Dilute to 1 liter with de-ionized water.

Operating Parameters

Instruments: ECIL AAS

Wave length: 248.3 nm

Slit setting: 0.2 nm

Light source: Hollow cathode lamp

Operating current: 5 mA

Flame type: Air-acetylene flame oxidizing (lean, blue)

Sensitivity

For the standard conditions, the sensitivity is about 0.09 μg/ml Fe for 1% absorption. A standard containing 4.0 μg/ml Fe will typically give an absorbance reading of about 0.19 absorbance units (about 35% absorption).

Linear Working Range

For the standard conditions, the working range for Fe is linear up to concentrations of approximately 4.0 μg/ml in aqueous solution.

Other Analytical Lines

Wave Length	*Slit*	*Relative Sensitivity*
248.3 nm	0.2 nm	1.0
392.0 nm	0.2 nm	270.0

Some essential knowledge about heavy metals is given below for basic setup and for understanding the sensitivity of each metal studied.

Table 9.5.1: Standard Criteria for Analyzing Heavy Metals by Atomic Absorption Spectrophotometer (AAS)

Sl.No.	*Name*	*Symbol*	*Wavelength nm*	*Flame Gases*	*Instrument Detection Limits Mg/l*	*Sensitivity Mg/l*	*Optimum Concentration Range Mg/l*
1.	Cadmium	Cd	228.8	A-Ac	0.002	0.025	0.05-2
2.	Copper	Cu	324.7	A-Ac	0.01	0.1	0.02-10
3.	Lead*	Pb	279.5	A-Ac	0.01	0.05	0.1-10
4.	Manganese	Mn	232.0	A-Ac	0.02	0.15	0.3-10
5.	Nickel	Ni	283.3	A-Ac	0.05	0.5	1-20
6.	Zinc	Zn	213.9	A-Ac	0.005	0.02	0.05-2
7.	Iron	Fe	248.3	A-Ac	0.02	0.12	0.3-10

A-Ac = Air-acetylene,

*: The more sensitive 217.0 nm wavelength is recommended for instruments with background correction capabilities (APHA, 1998).

Table 9.5.2: Periodic Position of Selected Heavy Metals

Sl.No.	*Name*	*Symbol*	*Atomic Number*	*Atomic Weight*
1.	Cadmium	Cd	48	112.411
2.	Copper	Cu	29	63.546
3.	Lead	Pb	82	207.2
4.	Manganese	Mn	25	54.93805
5.	Nickel	Ni	28	58.6934
6.	Zinc	Zn	30	65.39
7.	Iron	Fe	26	55.845

Source: IUPAC, 1994.

9.5.4 About AAS (4129 Model)

ECIL's Atomic Absorption Spectrophotometer, AAS 4129 is a PC based instrument for absorption and emission analysis. It is used for quantitative elemental analysis mainly like Copper, Iron, Zinc, Lead etc., by measuring the absorbance of a sample atomized in a flame. Some of the metals like Sodium, Potassium, Calcium, and Lithium are analyzed by emission method. PC does the data processing and partial control of the instrument.

The liquid sample is nebulised (reduce to a spray) by the support gas. The fuel gas is mixed and burnt over the burner head. A modulated light from Hollow Cathode lamp of a pre-selected element travels through the flame and enters the monochromator. The monochromator selects the appropriate resonance line of the selected element and directs it on to the PMT. The DC signal generated by the flame emission is rejected by FE compensation circuit and the original signal of the lamp is amplified, phase sensitively rectified averaged by an integrator to obtain sample signal. A computer processes the sample signal for photometric computations (% T, ABS or CONC). Instrument controls like wavelength, lamp current, gain, etc. are achieved and maintained by PC.

The cathode material of Hollow Cathode Lamp corresponds to the element of interest. ECIL's Atomic Absorption Spectrophotometer covers the complete range of Atomic Absorption applications. It incorporates State-of-the-art electronics, safety and operational convenience ensuring reliable and accurate analytical performance.

The data analysis and report making is done by the PC including selection of instrument parameters like wavelength, lamp current selection, and EHT to PMT at various wavelength. The software is user-friendly window based GUI interface using menus, function key, prompts, error messages, enabling ease of operation. Information is presented in easy read menus. In most cases recommended values are filled in.

The instrument was calibrated using regression techniques of linear and quadratic methods against standard solutions and concentration of unknown samples can be quantified. Instrument parameters and calibration parameters can be stored, as applications, which can be retrieved as and when, required. A hard copy of the results can be taken with the aid of a printer connected to one of the parallel ports of the PC.

Operating Steps of AAS

There are some main operating steps used in the operation of AAS (ECIL Instructions manual, 2004):

1. Switch on Stabilizer (Power) and computer.
2. Double click AAS NEW software icon on desktop and click power.
3. Select the required element from list.
4. Adjust selected element lamp on top position and switch on that lamp from instrument.
5. Click HC lamp current, 1, 2, 3, or 4.
6. Click peak, A and Bb options will appear, check the lamp before, if OK then click YES.
7. A peak will appear on screen, it should be sharp and compare element wavelength with present one, and the difference should not be more than ± 1 nm.
8. If peak is not OK or difference is > ±1 then click INDEX, after index again check the peak
9. If massage "*Signal is too high or too low for alignment*" appears, then check the lamp position, lamp and slit dial.
10. If peak is OK then align the burner with the help of line mark visiting card.
11. Switch on air compressor and open gas cylinder (pressure should be in green zone *i.e.* 5-10).
12. Open air from instant (pressure 15-20 LMP)
13. Open gas (Fuel) and adjust pressure 2-4 LMP and ignite immediately.
14. Switch On exhaust.
15. Click ANALYSIS.
16. Adjust HCL signal to green zone *i.e.* aprox. 3V with the help of EHT increase or decrease.
17. Feed blank in capillary and click zeroing.
18. Click CALIBRATION, and put the number of standard and cover of standard.
19. Feed blank in capillary and click zeroing.
20. Feed standard 1 in capillary and click READ.
21. Feed standard 2 in capillary and click READ.
22. Feed standard 3 in capillary and click READ.
23. Click CALIBRATION GRAPH and close, if graph is not OK then re-calibrate.
24. Click SAMPLE and put the number of samples and name of samples.
25. Feed blank in capillary and click zeroing.
26. Feed No. of samples one by one and click READ.

27. After taking the result of unknown click SAVE.
28. Click QUIT and close the gas cylinder tightly.
29. Switch of Air compressor and close gas from instrument.
30. Switch Off lamp 1, 2, 3 or 4.
31. Click POWER, switch of exhaust and click quit.
32. For print out results, double click AAS report, LOAD FILE, RES. OPEN, select the file and print result.
33. For print graph, load graph, print graph, res. open and print graph.
34. Now shut down PC, check the gas cylinder before closing the room and switch off printer and main power (stabilizer).

Precautions

Some precautions and highly attention is required during the handling of AAS 4129 and analyzing the heavy metals:

1. If the current wavelength is differed by ± 0.5 nanometers from the actual wavelength for any element after the peak search program, then the system needs INDEXING for correcting the ZERO error in the wavelength.
2. In case of any emergency while the Air – Acetylene Flame / N_2O–Acetylene is On, immediately put off the fuel switch and then turn the oxidant knob to off position.
3. While igniting $N_2O - C_2H_2$ flame ensure that the N_2O burner is fixed on the burner assembly.
4. Don't try to light up the flame without switching on the air.
5. Don't try to open or remove the Nebulizer when the flame is ON. Always ensure the Nebulizer is in locked position.
6. Always ensure the drain trap is filled with water to avoid back suction and also water drains out freely from spray chamber through the drain trap to the outlet.
7. Always switch on the exhaust system when the flame is ON.
8. Always keep ready your standards, samples, distilled water and then start working on AAS.
9. Check frequently for the gas leakage at the flow points with the soap solution.
10. After completing the analysis work, always ensure that the gas cylinder, compressor outlet is in closed position. Switch Off the power supplies.

9.5.5 Observations

Experimental Site

Heavy Metals in Textile Effluent

Cadmium (ppm)

The cadmium concentration in textile effluent was recorded maximum 0.052 ± 0.042 in summer 2005 and minimum 0.005 ± 0.004 in winter 2006-07 ranged between

0.001 to 0.1 ppm. The highest value of cadmium in textile effluent was found 0.1 ppm during June 2005 and lowest 0.001 ppm in November 2006.

Copper (ppm)

The concentration of copper in textile effluent was recorded maximum 0.44 ± 0.085 in summer 2005 and minimum 0.165 ± 0.066 in winter 2005-06 ranged between 0.1 to 0.49 ppm. The highest value of copper in textile effluent was found 0.49 ppm during March 2006 and lowest 0.1 ppm in November 2005.

Iron (ppm)

The concentration of iron in textile effluent was recorded maximum 0.543 ± 0.17 in summer 2006 and minimum 0.240 ± 0.10 in winter 2006-07 ranged between 0.12 to 0.78 ppm. The highest value of iron in textile effluent was found 0.78 ppm during May 2006 and lowest 0.12 ppm in September 2005.

Manganese (ppm)

The concentration of manganese in textile effluent was recorded maximum 0.310 ± 0.014 in summer 2006 and minimum 0.110 ± 0.02 in monsoon 2006 ranged between 0.09 to 0.32 ppm. The highest value of manganese in textile effluent was found 0.32 ppm during February 2007 and lowest 0.09 ppm in September 2005.

Nickel (ppm)

The concentration of nickel in textile effluent was recorded maximum 0.067 ± 0.037 in summer 2006 and minimum 0.007 ± 0.003 in monsoon 2006 ranged between 0.0012 to 0.061 ppm. The highest value of nickel in textile effluent was found 0.061 ppm during April 2006 and lowest 0.0012 ppm in July 2005.

Lead (ppm)

The concentration of lead in textile effluent was recorded maximum 0.500 ± 0.21 in summer 2005 and minimum 0.250 ± 0.085 in monsoon 2005 ranged between 0.21 to 0.81 ppm. The highest value of lead in textile effluent was found 0.81 ppm during June 2005 and lowest 0.21 ppm in September 2005.

Zinc (ppm)

The concentration of zinc in textile effluent was recorded maximum 0.338 ± 0.146 in winter 2006-07 and minimum 0.110 ± 0.012 in monsoon 2005 ranged between 0.09 to 0.51 ppm. The highest value of zinc in textile effluent was found 0.51 ppm during November 2006 and lowest 0.09 ppm in September 2005.

Heavy Metals in Surface Water

Cadmium (ppm)

The cadmium concentration in pond water was recorded maximum 0.012 ± 0.006 in summer 2006 and minimum 0.001 ± 0.002 in monsoon 2005 ranged between 0.00 to 0.02 ppm. The highest value of cadmium in pond water was found 0.02 ppm during June 2006 and lowest 0.00 ppm in August 2005.

Copper (ppm)

The concentration of copper in pond water was recorded maximum 0.427 ± 0.045 in summer 2005 and minimum 0.245 ± 0.07 in winter 2006-07 ranged between

1.9 to 13.2 ppm. The highest value of copper in pond water was found 13.2 ppm during April 2005 and lowest 1.9 ppm in October 2005.

Iron (ppm)

The concentration of iron in pond water was recorded maximum 9.70 ± 3.04 in summer 2005 and minimum 4.23 ± 1.45 in monsoon 2005 ranged between 0.09 to 0.6 ppm. The highest value of iron in pond water was found 0.6 ppm during May 2005 and lowest 0.09 ppm in December 2005.

Manganese (ppm)

The concentration of manganese in pond water was recorded maximum 0.530 ± 0.061 in summer 2005 and minimum 0.170 ± 0.059 in winter 2006-07 ranged between 0.09 to 0.6 ppm. The highest value of manganese in pond water was found 0.6 ppm during May 2005 and lowest 0.09 ppm in December 2005.

Nickel (ppm)

The concentration of nickel in pond water was recorded maximum 0.130 ± 0.014 in summer 2006 and minimum 0.047 ± 0.038 in winter 2006-07 ranged between 0.008 to 0.015 ppm. The highest value of nickel in pond water was found 0.15 ppm during May 2006 and lowest 0.008 ppm in November 2005.

Lead (ppm)

The concentration of lead in pond water was recorded maximum 1.80 ± 0.56 in summer 2005 and minimum 0.503 ± 0.346 in winter 2006-07 ranged between 0.05 to 2.3 ppm. The highest value of lead in pond water was found 2.3 ppm during May 2005 and lowest 0.05 ppm in October 2005.

Zinc (ppm)

The concentration of zinc in pond water was recorded maximum 195.0 ± 0.007 in summer 2007 and minimum 0.110 ± 0.02 in monsoon 2005 ranged between 0.05 to 0.21 ppm. The highest value of zinc in pond water was found 0.21 ppm during December 2006 and lowest 0.05 ppm in October 2005.

Heavy Metals in Groundwater

Cadmium (ppm)

The cadmium concentration in groundwater was recorded maximum 0.01 ± 0.002 in summer 2006 and minimum 0.002 ± 0.002 in monsoon 2006 ranged between 0.00 to 0.01 ppm. The highest value of cadmium in groundwater was found 0.01 ppm during March 2007 and lowest 0.00 ppm in August 2005.

Copper (ppm)

The concentration of copper in groundwater was recorded maximum 0.443 ± 0.067 in summer 2005 and minimum 0.288 ± 0.093 in winter 2006-07 ranged between 0.137 to 0.58 ppm. The highest value of copper in groundwater was found 0.58 ppm during July 2006 and lowest 0.137 ppm in October 2005.

Iron (ppm)

The concentration of iron in groundwater was recorded maximum 3.82 ± 0.59 in summer 2006 and minimum 1.50 ± 0.24 in monsoon 2005 ranged between 0.46 to 4.6

ppm. The highest value of iron in groundwater was found 4.6 ppm during April 2005 and lowest 0.46 ppm in October 2005.

Manganese (ppm)

The concentration of manganese in groundwater was recorded maximum 0.550 ± 0.08 in summer 2005 and minimum 0.284 ± 0.078 in winter 2005-06 ranged between 0.19 to 0.63 ppm. The highest value of manganese in groundwater was found 0.63 ppm during June 2006 and lowest 0.19 ppm in November 2005.

Nickel (ppm)

The concentration of nickel in groundwater was recorded maximum 0.153 ± 0.01 in summer 2006 and minimum 0.044 ± 0.035 in winter 2006-07 ranged between 0.009 to 0.16 ppm. The highest value of nickel in groundwater was found 0.16 ppm during May 2006 and lowest 0.009 ppm in November 2005.

Lead (ppm)

The concentration of lead in groundwater was recorded maximum 1.84 ± 0.31 in summer 2005 and minimum 0.850 ± 0.24 in winter 2005-06 ranged between 0.55 to 2.12 ppm. The highest value of lead in groundwater was found 2.12 ppm during May 2005 and lowest 0.55 ppm in October 2005.

Zinc (ppm)

The concentration of zinc in groundwater was recorded maximum 0.215 ± 0.03 in summer 2006 and minimum 0.126 ± 0.051 in winter 2006-07 ranged between 0.06 to 0.25 ppm. The highest value of zinc in groundwater was found 0.25 ppm during April 2005 and lowest 0.06 ppm in October 2005.

Heavy Metals in Effluent Drain Sediment

Cadmium (ppm)

The cadmium concentration in drain sediment was recorded maximum 5.78 ± 0.231 in summer 2005 and minimum 4.25 ± 0.544 in winter 2005-06 ranged between 3.54 to 6.12 ppm. The highest value of cadmium in drain sediment was found 6.12 ppm during June 2006 and lowest 3.54 ppm in November 2005.

Copper (ppm)

The concentration of copper in drain sediment was recorded maximum 54.83 ± 7.33 in summer 2006 and minimum 45.87 ± 5.82 in summer 2007 ranged between 37.85 to 55.36 ppm. The highest value of copper in drain sediment was found 55.36 ppm during April 2006 and lowest 37.85 ppm in August 2006.

Iron (ppm)

The concentration of iron in drain sediment was recorded maximum 8467.67 ± 2448.18 in summer 2005 and minimum 5656.0 ± 1216.72 in monsoon 2005 ranged between 4256.0 to 11235.0 ppm. The highest value of iron in drain sediment was found 11235.0 ppm during June 2005 and lowest 4256.0 ppm in August 2005.

Manganese (ppm)

The concentration of manganese in drain sediment was recorded maximum 1105.00 ± 107.08 in summer 2006 and minimum 791.33 ± 51.73 in monsoon 2005 ranged between 568.0 to 1105.0 ppm. The highest value of manganese in drain sediment was found 1105.0 ppm during April 2006 and lowest 568.0 ppm in August 2006.

Nickel (ppm)

The concentration of nickel in drain sediment was recorded maximum 75.00 ± 3.0 in summer 2005 and minimum 58.0 ± 3.0 in monsoon 2005 ranged between 49.0 to 79.0 ppm. The highest value of nickel in drain sediment was found 79.0 ppm during June 2006 and lowest 49.0 ppm in October 2006.

Lead (ppm)

The concentration of lead in drain sediment was recorded maximum 70.00 ± 4.36 in summer 2005 and minimum 47.20 ± 3.83 in winter 2005-06 ranged between 42.0 to 78.0 ppm. The highest value of lead in drain sediment was found 78.0 ppm during June 2006 and lowest 42.0 ppm in January 2006.

Zinc (ppm)

The concentration of zinc in drain sediment was recorded maximum 260.00 ± 83.54 in summer 2005 and minimum 143.50 ± 32.29 in winter 2006-07 ranged between 95.0 to 385.0 ppm. The highest value of zinc in drain sediment was found 385.0 ppm during June 2006 and lowest 95.0 ppm in October 2005.

Heavy Metals in Pond Sediment

Cadmium (ppm)

The cadmium concentration in pond sediment was recorded maximum 5.72 ± 0.45 in summer 2005 and minimum 4.05 ± 0.59 in winter 2005-06 ranged between 3.26 to 6.32 ppm. The highest value of cadmium in pond sediment was found 6.32 ppm during June 2006 and lowest 3.26 ppm in November 2005.

The concentration of copper in pond sediment was recorded maximum 52.46 ± 6.51 in summer 2006 and minimum 38.65 ± 9.23 in summer 2007 ranged between 24.45 to 57.21 ppm. The highest value of copper in pond sediment was found 57.21 ppm during May 2006 and lowest 24.45 ppm in January 2007.

Iron (ppm)

The concentration of iron in pond sediment was recorded maximum 6013.40 ± 856.58 in winter 2005-06 and minimum 3803.50 ± 113.84 in summer 2007 ranged between 3542.0 to 8514.0 ppm. The highest value of iron in pond sediment was found 8514.0 ppm during December 2006 and lowest 3542.0 ppm in April 2005.

Manganese (ppm)

The concentration of manganese in pond sediment was recorded maximum 942.00 ± 48.14 in summer 2005 and minimum 605.00 ± 161.71 in monsoon 2006 ranged between 465.0 to 998.0 ppm. The highest value of manganese in pond sediment was found 998.0 ppm during June 2006 and lowest 465.0 ppm in August 2006.

Nickel (ppm)

The concentration of nickel in pond sediment was recorded maximum 63.75 ± 11.12 in summer 2006 and minimum 49.0 ± 5.94 in winter 2006-07 ranged between

41.0 to 79.0 ppm. The highest value of nickel in pond sediment was found 79.0 ppm during June 2006 and lowest 41.0 ppm in October 2006.

Lead (ppm)

The concentration of lead in pond sediment was recorded maximum 69.00 ± 6.24 in summer 2005 and minimum 44.00 ± 5.39 in winter 2005-06 ranged between 37.0 to 75.0 ppm. The highest value of lead in pond sediment was found 75.0 ppm during June 2006 and lowest 37.0 ppm in January 2006.

Zinc (ppm)

The concentration of zinc in pond sediment was recorded maximum 240.00 ± 92.60 in summer 2005 and minimum 116.25 ± 32.76 in winter 2006-07 ranged between 75.0 to 321.0 ppm. The highest value of zinc in pond sediment was found 321.0 ppm during June 2006 and lowest 75.0 ppm in October 2006.

Control Site

Heavy Metals in Groundwater

Cadmium (ppm)

The cadmium concentration in groundwater on control site was recorded maximum 0.00 ± 0.00 and minimum 0.00 ± 0.00 ranged between 0.00 to 0.0005 ppm. The highest value of cadmium in groundwater was found 0.0005 ppm during June 2006 and lowest 0.00 ppm in April 2005 (mostly nil).

Copper (ppm)

The concentration of copper in groundwater on control site was recorded maximum 0.684 ± 0.80 in summer 2007 and minimum 0.90 ± 0.061 in winter 2005-06 ranged between 0.00 to 0.18 ppm. The highest value of copper in groundwater was found 0.18 ppm during May 2005 and lowest 0.00 ppm in December 2005.

Iron (ppm)

The concentration of iron in groundwater on control site was recorded maximum 0.868 ± 0.07 in summer 2006 and minimum 0.363 ± 0.128 in winter 2006-07 ranged between 0.18 to 0.99 ppm. The highest value of iron in groundwater was found 0.99 ppm during April 2005 and lowest 0.18 ppm in November 2005.

Manganese (ppm)

The concentration of manganese in groundwater on control site was recorded maximum 0.204 ± 0.03 in summer 2005 and minimum 0.075 ± 0.037 in winter 2006-07 ranged between 0.02 to 0.245 ppm. The highest value of manganese in groundwater was found 0.245 ppm during May 2006 and lowest 0.02 ppm in November 2005.

Nickel (ppm)

The concentration of nickel in groundwater on control site was recorded maximum 0.044 ± 0.011 in summer 2005 and minimum 0.00 ± 0.00 in winter 2005-06 ranged between 0.00 to 0.055 ppm. The highest value of nickel in groundwater was found 0.055 ppm during June 2006 and lowest 0.00 ppm in October 2005.

Lead (ppm)

The concentration of lead in groundwater on control site was recorded maximum 0.282 ± 0.013 in summer 2007 and minimum 0.178 ± 0.127 in winter 2006-07 ranged between 0.00 to 0.291 ppm. The highest value of lead in groundwater was found 0.291 ppm during February 2007 and lowest 0.00 ppm in October 2006.

Zinc (ppm)

The concentration of zinc in groundwater on control site was recorded maximum 0.099 ± 0.015 in summer 2005 and minimum 0.043 ± 0.013 in winter 2006-07 ranged between 0.02 to 0.112 ppm. The highest value of zinc in groundwater was found 0.112 ppm during April 2005 and lowest 0.02 ppm in December 2005.

Correlation Coefficient

Correlation between physico-chemical parameters and heavy metals of groundwater of 40 ft depth are given in tabular form for each metal. For cadmium correlation was found maximum 0.4400 with pH only. Correlation for copper was found maximum 0.7176 and 0.6712 with temperature and total solids respectively. Correlation for iron was found maximum 0.8102 and 0.6729 with pH and free carbon dioxide respectively. Correlation for manganese was found maximum 0.8508, 0.8001 and 0.8544 with total solids, total suspended solids and total dissolved solids respectively. Correlation for nickel was found maximum 0.8021 and 8021 with total dissolved solids and Electric conductivity respectively. Correlation for lead was found maximum 0.8593, 0.8340 and 0.8340 with pH, total dissolved solids and Electric conductivity respectively. Correlation for zinc was found maximum 0.7175 and 0.5164 with pH and free carbon dioxide respectively.

Correlation between physico-chemical parameters and heavy metals of groundwater of 80 ft depth are given tabular form for each metal. For cadmium correlation was found maximum 0.4448 and 0.5048 with pH and free carbon dioxide respectively. Correlation for copper was found maximum 0.7443 and 0.8099 with free carbon dioxide and total alkalinity respectively. Correlation for iron was found maximum 0.9188 and 0.8896 with temperature and total alkalinity. Correlation for manganese was found maximum 0.6930 and 0.7664 with free carbon dioxide and total alkalinity respectively. Correlation for nickel was found maximum 0.7536 and 0.7918 with free carbon dioxide and total alkalinity respectively. Correlation for lead was found maximum 0.6693 and 0.5841 with free carbon dioxide and total alkalinity respectively. Correlation for zinc was found maximum 0.6518 and 0.7069 with free carbon dioxide and total alkalinity respectively.

Correlation between physico-chemical parameters and heavy metals of deep groundwater of more than 120 ft depth are given in tabular form for each metal. For cadmium correlation was found maximum 0.2586 and 2761 with temperature and magnesium respectively. Correlation for copper was found maximum 0.6392 and 0.8666 with free carbon dioxide and total alkalinity respectively. Correlation for iron was found maximum 0.6815 and 0.8783 with free carbon dioxide and total alkalinity respectively. Correlation for manganese was found maximum 0.6144 and 0.8834 with temperature and total alkalinity respectively. Correlation for nickel was found maximum 0.7675 and 0.8302 with temperature and total alkalinity respectively.

Correlation for lead was found maximum 0.6347 and 0.7136 with free carbon dioxide and total alkalinity respectively. Correlation for zinc was found maximum 0.6340 and 0.8653 with free carbon dioxide and total alkalinity respectively.

Correlation between physico-chemical parameters and heavy metals of groundwater at control site are given in tabular form for each metal. For cadmium correlation was found maximum 0.3900 and 0.3991 with calcium and magnesium respectively. Correlation for copper was found maximum 0.1308 and 0.2028 with pH and total alkalinity respectively. Correlation for iron was found maximum 0.8049 and 0.8597 with free carbon dioxide and total alkalinity respectively. Correlation for manganese was found maximum 0.7006 and 0.8739 with temperature and total alkalinity respectively. Correlation for nickel was found maximum 0.8099 and 0.8175 with temperature and total alkalinity respectively. Correlation for lead was found maximum 0.8009 and 0.6927 with total alkalinity and free carbon dioxide respectively. Correlation for zinc was found maximum 0.6614 and 0.7411 with free carbon dioxide and total alkalinity respectively.

Transfer Factor (Coefficient) for Heavy Metals

From textile industrial effluent to groundwater, transfer factors for heavy metals are given in tabular form for experimental sites. Transfer factor for cadmium was found maximum 1.50 in winter 2006-07 and minimum 0.12 in monsoon 2005, while for copper transfer factor was found maximum 1.79 in winter 2005-06 and minimum 0.99 in summer 2006. Transfer factor for iron was found maximum 9.64 in summer 2007 and minimum 5.93 in monsoon 2005. Transfer factor for manganese was found maximum 4.12 in monsoon 2006 and minimum 1.27 in winter 2005-06. Transfer factor for nickel was found maximum 14.14 in monsoon 2006 and minimum 1.45 in winter 2005-06. Transfer factor for lead was found maximum 4.65 in monsoon 2005 and minimum 2.01 in winter 2005-06. Transfer factor for zinc was found maximum 1.21 in monsoon 2005 and minimum 0.38 in winter 2006-07.

From textile industrial effluent to pond water, transfer factors for heavy metals are given in tabular form.Transfer factor for cadmium was found maximum 0.83 in winter 2006-07 and minimum 0.05 in monsoon 2005, while for copper transfer factor was found maximum 1.53 in winter 2005-06 and minimum 0.97 in summer 2005. Transfer factor for iron was found maximum 25.0 in summer 2007 and minimum 15.93 in monsoon 2006. Transfer factor for manganese was found maximum 4.27 in monsoon 2006 and minimum0.77 in winter 2005-06. Transfer factor for nickel was found maximum 11.76 in monsoon 2006 and minimum 1.64 in winter 2006-07. Transfer factor for lead was found maximum 3.63 in summer 2006 and minimum 1.19 in winter 2005-06. Transfer factor for zinc was found maximum 1.00 in monsoon 2005 and minimum 0.54 in winter 2006-07.

From pond water to groundwater of 40 ft depth, transfer factors for heavy metals are given in tabular form. Transfer factor for cadmium was found maximum 2.20 in monsoon 2005 and minimum 0.87 in summer 2006, while for copper transfer factor was found maximum 1.17 in winter 2005-06 and minimum 0.97 in summer 2007. Transfer factor for iron was found maximum 0.40 in monsoon 2006 and minimum 0.34 in winter 2005-06. Transfer factor for manganese was found maximum 1.84 in winter 2006-07 and minimum 0.96 in monsoon 2006. Transfer factor for nickel was found maximum 1.29 in monsoon 2005 and minimum 0.83 in winter 2005-06. Transfer factor for lead was found maximum 1.91 in monsoon 2005 and minimum 1.02 in summer 2005. Transfer factor for zinc was found maximum 1.35 in monsoon 2006 and minimum 0.70 in winter 2006-07.

From pond water to deep groundwater of 120 ft depth, transfer factors for heavy metals are given in tabular form for various metals. Transfer factor for cadmium was found maximum 0.13 in summer 2006 and minimum 0.00 in monsoon 2005, while for copper transfer factor was found maximum 0.52 in winter 2006-07 and minimum 0.41 in monsoon 2005. Transfer factor for iron was found maximum 0.16 in monsoon 2006 and minimum 0.10 in winter 2005-06. Transfer factor for manganese was found maximum 0.75 in summer 2007 and minimum 0.40 in monsoon 2005. Transfer factor for nickel was found maximum 0.61 in monsoon 2005 and minimum 0.19 in winter 2006-07. Transfer factor for lead was found maximum 0.57 in winter 2005-06 and minimum 0.22 in summer 2005. Transfer factor for zinc was found maximum 0.74 in monsoon 2006 and minimum 0.25 in winter 2006-07.

Enrichment Factor for Heavy Metals

In the drain sediment, metal enrichment factor for heavy metals are given in tabular form. Enrichment factor for cadmium was found maximum 0.90 in monsoon 2005 and minimum 0.53 in winter 2005-06. For copper enrichment factor was found maximum 8.47 in summer 2006 and minimum 5.74 in winter 2005-06. Enrichment factor for iron was maximum 1000 due to the comparison base of study in the evaluation of enrichment factor of metals in drain sediment. For manganese enrichment factor was found maximum 175.63 in summer 2007 and minimum 109.92 in monsoon 2006. Enrichment factor for nickel was maximum 11.70 in summer 2007 and minimum 7.35 in winter 2006-07. For lead enrichment factor was found maximum 10.73 in monsoon 2005 and minimum 5.83 in winter 2005-06. Enrichment factor for zinc was found maximum 38.80 in summer 2006 and minimum 18.12 in winter 2006-07.

In the pond sediment, metal enrichment factor for heavy metals are given in tabular form. Metal enrichment factor for cadmium was found maximum 1.26 in summer 2007 and minimum 0.67 in winter 2005-06. For copper enrichment factor was found maximum 12.04 in summer 2006 and minimum 7.61 in winter 2006-07. Enrichment factor for iron was maximum 1000 due to the comparison base of study in the evaluation of enrichment factor of metals in pond sediment. For manganese enrichment factor was found maximum 243.85 in summer 2007 and minimum 139.09 in winter 2005-06. Enrichment factor for nickel was maximum 14.85 in summer 2007 and minimum 8.38 in winter 2006-07. For lead enrichment factor was found maximum 14.23 in summer 2006 and minimum 7.32 in winter 2005-06. Enrichment factor for zinc was found maximum 47.57 in summer 2006 and minimum 19.89 in winter 2006-07.

Geo-accumulation Index for Heavy Metals

Geo-accumulation index and values for heavy metals in effluent drain sediment are given tabular form for highest values. Value of cadmium in geo-accumulation index was found maximum 12.85 in summer 2005 and minimum 3.24 in winter

2005-06. For copper geo-accumulation index value was found maximum 0.81 in summer 2006 and minimum 0.68 in monsoon 2006. Geo-accumulation index value for iron was found maximum 0.12 in summer 2005 and minimum 0.08 in summer 2007. For manganese geo-accumulation index value was found maximum 0.87 in summer 2006 and minimum 0.62 in monsoon 2005. Geo-accumulation index value for nickel was found maximum 0.74 in summer 2005 and minimum 0.57 in monsoon 2005. For lead geo-accumulation index value was found maximum 2.33 in summer 2005 and minimum 1.57 in winter 2005-06. Geo-accumulation index value for zinc was maximum 1.82 in summer 2005 and minimum 1.01 in winter 2006-07.

Rank of cadmium in geo-accumulation index was found maximum 3.68 in summer 2005 and minimum 3.24 in winter 2005-06. For copper, iron, manganese and nickel geo-accumulation index rank was found in negative values below 0.00 For lead geo-accumulation index rank was found maximum 1.22 in summer 2005 and minimum 0.65 in winter 2005-06. Geo-accumulation index rank for zinc was maximum 0.87 in summer 2005 and minimum 0.01 in winter 2006-07. While for highest concentrations of heavy metals, highest values for cadmium, copper, iron, manganese, nickel, lead and zinc was found 13.60, 0.92, 0.16, 0.98, 0.77, 2.60 and 2.70 respectively. Geo-accumulation index rank was found 3.77, 1.38 and 1.43 for cadmium, lead and zinc respectively.

In pond sediment, geo-accumulation index and values of heavy metals are given in tabular form for highest values. Value of cadmium in geo-accumulation index was found maximum 12.70 in summer 2005 and minimum 9.01 in winter 2005-06. For copper geo-accumulation index value was found maximum 0.78 in summer 2006 and minimum 0.57 in summer 2007. Geo-accumulation index value for iron was found maximum 0.08 in winter 2005-06 and minimum 0.05 in summer 2007. For manganese geo-accumulation index value was found maximum 0.74 in summer 2005 and minimum 0.47 in monsoon 2006. Geo-accumulation index value for nickel was found maximum 0.63 in summer 2006 and minimum 0.48 in winter 2006-07. For lead geo-accumulation index value was found maximum 2.30 in summer 2005 and minimum 1.47 in winter 2005-06. Geo-accumulation index value for zinc was maximum 1.68 in summer 2005 and minimum 0.82 in winter 2006-07.

Rank of cadmium in geo-accumulation index was found maximum 3.67 in summer 2005 and minimum 3.17 in winter 2005-06. For copper, iron, manganese and nickel geo-accumulation index rank was found in negative values below 0.00 For lead geo-accumulation index rank was found maximum 1.20 in summer 2005 and minimum 0.55 in winter 2005-06. Geo-accumulation index rank for zinc was maximum 0.75 in summer 2005 and minimum 0.00 in monsoon 2005. While for highest concentrations of heavy metals, highest values for cadmium, copper, iron, manganese, nickel, lead and zinc was found 14.04, 0.85, 0.11, 0.78, 0.77, 2.50 and 2.25 respectively. Geo-accumulation index rank was found 3.81, 1.32 and 1.17 for cadmium, lead and zinc respectively.

Metal Accumulation Factor

In the present study of groundwater, metal accumulation factor for heavy metals are given in tabular form. Metal accumulation factor for cadmium was found maximum 250.00 in summer 2005 (almost infinite) and minimum 57.14 in summer 2006. For copper metal accumulation factor was found maximum 3.28 in winter 2005-06 and minimum 0.53 in summer 2007. Metal accumulation factor for iron was maximum 4.41 in summer 2005 and minimum 2.64 in monsoon 2005. For manganese metal accumulation factor was maximum 4.17 in winter 2006-07 and minimum 2.65 in summer 2006. Metal accumulation factor for nickel was found maximum 7.14 in summer 2007 and minimum 3.36 in summer 2005. For lead metal accumulation factor was found maximum 6.84 in summer 2006 and minimum 4.45 in winter 2005-06. Metal accumulation factor for zinc was maximum 3.00 in winter 2006-07 and minimum 2.02 in summer 2005.

9.5.6 Discussion

Heavy Metals in Textile Effluent, Surface Water, Groundwater, Control Groundwater, Effluent Drain Sediment and Pond Sediment

An increasing number of groundwater wells were found to be contaminated by chemical waste from point sources and also widespread known point source pollution from fertilizers was threatening the water resources in extensive areas (Lagas *et al.*, 1989 and Meier and Mull, 1989).

Wastewaters from textile industries have the high amount of the heavy metals entering them most hazardous for soil plant and other organisms including human beings (Sial *et al.*, 2006). Many effects of Cd action results from interactions of various micro and macro elements as it antagonizes to Cu, Zn and Fe and also interferes with Ca absorption. Cadmium found in a sample of Ca is likely in an inorganic form and may be relatively less toxic to flora and fauna, while same amount of Cd when present in zinc or phosphates may be highly toxic to plants and animals, especially in calcium deficiency in soil. The use of contaminated water into irrigation may be increase the cadmium status in agricultural soil (Mani *et al.*, 2005).

Cadmium concentrations in textile industrial effluent (0.005-0.052 ppm), pond water (0.001-0.012 ppm) and agricultural soil (0.7-3.4 ppm) turn down in rainy season due to the dilution factor, while in the groundwater system its impact seems after monsoon and cadmium concentration reduces. Cadmium slightly fluctuated and remains mostly constant in pond sediment (4.0-5.7 ppm) and drain sediment (4.2-5.8 ppm). Transfer factor for cadmium (0.12-1.5) from textile industrial effluent to groundwater was recorded high in winter months (after monsoon). In geo-accumulation index cadmium (3.77-3.81) laid in between 3 to 4 mean strongly polluted by cadmium. Metal accumulation factor for groundwater (57.1-250.0) was found mostly very high or infinite for cadmium, because in most samples of control sites cadmium was absent.

During the last decade, the industrial use of Cd has increased and can create both acute and chronic cases of clinically identifiable toxicity in humans. In human, absorption of dietary Cd is limited up to 15 % and that of inhaled Cd is high 40 % and not absorbed from skin (Mani *et al.*, 2005). When the animal kept on contaminated feed along with the industrial polluted environment for long time, they suffer from its toxicity symptoms which may be sub clinical or clinical. The retention time of Cd is quite high, half life being 40 years. Cadmium is produced as inevitable by-product of zinc (or occasionally lead) refining (lenntech.com). Cd was found slightly high in groundwater for drinking purposes, because it should not be more than 0.003 mg/l for health views, while it should be less than 1 µg/l generally in drinking water (WHO, 2006). Helena (1999), Umar and Ahmad (2000), Kumar *et al.*,(2001) and Yadav *et al.*,(2002) observed the high Cd concentrations in industrial area like the present study of groundwater, while Krebs *et al.* (1999), Singh *et al.*,(1994) and Fakayode and Oniyawa (2002) in soil and Bordas and Bourg (1998), Vazquez *et al.* (2007) and Korfali and Davies (2004) in sediment.

Concentrations of copper in textile industrial effluent are due to the residues of some dyes especially used for blue or green colours. Copper concentrations in textile industrial effluent (0.16-0.44 ppm) were found parallel or sometimes higher than iron. Most of the part of copper content reach in pond water (0.25-0.43 ppm) and rest settle down on drain sediment (45.8-54.8 ppm). Copper in pond sediment (38.6-52.4 ppm) also settled down after some time. Transfer factor of copper from pond water to groundwater (0.97-1.17) and groundwater to agricultural soil (0.45-0.82) was found higher than other microelement except cadmium. In geo-accumulation index copper was not recorded in polluted condition. Metal accumulation factor for copper was recorded high in winter season (3.28) for groundwater; while in agricultural soil high metal accumulation factor was found in summer months (1.20). Copper may accumulate in living organisms and their various body parts (Kudesia, 1992). High amount if heavy metals like cu and Zn may harm to living organism of existing ecosystem (Aslam *et al.*, 2004).

However, Cu concentration was not detected high in groundwater samples as described by WHO (2006) in drinking water *i.e.* 2.0 mg/l. The Cu concentrations level in study area have compared with those observed by Yusus and Sonibare (2004), Aslam *et al.* (2004), Helena (1999), Umar and Ahmad (2000), Kumar *et al.*,(2001) and Yadav *et al.*,(2002) in groundwater; Krebs *et al.* (1999), Singh *et al.*,(1994) and Fakayode and Oniyawa (2002) in soil and Bordas and Bourg (1998), Nasr *et al.*,(2006), Vazquez *et al.* (2007) and Korfali and Davies (2004) in sediments. Ather and Vohra (1985) reported that heavy metal enters in water system by various ways in natural resources like erosion, weathering, volcanic activities and anthropogenic activities that include direct emissions of heavy metal by different industries.

Iron is one of the most abundant elements of the rocks and soil, ranking fourth by weight. All kinds of waters including groundwater have appreciable quantities of iron. Iron has more solubility at acidic pH, therefore large quantities of iron are leached out from the soils by acidic waters. In the alkaline medium iron remain comparatively low in soluble phase. Excess calcium can reduced the activity of iron in soil and soil aeration may influence the availability of iron to plants (Miller and Turk, 2002).

In groundwaters most of the iron remains in ferrous state due to general lack of oxygen. In alkaline conditions in groundwaters, the iron is mostly ferrous bicarbonate, which is a colourless substance. When the groundwater with higher concentrations of iron is tapped, it quickly oxidizes to ferric state in the form of insoluble ferric hydroxide, a brown substance. If appreciable quantities of ferrous bicarbonates are present in groundwater, and they come in contact with oxygen at surface, the hydroxides are formed, CO_2 is released and hence it increases the pH, facilitating the oxidation processes (Minhas and Gupta, 1992). Generally, movement of iron compounds take place downward through the soil profile and reach in to groundwater table (Miller and Turk, 2002). However, iron was not found in high concentration in textile industrial effluents (0.24-0.54 ppm), but the high concentrations of iron were observed in effluent drain sediment (5656.0-8467.7 ppm) due to the continuous settlement and abundantly natural occurrence in earth crust materials. Iron in shallow groundwater samples (1.5-3.8 ppm) was found higher to textile effluents, while iron in deep groundwater (0.48-1.05 ppm) and control groundwater (0.363-0.868 mg/l) was not detected in high concentrations. Iron was present in high quantity in pond sediment (3803.5-6013.4 ppm) and effluent drain sediment (5656.0-8467.7 ppm). Iron concentration in agricultural soil was analyzed comparatively higher than other metals.

Iron's transfer factors were found very high from textile industrial effluent to groundwater (5.93-9.64), from textile industrial effluent to pond water up to 25.00, while iron was transferred from pond water to groundwater with highest 0.40 coefficient. However, transfer factor of iron was noticed low in comparison to other metals from shallow groundwater to agricultural soil. Metal enrichment factor in all seasons and in all sediment samples was calculated 1000.0 due to the comparative parameter for other metals for determination metals enrichment factor. In geo-accumulation index for drain sediment and pond sediment iron was not indexed at very high rank, it was found very low because the natural occurrence of iron in earth crust shale was very high, so iron was not a pollution causing agent in industrial area during the present study. Metal accumulation factor of iron was found from 2-4 for groundwater in Panipat region. Iron was detected in groundwater with 2-4 times high quantities in comparison to control site's groundwater. Iron in textile industrial effluent and pond water was found very high, while in groundwater samples it was also found very high for drinking purposes (WHO, 2006) Helena (1999), Yusus and Sonibare (2004), Umar and Ahmad (2000), Kumar *et al.*,(2001) and Yadav *et al.*,(2002) observed the similar trends of iron concentrations in groundwater and Singh *et al.*,(1994) in agricultural soil of industrial area.

Manganese was found as a second abundant element in the effluent drain and pond sediment after iron. However, manganese was comparatively low in textile industrial effluent (0.11-0.31 ppm) and very low in groundwater samples (0.28-0.55 ppm). In groundwater samples manganese remains below 1.0 during the study even in shallow aquifer. In agricultural soil, manganese was comparatively low in concentrations (5.8-13.6 ppm) regarding other metals. Manganese was third most enriched element in groundwater samples. Mn was found slightly high at experimental sites in the case of soil samples. Manganese has positive relationship with all the physico-chemical parameters of groundwater as correlated with temperature (0.6892), total solids (0.8508) electric conductivity (0.8544), total alkalinity (0.7074) except dissolved oxygen.

Transfer factor of Mn from textile industrial effluent to pond water was noticed from 1to 4 almost in all seasons, while below 1 in winter season. Transfer factor was calculated near 1 in all seasons from pond water to groundwater. Transfer factor from groundwater to agricultural soil was noticed very low at experimental sites as well as at control site. Enrichment factor of Mn was found around 100-200, highest after Fe in drain sediment, while enrichment factor was noticed higher in pond sediment. The value of Mn in geo-accumulation index was noticed always below 1 with negative rank even highest value in drain sediment as well as pond sediment due to the high natural shale value of Mn in earth crust. Metal accumulation factor of Mn in groundwater was high and ranged between 2 to 4, while in soil environment it was found below 2 always. Mn was found slightly high in groundwater for drinking purposes, because it should not be more than 0.5 mg/l for health views in drinking water (WHO, 2006).

Mathess (1974) reported that fresh groundwater constitutes 0.00-0.007 ppm cadmium, WHO (1984) recommended Cd concentration should not exceed maximum of 0.01 ppm in raw drinking water supply, 0.5 ppm in irrigation water. USEPA (1990) recommended maximum permissible Cd concentration as 0.04 and 0.02 ppm to protect aquatic life including fish. Hart (1982) reported a concentration range of Pb 0.0003-0.03 ppm in natural freshwater, while Frostner and Wittman (1979) the likely level as 0.002 ppm. Siddiqui and Pathania (2002) reported that the high value of Pb, Cr and other trace metals in groundwater in Jalandhar and Ludiana industrial area.

Nickel is one of the second trace elements of the present study after cadmium. As it is very toxic to plants and animals in low concentrations and has a tendency to accumulate in body parts. However Ni was presented in very minor concentrations in textile industrial effluent (0.007-0.067 ppm), and surface water (0.047-0.13 ppm), it was found comparatively high due to the regular input. Ni concentrations in pond were noticed higher during the summer season due to the loss of water by vaporization from pond system. About similar conditions were observed in groundwater samples. In deep groundwater, Ni was almost absent like cadmium. In agricultural soil all metals were found higher than groundwater so, nickel was also found high (5.3-10.5 ppm). Ni was found very high like other metals due to the settling of metals on bottom beds in pond sediment (49.0-63.7 ppm) and drain sediment (58.0-75.0 ppm). Nickel has no positive correlations with any physico-chemical parameter of soil and water except total alkalinity, Calcium, electric conductivity and water holding capacity. Highest transfer factor of Ni from textile industrial effluent to pond water and groundwater (14.14) was found in monsoon seasons. However, transfer factor from pond water to groundwater (0.83-1.29) was not found effective. Like cadmium, Ni was sometimes found infinitive in winter seasons.

Enrichment factor of Ni (7.35-11.7) was not effective in comparison to iron in drain sediment, but in pond sediment (8.38-14.85) it was slightly high due to the high retention time of wastewater in pond. The observations of present study reveals that Ni never reflected the pollution load in drain or pond sediment through the geo-accumulation index because it was found always below than 1. Metal accumulation factor in groundwater was found slightly high or sometimes infinitive. Ni was found high in groundwater for drinking purposes, because it should not be more than 0.07

mg/l for health views, while it should be less than 0.02 mg/l generally in drinking water (WHO, 2006). Nickel may accumulate in aquatic life but its presence is not magnified along food chains (lenntech.com). So, there is not so big fear of nickel toxicity to higher animals including human beings, but agricultural plant health will be affected in contaminated agricultural soil. This trend of Ni concentrations in present study have been supported on the basis of recommendation of Kumar *et al.* (2001) and Yadav *et al.*,(2002) in groundwater, Kasem and Singh (1999), Singh *et al.*,(1994) and Fakayode and Oniyawa (2002) in soil and Nasr *et al.* (2006) in sediment. Jayabaskeran and Sree Ramulu (1996) observed a great heavy metal movement in sewage irrigating light textured soil than in heavy textured soil. It may be pointed out that the builds up of heavy metal like Cr, Pb, Ni warrant toward continuous monitoring and suitable measures are needed before these become toxic.

Lead was found highest in textile industrial effluent, but it accumulated in drain sediment in comparatively less quantity. Lead mostly remained in effluent (0.25-0.50 ppm) and fluctuated in pond (0.5-1.8 ppm). Rest quantity of lead settled down on bed sediment of drain and pond, so, the lead concentration was found low in pond sediment (44.0-69.0 ppm) and high in drain sediment (47.2-70.0 ppm). Lead was the second most abundant metal species after iron. Lead was found in high concentrations in shallow groundwater (0.85-1.84 ppm) in comparison to deep groundwater (0.28-0.41 ppm). Lead is deposited mostly in bones and some soft tissues. High concentrations of lead may create toxicity in human (Kudesia, 1992).

Pb was found slightly high in groundwater (0.85-1.84 ppm) for drinking purposes and also in pond water (0.50-1.8 ppm), because it should not be more than 0.01 mg/l for health views, while it should be less than 0.1 mg/l generally in drinking water (WHO, 2006). Helena (1999), Umar and Ahmad (2000), Kumar *et al.*,(2001) and Yadav *et al.*,(2002) were observed the same trend of occurrence of Pb concentrations in groundwater, Fakayode and Oniyawa (2002), Krebs *et al.* (1999) and Singh *et al.*,(1994) in soil environment and Bordas and Bourg (1998), Nasr *et al.*,(2006) and Vazquez *et al.* (2007) in sediment.

However, zinc was not found so high in textile industrial effluent (0.11-0.34 ppm) in comparison to lead, but it was found in very high concentrations in drain sediment (143.5-260.0 ppm). Similarly, it was found in less quantity in pond water (0.11-0.2 ppm) and accumulated in very high quantity in bed sediment (116.2-240.0 ppm) of pond. Zinc concentration was fluctuated in pond sediment (116.2-240.0 ppm) season to season, while in drain sediment (143.5-260.0 ppm) the fluctuation of zinc concentrations was not observed in high concentration. Zinc concentration (0.13-0.22 ppm) was found at fifth position in groundwater samples among the all seven metals among all metals studied. Positive relationship was noticed between heavy metals of groundwater with Zn. Transfer factor of zinc from textile industrial effluent to pond water was not found more than 1. However, transfer factor of Zn was found more than 1 from pond water to groundwater during almost all seasons.

Enrichment factor of zinc in drain sediment was ranked at third position, while it was noticed slightly high in pond sediment due to the long retention time. In geo-accumulation index, the value of zinc was found more than 1.0 in all seasons, and ranked below 1 in geo-accumulation index in drain sediment.

Metal accumulation factor of Zn was calculated between 2 to 3 in groundwater samples. Zn was found low in groundwater and in pond water for drinking purposes, because it should not be more than 3.0 mg/l for health views, while it should be less than 5.0 mg/l generally in drinking water (WHO, 2006).

Zinc salts are relatively non-toxic, but high concentrations may cause health problems like vomiting, renal damage, etc. (Kudesia, 1992). High amount of Zn may harm to living organism of that ecosystem (Aslam *et al.*, 2004). Helena (1999), Umar and Ahmad (2000), Kumar *et al.*,(2001), Yadav *et al.*,(2002), Yusus and Sonibare (2004) and Aslam *et al.* (2004) reported the same fluctuations of Zn concentrations in groundwater, Singh *et al.*,(1994), Krebs *et al.* (1999) and Fakayode and Oniyawa (2002) in soil and Bordas and Bourg (1998), Nasr *et al.*,(2006), Vazquez *et al.* (2007) and Korfali and Davies (2004) in sediment. It is urgently required that industries should continuously monitor textile effluent and take necessary actions to properly treat waste water prior their disposal to water bodies and save already depleting natural water resources (Aslam *et al.*, 2004).

9.5.7 Transfer of Heavy Metals

In the recent years there has been a growing concern with environmental protection. This can be achieved either by decreasing the afflux of pollutants to the environment or by their removal from contaminated media. The former is a feasible choice only for pollutants of anthropogenic origin, whereas, the latter is unavoidable for those of natural origin (Gomez-Serrano *et al.*, 1998). The presence of heavy metals in the aquatic environment has been of great concern to scientists and engineers because of their increased discharge, toxic nature, and other adverse effects on receiving waters (Singh, 2006).

In heavy metals analysis, the total concentrations of the metals are often determined (Okonwo *et al.*, 1999, 2001; Castro Dentros *et al.*, 2003). However, total concentration of trace metals provides no information concerning the fate of the metal in the terms of its interaction with sediments, its mobility, bioavailability, or resultant toxicity (Christie, 1995). It is now widely accepted that measuring total metal concentrations cannot fully assess the role of aquatic sediments as a sink or as a source of pollutants. In addition, determination of total elements does not given an accurate estimate of the likely environmental impact. Instead, it is desirable to have information on the potential availability of metals (whether toxic or essential) to biota under various environmental conditions. Since the mobility of heavy metals, as well as their bioavailability and related eco-toxicity to plants, critically depends upon chemical forms in which, a metal is present in the sediment, considerable interest exists in trace element speciation (Davidson *et al.*, 1994).

Heavy metals are introduced into aquatic system from various anthropogenic sources. Heavy metals constitute a special group of contaminants of aquatic systems and deserve special attention. Since metals are not removed by natural degradation processes, they may become enriched in sediments over time. Metal contamination of sediments is an issue of growing concerns worldwide (NRC, 1989). Both natural processes and anthropogenic activities are responsible for introducing metals in to the aquatic system (Nriagu, 1989). Many contaminants discharged into surface waters rapidly become associated with the particulate matter and incorporated in sediments. Metals in aquatic systems become part of the water-sediment system and their distribution is controlled by a dynamic set of physical-chemical interactions and equilibrium, largely governed by pH and type of legends and chelating agents, oxidation state of the mineral components and the redox conditions of the system. Metal contaminated sediments may release heavy metals back to the overlying water column and, thus, pose risk to aquatic life and ecosystems. Due to their particle reactivity, heavy metals tend to accumulate in sediment as a result may persist in the environment long after their primary sources have been removed (Forstner and Wittman, 1981).

Heavy metals travel from one level to another in the ecological system due to the accumulation in abiotic and biotic components. In the study area, basically anthropogenic source of heavy metals are the dye houses in textile industrial area. Heavy metals reach in effluent drain and also its bottom sediment and further into pond and bed sediment of pond near village Binjhole adjoining to textile industrial area of Panipat. Heavy metals percolate slowly from the bed sediment of Binjhole pond towards the groundwater table and there may be a threat to deep aquifers also by leaching process of metals. As the groundwater was mostly used in irrigation and drinking purposes in most rural parts of Haryana, which have affected the agricultural soil health after irrigation by contaminated groundwater and ultimately influence on the agricultural productivity, vegetation health and grain quality also. The use of groundwater for drinking purposes of human and cattle in contaminated conditions, a threat of various health hazards and diseases have occurred to public at present. Some of the diseases caused by toxic heavy metals have been lethal to living organisms.

9.5.8 Accumulation of Heavy Metals

The development and pollution are the two faces of the same coin having the forever positive relationship between each other. Due to the industrialization, a huge quantity of waste materials discarded outside from the industries, in which various toxic substances including heavy metals are present. These large quantities of discarded heavy metals have been created havoc in the environmental ecosystem and affected all biotic components of the surrounding water and agricultural system.

The accumulating processes of run-off derived metals from the point and non-point pollution sources and their significant accumulation in the sediment of drain and pond with furthermore retention in agricultural soil has been observed by many investigators (Harper *et al.*, 1984; Nightangle, 1987 and Yusuf *et al.*, 1986). The extent of contamination due to heavy metal deposition in different industrial sites in relation to quite vulnerable metal toxicity among soil biota and plants have been investigated by Moon *et al.* (1991) and recorded Cd, Cu, Pb, Zn level in the industrial drain and top soil of agricultural fields.

Heavy metals have a tendency to accumulate and store in a component or trophic levels. The storage of heavy metals has created harmful effects for biotic components. The heavy metals accumulated in sediment and percolated down in to groundwater known as bio-accumulation of metal. From groundwater, heavy metals may turn into two ways; one is though irrigation and second is through drinking by human beings.

Table 9.5.3: Seasonal Variation of Heavy Metals in Groundwater at 40 ft Depth from Hand Pump in Village Binjhole

Heavy Metals	*Unit*	*Summer 2005*		*Monsoon 2005*		*Winter 2005-06*		*Summer 2006*		*Monsoon 2006*		*Winter 2006-07*		*Summer 2007*	
		Mean	*SD*	*Mean*	*SD*	*Mean*	*SD*	*Mean*	*SD*	*Mean*	*SD*	*Mean*	*SD*	*Mean*	*SD*
Cadmium (Cd)	ppm	0.008	0.002	0.003	0.003	0.007	0.001	0.010	0.002	0.002	0.002	0.007	0.002	0.010	0.000
Copper (Cu)	ppm	0.443	0.067	0.413	0.142	0.296	0.094	0.425	0.068	0.423	0.150	0.288	0.093	0.360	0.028
Iron (Fe)	ppm	3.777	0.891	1.503	0.235	1.628	0.922	3.820	0.589	1.840	0.265	1.513	0.645	3.375	0.389
Manganese (Mn)	ppm	0.550	0.079	0.373	0.146	0.284	0.078	0.530	0.083	0.453	0.117	0.313	0.049	0.430	0.028
Nickel (Ni)	ppm	0.147	0.015	0.094	0.020	0.045	0.036	0.153	0.010	0.099	0.012	0.044	0.035	0.125	0.007
Lead (Pb)	ppm	1.840	0.308	1.163	0.214	0.850	0.235	1.820	0.275	1.270	0.401	0.948	0.142	1.295	0.021
Zincppm (Zn)	0.200	0.046	0.133	0.021	0.126	0.051	0.215	0.025	0.153	0.031	0.128	0.043	0.200	0.014	

Table 9.5.4: Seasonal Variation of Heavy Metals in Groundwater at 80 ft Depth from Tube Well and Deep Hand Pump

Heavy Metals	*Unit*	*Summer 2005*		*Monsoon 2005*		*Winter 2005-06*		*Summer 2006*		*Monsoon 2006*		*Winter 2006-07*		*Summer 2007*	
		Mean	*SD*	*Mean*	*SD*	*Mean*	*SD*	*Mean*	*SD*	*Mean*	*SD*	*Mean*	*SD*	*Mean*	*SD*
Cadmium (Cd)	ppm	0.006	0.002	0.001	0.001	0.004	0.002	0.006	0.001	0.000	0.001	0.004	0.001	0.006	0.000
Copper (Cu)	ppm	0.288	0.035	0.219	0.030	0.152	0.024	0.288	0.049	0.218	0.029	0.158	0.025	0.212	0.054
Iron (Fe)	ppm	1.880	0.397	1.657	0.362	0.668	0.224	1.788	0.572	1.783	0.325	0.783	0.311	1.065	0.191
Manganese (Mn)	ppm	0.294	0.021	0.215	0.031	0.149	0.047	0.286	0.041	0.228	0.036	0.150	0.036	0.225	0.007
Nickel (Ni)	ppm	0.098	0.017	0.059	0.018	0.016	0.013	0.099	0.028	0.063	0.020	0.013	0.004	0.052	0.013
Lead (Pb)	ppm	0.863	0.076	0.627	0.146	0.530	0.175	0.850	0.130	0.660	0.101	0.505	0.152	0.740	0.014
Zinc (Zn)	ppm	0.163	0.015	0.133	0.025	0.069	0.032	0.170	0.022	0.127	0.021	0.078	0.026	0.135	0.021

Table 9.5.5: Seasonal Variation of Heavy Metals in Groundwater (more than 120 ft depth) of Tube Well

Heavy Metals	*Unit*	*Summer 2005*		*Monsoon 2005*		*Winter 2005-06*		*Summer 2006*		*Monsoon 2006*		*Winter 2006-07*		*Summer 2007*	
		Mean	*SD*	*Mean*	*SD*	*Mean*	*SD*	*Mean*	*SD*	*Mean*	*SD*	*Mean*	*SD*	*Mean*	*SD*
Cadmium (Cd)	ppm	0.000	0.001	0.000	0.000	0.000	0.000	0.002	0.002	0.000	0.000	0.000	0.000	0.000	0.000
Copper (Cu)	ppm	0.200	0.015	0.163	0.008	0.124	0.025	0.206	0.022	0.169	0.017	0.129	0.015	0.168	0.004
Iron (Fe)	ppm	1.017	0.168	0.673	0.117	0.478	0.241	1.048	0.101	0.730	0.092	0.483	0.210	1.030	0.099
Manganese (Mn)	ppm	0.290	0.022	0.187	0.053	0.095	0.066	0.287	0.046	0.209	0.048	0.092	0.051	0.222	0.041
Nickel (Ni)	ppm	0.068	0.014	0.044	0.019	0.009	0.009	0.066	0.020	0.050	0.022	0.009	0.012	0.039	0.009
Lead (Pb)	ppm	0.402	0.069	0.287	0.026	0.289	0.098	0.414	0.029	0.295	0.035	0.281	0.085	0.405	0.030
Zinc (Zn)	ppm	0.113	0.016	0.078	0.007	0.047	0.028	0.117	0.015	0.084	0.008	0.047	0.020	0.103	0.017

Table 9.5.6: Seasonal Variation of Heavy Metals in Soil Near Textile Industries

Heavy Metals	*Unit*	*Summer 2005*		*Monsoon 2005*		*Winter 2005-06*		*Summer 2006*		*Monsoon 2006*		*Winter 2006-07*		*Summer 2007*	
		Mean	*SD*	*Mean*	*SD*	*Mean*	*SD*	*Mean*	*SD*	*Mean*	*SD*	*Mean*	*SD*	*Mean*	*SD*
Cadmium (Cd)	ppm	3.533	0.586	0.773	0.560	1.920	0.396	3.350	0.597	1.133	0.651	2.100	0.432	2.800	0.424
Copper (Cu)	ppm	36.867	7.407	31.300	4.652	15.400	5.439	33.925	9.215	32.233	4.644	16.800	4.574	24.200	2.970
Iron (Fe)	ppm	77.267	14.408	32.700	11.701	28.460	12.233	76.450	10.959	39.000	12.957	25.450	5.298	58.650	12.516
Manganese (Mn)	ppm	13.767	0.907	10.967	2.501	6.540	2.221	13.175	2.451	11.833	2.219	7.375	1.417	10.350	1.202
Nickel (Ni)	ppm	10.400	1.179	7.567	1.079	5.940	1.242	10.675	1.670	8.400	1.015	5.975	0.670	8.150	0.919
Lead (Pb)	ppm	62.467	9.804	40.833	11.545	26.820	9.166	60.750	9.793	46.167	13.674	27.075	7.168	47.550	3.182
Zinc (Zn)	ppm	11.267	2.950	16.967	3.037	9.580	2.647	11.675	3.914	17.467	1.966	10.975	2.579	8.000	1.131

Table 9.5.7: Seasonal Variation of Heavy Metals in Groundwater of 80 ft at Control Site

Heavy Metals	*Unit*	*Summer 2005*		*Monsoon 2005*		*Winter 2005-06*		*Summer 2006*		*Monsoon 2006*		*Winter 2006-07*		*Summer 2007*	
		Mean	*SD*	*Mean*	*SD*	*Mean*	*SD*	*Mean*	*SD*	*Mean*	*SD*	*Mean*	*SD*	*Mean*	*SD*
Cadmium (Cd)	ppm	0.000	0.000	0.000	0.000	0.000	0.000	0.000	0.000	0.000	0.000	0.000	0.000	0.000	0.000
Copper (Cu)	ppm	0.157	0.032	0.149	0.012	0.090	0.052	0.152	0.032	0.149	0.007	0.090	0.061	0.684	0.800
Iron (Fe)	ppm	0.857	0.119	0.570	0.122	0.400	0.194	0.868	0.070	0.593	0.074	0.363	0.128	0.800	0.071
Manganese (Mn)	ppm	0.204	0.030	0.135	0.026	0.079	0.053	0.200	0.041	0.140	0.024	0.075	0.037	0.148	0.004
Nickel (Ni)	ppm	0.044	0.011	0.026	0.017	0.000	0.000	0.043	0.011	0.027	0.010	0.000	0.000	0.018	0.025
Lead (Pb)	ppm	0.265	0.015	0.203	0.028	0.191	0.112	0.266	0.012	0.210	0.034	0.178	0.127	0.282	0.013
Zinc (Zn)	ppm	0.099	0.015	0.065	0.005	0.044	0.021	0.099	0.008	0.072	0.008	0.043	0.013	0.087	0.016

Table 9.5.8: Mean Values (±SD) of Heavy Metals in Groundwater at Control and Experiment Sites

Heavy Metals	*Unit*	*2005-06*				*2006-07*			
		Control Site	*SD*	*Experimental sites*	*SD*	*Control Site*	*SD*	*Experimental sites*	*SD*
Cadmium (Cd)	ppm	0	0	0.004	0.002	0.0001	0.0002	0.004	0.003
Copper (Cu)	ppm	0.123	0.047	0.244	0.069	0.223	0.327	0.254	0.071
Iron (Fe)	ppm	0.597	0.25	1.414	0.719	0.618	0.231	1.562	0.697
Manganese (Mn)	ppm	0.13	0.063	0.257	0.101	0.139	0.061	0.283	0.093
Nickel (Ni)	ppm	0.022	0.021	0.059	0.038	0.023	0.021	0.066	0.04
Lead (Pb)	ppm	0.218	0.077	0.735	0.248	0.226	0.082	0.785	0.237
Zinc (Zn)	ppm	0.067	0.028	0.115	0.045	0.072	0.026	0.126	0.042

Table 9.5.10: Correlation Between Heavy Metals and Physico-chemical Parameters of Groundwater at 40 ft Depth

Parameters	Temperature	pH	TS	TSS	TDS	EC	DO	Free CO_2	BOD	COD	Total Alkalinity	Ca	Mg	K	Cl	Na
Cadmium (Cd)	-0.4720	0.4400	-0.0844	-0.1491	-0.0780	-0.0780	-0.4459	0.4060	-0.3829	-0.3896	-0.2270	-0.5395	-0.4221	-0.8034	-0.7787	-0.5654
Copper (Cu)	0.7176	0.6031	0.6712	0.6589	0.6714	0.6714	-0.4396	0.5115	0.5203	0.4632	0.6306	0.6677	0.6445	0.1376	0.2027	0.5021
Iron (Fe)	0.1340	0.8102	0.4987	0.4064	0.5069	0.5069	-0.6278	0.6729	0.0648	0.0647	0.2490	0.0946	0.0987	-0.5786	-0.4117	0.0366
Manganese (Mn)	0.6892	0.7867	0.8508	0.8001	0.8544	0.8544	-0.6314	0.6306	0.5396	0.5222	0.7074	0.6099	0.6586	0.0178	0.1352	0.5094
Nickel (Ni)	0.4747	0.7167	0.7983	0.7469	0.8021	0.8021	-0.4856	0.5276	0.3021	0.3030	0.6393	0.4971	0.4080	-0.1919	-0.0715	0.4255
Lead (Pb)	0.6106	0.8593	0.8296	0.7709	0.8340	0.8340	-0.6519	0.6839	0.4734	0.4754	0.5818	0.5440	0.6065	-0.0930	0.0378	0.4703
Zinc	0.1239	0.7175	0.4302	0.3529	0.4370	0.4370	-0.4412	0.5164	0.0132	-0.0055	0.2999	0.1556	0.0547	-0.5448	-0.4111	0.0297

Table 9.5.11: Correlation Between Heavy Metals and Physico-chemical Parameters of Ground Water at 80 ft Depth

Parameters	*Temperature*	*pH*	*TS*	*TSS*	*TDS*	*EC*	*DO*	*Free CO_2*	*BOD*	*COD*	*Total Alkalinity*	*Ca*	*Mg*	*K*	*Cl*	*Na*
Cadmium (Cd)	-0.4249	0.4498	-0.7675	-0.7338	-0.7699	-0.7699	-0.5169	0.5048	-0.3579	-0.3655	0.0237	-0.6322	-0.4514	-0.8700	-0.7527	-0.4974
Copper (Cu)	0.6860	-0.6296	-0.3314	-0.3518	-0.3288	-0.3288	-0.7029	0.7443	0.5230	0.5269	0.8099	0.5265	0.6353	-0.0677	-0.4178	0.6069
Iron (Fe)	0.9188	-0.8515	0.0718	0.0396	0.0750	0.0750	-0.4897	0.5458	0.7191	0.7550	0.8896	0.8398	0.8894	0.3575	-0.0309	0.8503
Manganese (Mn)	0.6670	-0.6006	-0.4141	-0.4318	-0.4116	-0.4116	-0.6248	0.6930	0.4701	0.4793	0.7664	0.4874	0.5708	-0.1260	-0.4779	0.5763
Nickel (Ni)	0.7044	-0.7071	-0.2883	-0.3056	-0.2860	-0.2860	-0.7447	0.7536	0.5755	0.5795	0.7918	0.5774	0.6618	-0.0759	-0.3709	0.6491
Lead (Pb)	0.4699	-0.3677	-0.6339	-0.6469	-0.6316	-0.6316	-0.5968	0.6693	0.3066	0.2903	0.5841	0.2398	0.3342	-0.3304	-0.7127	0.3610
Zinc (Zn)	0.6489	-0.7275	-0.2520	-0.2637	-0.2504	-0.2504	-0.6222	0.6518	0.5733	0.5755	0.7069	0.5727	0.5782	-0.1022	-0.2697	0.6108

Table 9.5.12: Correlation Between Heavy Metals and Physico-chemical Parameters of Groundwater (more than 120 ft)

Parameters	*Temperature*	*pH*	*TS*	*TSS*	*TDS*	*EC*	*DO*	*Free CO_2*	*BOD*	*COD*	*Total Alkalinity*	*Ca*	*Mg*	*K*	*Cl*	*Na*
Cadmium (Cd)	0.2586	-0.1922	-0.1886	-0.1927	-0.1882	-0.1882	-0.1208	0.1808	0.1577	0.1501	0.1851	0.2236	0.2761	0.0105	-0.1648	0.2274
Copper (Cu)	0.5657	-0.7221	-0.7972	-0.7977	-0.7970	-0.7970	-0.5948	0.6392	0.5026	0.5084	0.8666	0.4787	0.4949	-0.3674	-0.3668	0.5099
Iron (Fe)	0.3286	-0.3743	-0.9582	-0.9592	-0.9579	-0.9579	-0.6330	0.6815	0.1580	0.1551	0.8783	0.1801	0.1629	-0.6196	-0.6129	0.2244
Manganese (Mn)	0.6144	-0.6217	-0.9099	-0.9097	-0.9098	-0.9098	-0.6125	0.6554	0.4566	0.4558	0.8834	0.4620	0.4791	-0.4055	-0.4809	0.5253
Nickel (Ni)	0.7675	-0.7133	-0.7984	-0.7932	-0.7988	-0.7988	-0.5782	0.5974	0.5868	0.5877	0.8302	0.6059	0.6627	-0.2177	-0.3703	0.6663
Lead (Pb)	0.0368	-0.0109	-0.8292	-0.8222	-0.8297	-0.8297	-0.6002	0.6347	-0.1034	-0.0908	0.7136	-0.1830	-0.1350	-0.7297	-0.7721	-0.0983
Zinc (Zn)	0.4445	-0.6682	-0.8084	-0.8107	-0.8080	-0.8080	-0.5886	0.6340	0.3849	0.3854	0.8653	0.3815	0.3368	-0.4709	-0.3812	0.3780

Table 9.5.13: Correlation Between Heavy Metals and Physico-chemical Parameters of Groundwater at Control Site

Parameters	*Temperature*	*pH*	*TS*	*TSS*	*TDS*	*EC*	*DO*	*Free CO_2*	*BOD*	*COD*	*Total Alkalinity*	*Ca*	*Mg*	*K*	*Cl*	*Na*
Cadmium (Cd)	0.3314	-0.3195	-0.1977	-0.1917	-0.1982	-0.1982	-0.1820	0.1921	0.2838	0.2944	0.3888	0.3900	0.3991	0.0728	-0.2197	0.3398
Copper (Cu)	0.0236	0.1308	-0.1525	-0.1720	-0.1505	-0.1505	-0.0006	0.0907	0.0053	-0.0221	0.2028	-0.1738	-0.1293	-0.1285	-0.1667	-0.0372
Iron (Fe)	0.5000	-0.1850	-0.9750	-0.9773	-0.9745	-0.9745	-0.7472	0.8049	0.2986	0.3181	0.8597	0.2190	0.1777	-0.4871	-0.7837	0.2632
Manganese (Mn)	0.7006	-0.3744	-0.8475	-0.8573	-0.8464	-0.8464	-0.5798	0.6515	0.4829	0.5029	0.8739	0.4496	0.4510	-0.2603	-0.6374	0.5588
Nickel (Ni)	0.8099	-0.5217	-0.7634	-0.7685	-0.7627	-0.7627	-0.5530	0.6664	0.6405	0.6720	0.8175	0.5739	0.6263	-0.0985	-0.5878	0.6268
Lead (Pb)	0.2533	0.3462	-0.6613	-0.6535	-0.6619	-0.6619	-0.5997	0.6927	-0.1630	-0.1323	0.8009	-0.1149	-0.1161	-0.4930	-0.8937	-0.0558
Zinc (Zn)	0.5352	-0.4305	-0.8369	-0.8382	-0.8365	-0.8365	-0.6323	0.6614	0.5439	0.5513	0.7411	0.3509	0.3381	-0.3646	-0.5368	0.4302

Table 9.5.14: Correlation Between Heavy Metals and Physico-chemical Parameters of Textile Effluents

Parameters	*Temperature*	*pH*	*TS*	*TSS*	*TDS*	*EC*	*DO*	*Free CO_2*	*BOD*	*COD*	*Total Alkalinity*	*Ca*	*Mg*	*K*	*Cl*	*Na*
Cadmium (Cd)	0.5954	0.2054	0.4065	0.1194	0.4967	0.4949	-0.6152	0.6627	0.4508	0.4810	0.5408	0.4782	0.4821	0.2125	0.0739	0.0502
Copper (Cu)	0.5386	-0.0945	0.6047	0.2598	0.6126	0.5849	-0.5741	0.6112	0.2584	0.2011	0.5988	0.4728	0.3539	0.0231	-0.0995	0.1084
Iron (Fe)	0.4191	-0.2336	0.3555	-0.0584	0.6848	0.6947	-0.8010	0.7573	0.3639	0.1431	0.3816	0.3389	0.3894	-0.1857	-0.2576	-0.1650
Manganese (Mn)	-0.7252	-0.5784	-0.5025	-0.7485	0.3101	0.2820	0.1536	-0.0984	-0.3822	-0.7932	-0.6307	-0.6879	-0.8048	-0.7144	-0.8178	-0.7276
Nickel (Ni)	-0.1097	-0.4854	-0.1497	-0.3875	0.3455	0.3433	-0.4807	0.4410	0.0597	-0.2737	-0.0827	-0.1454	-0.0609	-0.5091	-0.5042	-0.4635
Lead (Pb)	0.1387	-0.1111	0.1279	-0.3402	0.7373	0.7303	-0.2132	0.3252	-0.0972	-0.1625	0.0515	-0.0132	-0.0200	-0.0134	-0.2652	-0.2585
Zinc (Zn)	-0.4590	-0.1986	-0.4412	-0.5178	0.0579	0.0003	0.0685	-0.0395	-0.0593	-0.2533	-0.4103	-0.4126	-0.3176	-0.3053	-0.2827	-0.3781

Table 9.5.15: Correlation Between Heavy Metals of Textile Effluents and Heavy Metals of Pond Water

	Cadmium (Cd)	*Copper (Cu)*	*Iron (Fe)*	*Manganese (Mn)*	*Nickel (Ni)*	*Lead (Pb)*	*Zinc (Zn)*
Cadmium (Cd)	0.3867	0.6257	0.3811	0.5244	0.4933	0.3803	-0.1229
Copper (Cu)	0.4993	0.7851	0.6926	0.7488	0.7762	0.7975	0.0633
Iron (Fe)	0.7229	0.6959	0.7251	0.6304	0.8110	0.8506	0.2362
Manganese (Mn)	0.1607	-0.1164	0.4070	-0.5011	0.2191	0.1712	0.8434
Nickel (Ni)	0.5772	0.2261	0.5584	0.2070	0.5204	0.5855	0.4325
Lead (Pb)	0.6835	0.4987	0.5301	0.0962	0.5946	0.4128	0.4019
Zinc (Zn)	0.0683	-0.2977	-0.1108	-0.4107	-0.2036	-0.1970	0.4195

Table 9.5.16: Correlation Between Heavy Metals of Pond Water and Heavy Metals of Groundwater

	Cadmium (Cd)	*Copper (Cu)*	*Iron (Fe)*	*Manganese (Mn)*	*Nickel (Ni)*	*Lead (Pb)*	*Zinc (Zn)*
Cadmium (Cd)	0.5955	0.4925	0.7118	0.7155	0.6233	0.7618	0.5954
Copper (Cu)	-0.0073	0.9116	0.5612	0.8907	0.7902	0.8271	0.6287
Iron (Fe)	0.6647	0.4978	0.9580	0.6654	0.8211	0.7114	0.9422
Manganese (Mn)	-0.1682	0.6457	0.5135	0.7864	0.8076	0.7998	0.4612
Nickel (Ni)	0.4472	0.6508	0.8689	0.7913	0.9223	0.8042	0.9085
Lead (Pb)	0.5029	0.5822	0.9387	0.7889	0.8411	0.8863	0.8754
Zinc (Zn)	0.6681	0.1114	0.4908	0.0796	0.0789	0.1328	0.5405

Table 9.5.17: Correlation Between Heavy Metals of Groundwater at 40 ft Depth

	Cadmium (Cd)	*Copper (Cu)*	*Iron (Fe)*	*Manganese (Mn)*	*Nickel (Ni)*	*Lead (Pb)*	*Zinc (Zn)*
Cadmium (Cd)	1						
Copper (Cu)	-0.0297	1					
Iron (Fe)	0.6622	0.4766	1				
Manganese (Mn)	0.1973	0.8465	0.7032	1			
Nickel (Ni)	0.3374	0.5842	0.8490	0.8207	1		
Lead (Pb)	0.2640	0.7652	0.7915	0.9365	0.8564	1	
Zinc (Zn)	0.5500	0.5634	0.9363	0.6657	0.8227	0.73721449	1

Table 9.5.18: Correlation Between Heavy Metals of Groundwater at 80 ft Depth

	Cadmium (Cd)	*Copper (Cu)*	*Iron (Fe)*	*Manganese (Mn)*	*Nickel (Ni)*	*Lead (Pb)*	*Zinc (Zn)*
Cadmium (Cd)	1						
Copper (Cu)	0.2862	1					
Iron (Fe)	-0.1759	0.8387	1				
Manganese (Mn)	0.2938	0.9623	0.8108	1			
Nickel (Ni)	0.2378	0.9548	0.8665	0.9446	1		
Lead (Pb)	0.4973	0.8559	0.5784	0.9195	0.8326	1	
Zinc (Zn)	0.1943	0.9000	0.8367	0.9207	0.9394	0.784857601	1

Table 9.5.19: Correlation Between Heavy Metals of Groundwater (more than 120 ft depth)

	Cadmium (Cd)	*Copper (Cu)*	*Iron (Fe)*	*Manganese (Mn)*	*Nickel (Ni)*	*Lead (Pb)*	*Zinc (Zn)*
Cadmium (Cd)	1						
Copper (Cu)	0.3286	1					
Iron (Fe)	0.2481	0.8289	1				
Manganese (Mn)	0.3517	0.9427	0.9104	1			
Nickel (Ni)	0.3877	0.9122	0.7884	0.9536	1		
Lead (Pb)	0.1820	0.5557	0.8446	0.6508	0.5299	1	
Zinc (Zn)	0.3245	0.9509	0.8660	0.9143	0.8346	0.578293375	1

Table 9.5.20: Correlation Between Heavy Metals of Pond Sediment and Heavy Metals of Drain Sediment

	Cadmium (Cd)	*Copper (Cu)*	*Iron (Fe)*	*Manganese (Mn)*	*Nickel (Ni)*	*Lead (Pb)*	*Zinc (Zn)*
Cadmium (Cd)	0.9493	0.2589	0.0530	0.2225	0.4803	0.7144	0.5922
Copper (Cu)	0.3647	0.9273	0.2261	0.2643	0.1140	0.2962	0.0239
Iron (Fe)	-0.1269	0.0944	0.9466	0.1694	-0.0400	-0.0980	0.0671
Manganese (Mn)	0.1856	0.3550	0.2388	0.9223	0.5129	0.0492	0.1831
Nickel (Ni)	0.5374	0.0246	0.2511	0.2658	0.8060	0.6183	0.9359
Lead (Pb)	0.6434	0.3742	0.0489	0.1409	0.3669	0.9388	0.4618
Zinc (Zn)	0.6764	-0.0189	0.2305	0.2456	0.7559	0.6630	0.9563

Table 9.5.21: Correlation Between Physico-chemical Parameters and Heavy Metals of Effluent Drain Sediment

Parameters	*Temperature*	*WHC*	*Bulk Density*	*Soil Moisture*	*pH*	*EC*	*Cl*	*Na*	*K*
Cadmium (Cd)	0.6827	0.4937	0.7226	-0.0967	-0.7117	0.7258	0.6894	0.2038	-0.0080
Copper (Cu)	0.2637	-0.0428	0.3623	-0.2021	-0.3459	0.2671	0.2181	-0.0577	0.0405
Iron (Fe)	-0.0671	0.0108	-0.0119	-0.3035	-0.0500	-0.1298	0.1399	-0.1357	0.1114
Manganese (Mn)	-0.2886	0.4659	-0.2402	-0.8078	-0.1016	-0.1484	-0.2057	0.6220	0.7253
Nickel (Ni)	0.3379	0.8752	0.2655	-0.6915	-0.5829	0.4826	0.3521	0.7610	0.5300
Lead (Pb)	0.8233	0.3379	0.8137	0.0752	-0.8377	0.8331	0.8293	-0.0199	-0.3465
Zinc (Zn)	0.6377	0.7598	0.5957	-0.2807	-0.7645	0.6900	0.7570	0.3600	0.0915

Table 9.5.22: Correlation Between Heavy Metals of Effluent Drain Sediment

	Cadmium (Cd)	*Copper (Cu)*	*Iron (Fe)*	*Manganese (Mn)*	*Nickel (Ni)*	*Lead (Pb)*	*Zinc (Zn)*
Cadmium (Cd)	1						
Copper (Cu)	0.3195	1					
Iron (Fe)	-0.0188	0.1213	1				
Manganese (Mn)	0.1399	0.3559	0.2154	1			
Nickel (Ni)	0.4724	0.1088	0.1213	0.5474	1		
Lead (Pb)	0.7101	0.2241	-0.0060	0.0275	0.4277	1	
Zinc (Zn)	0.6378	-0.0334	0.1473	0.1706	0.7211	0.6439	1

Table 9.5.23: Correlation Between Physico-chemical Parameters and Heavy Metals of Pond Sediment

Parameters	*Temperature*	*WHC*	*Bulk Density*	*Soil Moisture*	*pH*	*EC*	*Cl*	*Na*	*K*
Cadmium (Cd)	0.5929	0.4568	0.5963	-0.0794	-0.6108	0.6199	0.6032	0.1886	0.1151
Copper (Cu)	0.3937	-0.0270	0.2926	-0.1381	-0.3878	0.3652	0.2819	-0.0854	0.0318
Iron (Fe)	-0.1524	-0.1202	-0.0516	-0.1906	0.0855	-0.2443	0.0477	-0.2204	-0.0107
Manganese (Mn)	-0.2233	0.3758	-0.2722	-0.7337	0.0100	-0.1751	-0.2210	0.6170	0.7442
Nickel (Ni)	0.5642	0.8307	0.6211	-0.4386	-0.6914	0.6017	0.6717	0.4295	0.3376
Lead (Pb)	0.7460	0.2088	0.6861	0.0758	-0.7389	0.7095	0.7158	-0.0899	-0.2138
Zinc (Zn)	0.6040	0.8126	0.6614	-0.3505	-0.7260	0.6359	0.7137	0.3865	0.2800

Table 9.5.24: Correlation Between Heavy Metals of Pond Sediment

	Cadmium (Cd)	*Copper (Cu)*	*Iron (Fe)*	*Manganese (Mn)*	*Nickel (Ni)*	*Lead (Pb)*	*Zinc (Zn)*
Cadmium (Cd)	1						
Copper (Cu)	0.3044	1					
Iron (Fe)	-0.0569	0.2003	1				
Manganese (Mn)	0.2751	0.3340	0.1939	1			
Nickel (Ni)	0.5113	0.0523	0.1490	0.2330	1		
Lead (Pb)	0.7033	0.4419	-0.0253	0.1549	0.4747	1	
Zinc (Zn)	0.6544	0.0345	0.1314	0.2260	0.9485	0.524939198	1

Table 9.5.25: Transfer Factor for Heavy Metals from Textile Effluent to Groundwater in Experimental Sites

	Summer 2005	*Monsoon 2005*	*Winter 2005-06*	*Summer 2006*	*Monsoon 2006*	*Winter 2006-07*	*Summer 2007*
Cadmium (Cd)	0.16	0.12	0.62	0.36	0.19	1.50	0.53
Copper (Cu)	1.01	1.20	1.79	0.99	1.15	1.60	1.06
Iron (Fe)	7.17	5.93	6.12	7.04	6.42	6.30	9.64
Manganese (Mn)	3.59	2.95	1.27	3.01	4.12	1.45	1.39
Nickel (Ni)	3.93	5.83	1.45	2.28	14.14	1.52	2.78
Lead (Pb)	3.68	4.65	2.01	3.83	3.85	2.33	2.67
Zinc (Zn)	1.16	1.21	0.53	0.97	0.93	0.38	0.73

Table 9.5.26: Transfer Factor for Heavy Metals from Textile Effluent to Pond Water in Experimental Sites

	Summer 2005	*Monsoon 2005*	*Winter 2005-06*	*Summer 2006*	*Monsoon 2006*	*Winter 2006-07*	*Summer 2007*
Cadmium (Cd)	0.17	0.05	0.32	0.41	0.19	0.83	0.37
Copper (Cu)	0.97	1.16	1.53	0.98	1.10	1.36	1.09
Iron (Fe)	18.42	16.71	18.12	17.42	15.93	16.04	25.00
Manganese (Mn)	3.46	3.66	0.77	2.78	4.27	0.79	0.95
Nickel (Ni)	3.39	4.52	1.74	1.95	11.76	1.64	2.56
Lead (Pb)	3.60	2.44	1.19	3.63	2.20	1.23	2.40
Zinc (Zn)	0.90	1.00	0.66	0.74	0.69	0.54	0.71

Table 9.5.27: Transfer Factor for Heavy Metals from Pond Water to Groundwater (40ft) in Experimental Sites

	Summer 2005	*Monsoon 2005*	*Winter 2005-06*	*Summer 2006*	*Monsoon 2006*	*Winter 2006-07*	*Summer 2007*
Cadmium (Cd)	0.93	2.20	1.93	0.87	1.00	1.80	1.43
Copper (Cu)	1.04	1.04	1.17	1.01	1.05	1.17	0.97
Iron (Fe)	0.39	0.36	0.34	0.40	0.40	0.39	0.39
Manganese (Mn)	1.04	0.81	1.65	1.08	0.96	1.84	1.46
Nickel (Ni)	1.16	1.29	0.83	1.17	1.20	0.93	1.09
Lead (Pb)	1.02	1.91	1.69	1.06	1.75	1.89	1.11
Zinc (Zn)	1.28	1.21	0.80	1.30	1.35	0.70	1.03

Table 9.5.28: Transfer Factor for Heavy Metals from Pond Water to Groundwater (80ft) in Experimental Sites

	Summer 2005	*Monsoon 2005*	*Winter 2005-06*	*Summer 2006*	*Monsoon 2006*	*Winter 2006-07*	*Summer 2007*
Cadmium (Cd)	0.64	0.50	1.05	0.53	0.18	1.11	0.82
Copper (Cu)	0.68	0.55	0.60	0.68	0.54	0.64	0.57
Iron (Fe)	0.19	0.39	0.14	0.19	0.39	0.20	0.12
Manganese (Mn)	0.55	0.46	0.87	0.58	0.48	0.88	0.76
Nickel (Ni)	0.77	0.82	0.29	0.76	0.77	0.27	0.45
Lead (Pb)	0.48	1.03	1.05	0.49	0.91	1.00	0.64
Zinc (Zn)	1.05	1.21	0.44	1.03	1.12	0.43	0.69

Table 9.5.29: Transfer Factor for Heavy Metals from Pond Water to Groundwater (deep than 120 ft) in Experimental Sites

	Summer 2005	*Monsoon 2005*	*Winter 2005-06*	*Summer 2006*	*Monsoon 2006*	*Winter 2006-07*	*Summer 2007*
Cadmium (Cd)	0.04	0.00	0.00	0.13	0.00	0.00	0.00
Copper (Cu)	0.47	0.41	0.49	0.49	0.42	0.52	0.45
Iron (Fe)	0.10	0.16	0.10	0.11	0.16	0.13	0.12
Manganese (Mn)	0.55	0.40	0.55	0.58	0.44	0.54	0.75
Nickel (Ni)	0.54	0.61	0.17	0.51	0.60	0.19	0.33
Lead (Pb)	0.22	0.47	0.57	0.24	0.41	0.56	0.35
Zinc (Zn)	0.72	0.71	0.29	0.71	0.74	0.25	0.53

Table 9.5.30: Enrichment Factor for Various Metals in Drain Sediment

	Summer 2005	*Monsoon 2005*	*Winter 2005-06*	*Summer 2006*	*Monsoon 2006*	*Winter 2006-07*	*Summer 2007*
Cadmium (Cd)	0.68	0.90	0.53	0.85	0.81	0.65	0.86
Copper (Cu)	5.82	8.11	5.74	8.47	7.47	6.24	7.89
Iron (Fe)	1000.00	1000.00	1000.00	1000.00	1000.00	1000.00	1000.00
Manganese (Mn)	123.69	139.91	120.96	170.80	109.92	129.81	175.63
Nickel (Ni)	8.86	10.25	7.49	11.48	9.22	7.35	11.70
Lead (Pb)	8.27	10.73	5.83	9.89	9.54	6.63	8.51
Zinc (Zn)	30.71	36.78	18.71	38.80	27.45	18.12	33.71

Table 9.5.31: Enrichment Factor for Various Metals in Pond Sediment

	Summer 2005	*Monsoon 2005*	*Winter 2005-06*	*Summer 2006*	*Monsoon 2006*	*Winter 2006-07*	*Summer 2007*
Cadmium (Cd)	1.01	1.11	0.67	1.24	1.20	0.87	1.26
Copper (Cu)	9.13	10.17	7.29	12.04	10.46	7.61	10.16
Iron (Fe)	1000.00	1000.00	1000.00	1000.00	1000.00	1000.00	1000.00
Manganese (Mn)	167.01	167.88	139.09	213.02	145.51	151.18	243.85
Nickel (Ni)	11.29	12.13	8.78	14.63	13.07	8.38	14.85
Lead (Pb)	12.23	12.83	7.32	14.23	13.79	8.43	11.70
Zinc (Zn)	42.55	33.00	20.49	47.57	36.96	19.89	43.78

Table 9.5.32: Geo-accumulation Index for Various Metals in Drain Sediment Samples

Parameters	Summer 2005		Monsoon 2005		Winter 2005-06		Summer 2006		Monsoon 2006		Winter 2006-07		Summer 2007	
	Value	Igeo	Value	Igeo	Value	Igeo	Value	Igeo	Value	Igeo	Value	Igeo	Value	Igeo
Cadmium (Cd)	12.85	3.68	11.34	3.50	9.44	3.24	12.15	3.60	11.46	3.52	11.36	3.51	11.16	3.48
Copper (Cu)	0.73	-0.45	0.68	-0.56	0.69	-0.54	0.81	-0.30	0.70	-0.51	0.73	-0.45	0.68	-0.56
Iron (Fe)	0.12	-3.06	0.08	-3.65	0.11	-3.13	0.09	-3.45	0.09	-3.48	0.11	-3.16	0.08	-3.61
Manganese (Mn)	0.82	-0.28	0.62	-0.69	0.77	-0.38	0.87	-0.21	0.55	-0.87	0.81	-0.31	0.80	-0.32
Nickel (Ni)	0.74	-0.44	0.57	-0.81	0.59	-0.75	0.73	-0.46	0.58	-0.80	0.57	-0.81	0.67	-0.58
Lead (Pb)	2.33	1.22	2.02	1.02	1.57	0.65	2.13	1.09	2.02	1.02	1.75	0.81	1.65	0.72
Zinc (Zn)	1.82	0.87	1.46	0.55	1.06	0.09	1.76	0.82	1.23	0.29	1.01	0.01	1.38	0.46

Table 9.5.33: Geo-accumulation Index for Highest Value of Metals in Drain Sediment Samples

	2005-06		2006-07	
	Value	Igeo	Value	Igeo
Cadmium (Cd)	13.22	3.72	13.60	3.77
Copper (Cu)	0.79	-0.33	0.92	-0.12
Iron (Fe)	0.16	-2.66	0.15	-2.76
Manganese (Mn)	0.89	-0.17	0.98	-0.03
Nickel (Ni)	0.76	-0.39	0.77	-0.37
Lead (Pb)	2.43	1.28	2.60	1.38
Zinc (Zn)	2.40	1.26	2.70	1.43

Table 9.5.34: Geo-accumulation Index for Various Metals in Pond Sediment Samples

Parameters	Summer 2005		Monsoon 2005		Winter 2005-06		Summer 2006		Monsoon 2006		Winter 2006-07		Summer 2007	
	Value	Igeo	Value	Igeo	Value	Igeo	Value	Igeo	Value	Igeo	Value	Igeo	Value	Igeo
Cadmium (Cd)	12.70	3.67	10.62	3.41	9.01	3.17	12.02	3.59	11.10	3.47	11.27	3.49	10.66	3.41
Copper (Cu)	0.76	-0.39	0.65	-0.62	0.65	-0.62	0.78	-0.36	0.64	-0.63	0.66	-0.60	0.57	-0.80
Iron (Fe)	0.08	-3.65	0.06	-4.04	0.08	-3.56	0.06	-4.02	0.06	-4.09	0.08	-3.60	0.05	-4.22
Manganese (Mn)	0.74	-0.44	0.57	-0.82	0.66	-0.61	0.73	-0.46	0.47	-1.08	0.69	-0.53	0.73	-0.46
Nickel (Ni)	0.62	-0.68	0.51	-0.96	0.52	-0.95	0.63	-0.68	0.53	-0.91	0.48	-1.06	0.55	-0.85
Lead (Pb)	2.30	1.20	1.84	0.88	1.47	0.55	2.07	1.05	1.91	0.93	1.64	0.72	1.48	0.57
Zinc (Zn)	1.68	0.75	1.00	0.00	0.86	-0.21	1.45	0.54	1.08	0.11	0.82	-0.29	1.17	0.22

Table 9.5.35: Geo-accumulation Index for Highest Value Metals in Pond Sediment Samples

	2005-06		2006-07	
	Value	Igeo	Value	Igeo
Cadmium (Cd)	13.67	3.77	14.04	3.81
Copper (Cu)	0.82	-0.28	0.85	-0.24
Iron (Fe)	0.11	-3.17	0.00	-9.70
Manganese (Mn)	0.77	-0.37	0.78	-0.35
Nickel (Ni)	0.70	-0.52	0.77	-0.37
Lead (Pb)	2.47	1.30	2.50	1.32
Zinc (Zn)	2.18	1.12	2.25	1.17

Table 9.5.36: Metal Accumulation Factor for the Groundwater of Panipat Region

	Summer 2005	*Monsoon 2005*	*Winter 2005-06*	*Summer 2006*	*Monsoon 2006*	*Winter 2006-07*	*Summer 2007*
Cadmium (Cd)	250.00	α	α	57.14	α	α	α
Copper (Cu)	2.83	2.76	3.28	2.80	2.84	3.20	0.53
Iron (Fe)	4.41	2.64	4.07	4.40	3.10	4.17	4.22
Manganese (Mn)	2.70	2.76	3.59	2.65	3.24	4.17	2.91
Nickel (Ni)	3.36	3.60	á	3.59	3.67	á	7.14
Lead (Pb)	6.93	5.73	4.45	6.84	6.06	5.32	4.59
Zinc (Zn)	2.02	2.05	2.86	2.17	2.12	3.00	2.31

α: infinite.

The accumulation of heavy metals through the food chain is called the biomagnifications. The concentrations of metal increased at every next trophic level, whereas metals can cause various harmful effects on irrigated agricultural soil, human beings and livestock by alteration in some biochemical reaction in body cells (De, 2002).

In the present study, heavy metals in pond water were observed slightly lower than textile industrial effluents, whereas the heavy metal concentrations in effluent drain were higher than pond sediment. Shallow groundwater of about 40 ft depth was highly polluted in comparison to increasing depth of water table. Although the effect of spatial variation was also found in the study, when the heavy metals concentrations in groundwater at control site were presented comparatively in less or very less quantities. Some metals like cadmium and nickel were not detected in groundwater at control site. After all, if the conditions will be same in textile industrial area then definitely there is a fear to contamination of groundwater into horizontal direction also and this will affect the groundwater of surroundings and deep aquifers with the time.

9.5.9 Conclusion

The present study reveals that there was heavy metals pollution in pond water and sediment, which affected the groundwater of the industrial area of Panipat region. Beside this, the bottom sediment of common effluent drain stored the heavy metals in high quantities, which have no secure or pre-managed future. Thus, textile industrial effluents discharging from dye houses contaminated the surface water, drain sediment, pond sediment and groundwater also. Furthermore, the impact of heavy metals reflected negative impacts on agricultural soil after irrigation by contaminated groundwater. Heavy metals remained in upper part of soil horizons mostly but moved in to lower soil layers probably after a long time due to slow adsorption (Alumaa *et al.*, 2001). Heavy metals strongly absorbed by first component to which they make contact and plants uptake them. So there is a fear to accumulate the heavy metals in different body parts of vegetation. High quantity of heavy metals accumulated in organisms may be harmful for health of organisms and create various diseases, which may magnify through food web of the water and agricultural ecosystems.

Heavy metals from textile industries affected the shallow groundwater quality in shallow badly, while deep groundwater affected slightly. Vertically, heavy metals contamination decreased with the increasing depth of water table. In the case of horizontal distribution, the heavy metal concentrations decrease with increasing distance from pollution source. In the circle of 1 Km from pollution source almost heavy metals level was found higher than the outer wide circle in the industrial area. Heavy metals contamination was found to be low in soil at control site and also in outer circle of textile industrial area. However, the area of around 1 Km from textile industrial area was found highly affected by heavy metals in Panipat region. Textile industrial effluent or contaminated groundwater can also altered the physico-chemical parameters of agricultural soil after repeated irrigation by contaminated groundwater. So, some appropriate measures for the amendment and control of textile pollution should be adopted by industrialists, municipality, government, NGOs and local people also at various levels for the protection of environmental components.

It is evident from the data that the physico-chemical characteristics of effluents exceed the prescribed Indian standards. It is therefore obvious that scientific treatment is necessary to minimize the pollution effects before textile industrial effluent is discharge on the land. But disposal of these effluents after proper dilution may be a favourable approach. After dilution, the effluent characteristics come within the prescribed disposal limits and the pollution load per unit effluent volume is decreases.

Effective steps should be taken for improving water use efficiency, as the integrated management of water resources should be based on the treatment of wastewater as an integral part of ecosystem and as a natural resource whose quantity and quality determine the nature of its utilization. Wastewater use in turn has its impact on the water quality and therefore utilization of water has to be managed as not to contribute to the deterioration of water quality. Secondly, conjunctive use of groundwater and surface water resources needs to be planned in the irrigation project from the beginning. There is a need to take effective steps for improving wastewater use efficiency through renovation and modernization of recycling treatments of wastewater.

Different guidelines and standards limits should be immediately applied in small scale textile industries for utilization of groundwater and open discharging the effluents into surface water or on land. A regular bio-monitoring should be applied for the assessment of effluent quality of every dye house outlet. An effluent treatment plant of appropriate capacity must be installed in the industrial area for the primary and biological treatment of for composite effluent from textile industries. Unlike most organic pollutants, heavy metals are generally refectory and cannot be degraded or readily detoxified biologically. Hence the safe and effective disposal of wastewater containing heavy metals is always a challenge to industrialists and environmentalists, since cost-effective treatment alternative are not available (Manahan, 1984). However, some researchers like Singh (2006) developed a low cost adsorbent of heavy metals from some cheap byproducts.

Beside this, water supply of the industrial sector should be managed and regularly analyzed the suitability of drinking water quality. Groundwater safety measures are immediately necessary in the industrial region. Restoration of affected agricultural soil is still an environmental aspect for Haryana state. All the above observation and data indicated that the qualities of effluents sometimes do not meet the CPCB, BIS, MINAS and WHO specified norms. The effluents may also cause various health problems among the human being through contaminated groundwater supply by municipal tube wells water scheme. In order to achieve the standards it is suggested to install the effluent treatment plants for the treatment of composite effluents of the textile industries.

Glossary

Arid: Said of a climate characterized by dryness, variously defined as rainfall insufficient for plant life or less than 250 mm of annual rainfall.

Base flow: Stream flow derived mainly from groundwater seepage into the stream.

Bomb tracer: A tracer resulting from nuclear testing, such as tritium or chlorine-36.

Boiling: Boiling is a very effective method of purification and very simple to carry out. To remove all biological contaminants, boiling water for 10 – 20 minutes is enough.

Chlorination: Chlorination is done with stabilized calcium hypochlorite – $CaOCl_2$ (Bleaching powder) – a mixture of chlorine and lime. Chlorination can kill all type of bacteria and make water safe for drinking purposes. About 1 gm (1/4 tea spoon) of bleaching powder is enough to treat 200 litres of water.

Charcoal filter: Simply, a charcoal water filter can be made in a drum or an earthen pot. The filter is made of gravel, sand and charcoal, which are easily available.

Ceramic filter: Commercially, these filters are manufactured on a wide scale. Most of the water purifiers available in the market are of this type.

Capillary flow: The flow that takes place in pores with a diameter less than approximately 3 mm in which capillary forces, together with gravity, determine the flow process.

Catchment: *See* watershed.

Catchment's runoff type: I – From paved surfaces (Roofs and courtyards), II–From unpaved surfaces (Lawns and playgrounds).

Conceptual model: An interpretation or working description of the characteristics and dynamics of a physical system.

Confining bed: A geological unit of significantly lower hydraulic conductivity than an aquifer stratigraphically adjacent to one or more aquifers.

Deep drainage: Drainage of water below the root zone.

Diffuse recharge: Water added to the water table by vertical percolation of precipitation through the unsaturated zone. Also known as direct recharge.

Discharge area: An area in which water is lost naturally from the saturated zone.

Enrichment factor: The primary objectives of the sediment sampling study were to estimate how sediment chemistry changes throughout a watershed and to relate these changes to natural and manmade sources of pollution. Environmental factor is a general factor (coefficient) comparatively with iron for every metal ranging between from 1 to 1000 on a simple scale.

Fallow: The period during which land is left to recover its productivity after cropping, mainly through accumulation of water and nutrients, attrition of pathogens, or a combination of these factors.

Fingered flow: Unstable flow whereby the percolating water may concentrate at certain points to break into the sublayer in the form of fingerlike or tongue-like protrusions.

Flow path: The route groundwater takes to a distant point.

Flow net: The set of intersecting lines of equal hydraulic head values and flow lines representing two-dimensional steady flow through a porous medium.

Geographic Information Systems (GIS): Computer-based systems for storing and manipulating geographic (spatial) information.

Geo-accumulation index: To assess the anthropogenic influence in the study area, the evaluation of sediments contamination with heavy metals was made using the index of accumulation, I_{geo} which permits assessment of the extent of sediment contamination with respect to the global standards.

Groundwater flow system: A set of groundwater flow paths with common recharge and discharge areas. Flow systems are dependent on both the hydrogeologic characteristics of the soil/rock material and landscape position. Areas of steep or undulating relief tend to have dominant local flow systems (discharging in nearby topographic lows such as ponds or streams). Areas of gently sloping or nearly flat relief tend to have dominant regional flow systems (discharging at much greater distances than local systems in major basin topographic lows or oceans).

Hydrogeologic environment: The physical and chemical conditions resulting from the combination of topography, geology, and climate.

Hydrologic budget or water balance: An accounting of the inflow to, outflow from, and storage in a hydrologic unit such as a drainage basin, aquifer, soil zone, lake, or reservoir.

Indirect recharge: Recharge that results from percolation to the water table following runoff and localization in joints, as ponding in lowlying areas and lakes, or through the beds of surface water courses.

Induced recharge: Recharge to groundwater by infiltration, either natural or anthropogenic, from a body of surface water as a result of the lowering of the groundwater level below the surface-water level.

Interflow: Subsurface lateral flow that can enter streams quickly enough to contribute to the rising streamflow hydrograph response to a storm.

Localized recharge: Recharge that results from horizontal surface concentration of water in the absence of well-defined channels, such as sloughs, potholes, and playas. Also called focused or depression-focused recharge.

Macropore flow: The flow that takes place in a wide range of large pores such as cracks in clay soils, rock fractures, fissures in sediments, worm holes, and old root channels. Preferential and by-pass flow are alternative names for macropore flow.

Matric suction: Soil-water potential (energy) resulting from the capillary and absorptive forces due to the soil matrix.

Metal accumulation factor: Toxic pollutants especially pesticides and heavy metals have a tendency to accumulate in various interrelated environmental components and also at different trophic levels of food chain of biological system. Metal accumulation index indicates the degree of metal pollution in the experimental component by comparing the control site. Metal accumulation factor 1 indicates the 100 percent similarity in the metal concentrations in experimental and control sites, while accumulation factor 2 indicates the two-fold contamination of metal on experimental site in comparison with control.

Mountain front recharge: Recharge that involves complex processes of unsaturated and saturated flow in fractured rocks, as well as infiltration along channels flowing across alluvial fans.

Natural recharge: Naturally occurring water added to an aquifer. Natural recharge generally results from snowmelt and precipitation or storm runoff.

Perched groundwater; perching: A superficial body of groundwater separated from an underlying main body of groundwater by an unsaturated zone due to a sufficiently low hydraulic conductivity layer that supports this body of perched groundwater; the act of causing a body of groundwater to form above a low-permeability layer in an unsaturated zone.

Piston flow or plug flow: Purely advective flow without dispersion or diffusion of the dissolved components.

Potential energy: The energy deriving from elevation and/or pressure.

Potential recharge: Soil-water that percolates below the root zone and has the potential of reaching the aquifer, whereas actual recharge is soil-water that actually reaches the aquifer.

Preferential recharge: Recharge that takes place preferentially through macropores, as opposed to diffuse recharge, which takes place through the entire vadose porous medium.

Parameters for collection of rainwater: 1: Average annual rainfall; 2: Size of the catchment; 3: Drinking water requirement.

Purpose of harvesting: I: Direct use – stored for ready use in containers above ground or below ground. II: Groundwater recharging – charged into soil for withdrawal later.

Rainwater harvesting: Collection of rainwater from paved or unpaved area for various daily needs.

Rainwater endowment: Total amount of received rainfall of area.

Recharge area: The area that contributes water to an aquifer. Normally considered to be the natural area of recharge, as contrasted with a constructed recharge basin.

Rejected recharge: Potential recharge that exceeds the rate of flow through an aquifer that is already overfull, and as a result is rejected.

Residence time: The length of time between the input of water as infiltration or recharge and its output as runoff or discharge. Also known as transit time or turnover time.

Residual: In the case of recharge, the remainder of all other hydrologic components in the water balance equation.

Runoff coefficient: Runoff coefficient is a factor, which accounts for the fact that all the rainfall falling on a catchment cannot be collected. Some rainfall will be lost from the catchment by evaporation and retention on the surface itself.

Sand filter: Sand filters are easy and cheap to construct having commonly available sand as filter media. These filters can be employed for treatment of water to effectively remove turbidity (suspended matters as silt and clay), colour and microorganisms from the water.

Semiarid: Said of a type of climate in which there is slightly more precipitation (250 to 500 mm) than in an arid climate, and in which sparse grasses are the characteristic vegetation.

Sensitivity (analysis): In model application, the degree to which the model result is affected by changes in a selected model input representing hydrogeologic framework, hydraulic properties, and boundary conditions.

Transmission losses: Streamflow losses through seepage in ephemeral streams.

Transfer factor (Coefficient): Transfer coefficient is the indication of metal deposition or transportation rate of any metal from one medium to another. Metals have a tendency to accumulate or migrate from one component to other component. Accumulation period or rate may influence the metal availability and balance among both components. In the present study, abiotic components such as textile industrial effluent, pond water, groundwater, agricultural soils and bed sediments of pond and drain are taken for the evaluation of transfer factor.

Unconfined (or water table) aquifer: An aquifer in which the water table is at the upper boundary of the groundwater flow system that is at atmospheric pressure.

Unsaturated or vadose zone: The unsaturated (*i.e.* not completely filled with water) zone lying between the Earth's surface and the top of the groundwater.

Water table: The upper boundary of an unconfined aquifer at atmospheric pressure.

Watershed: That surface area which drains to a specified point on a watercourse, usually a confluence of streams or rivers.

Water harvesting potential: Amount that can be effectively harvested.

Water harvesting potential formula (Annually from 100 sq. m. roof): = $A \times R \times C$

A = Area of Catchment,
R = Average annual rainfall,
C = Runoff coefficient (0.85)

Reference

Aboulhassan, M.A.; Souabi, S.; Yaacoubi, A. and Baudu, M. (2005): Treatment of textile wastewater using a natural flocculants, *Environmental Technology*. 26: 705-711.

Abson, J.N.; Furness, C.D. and Howe, C. (1967): Development of the simicar resipirometer and its application to waste treatment, *Waste Poll. Control*, 66: 607.

Aggarwal, R.R. and Mehrotra, R.R. (1952): Soil survey and soil water in Uttar Pradesh, *Suptd. Printing and Stationery*, Aallahabad, pp: 361-372.

Ajmal, M. and Khan, A.U. (1985): Effects of a textile factory effluent on soil and crop plants, *J. Env. Poll.*, 37(2): 131-137.

Al-Degs, Y.; Khraisheh, M.A.M.; Allen, S.J. and Ahmed, M.N. (2000): Effect of carbon surface chemistry on the removal of reactive dyes from textile effluent, *Water Research*, 34(3): 927-935.

Alumaa, P.; Steinnes, E.; Kirso, U. and Petersell, V. (2001): Heavy metal sorption by different Estonian soil types at low equilibrium solution concentrations, *Proc. Estonian Acad. Sci. Chem.*, 50(2): 104–115.

Ameta Suresh C., Punjabi Pinki Bala, Kothari Shilpa, Sancheti Anjali (2003): Effect of untreated and photocatalytically treated dyeing industry effluent on growth and biochemical parameters of *Allium cepa* (Onion), *Poll. Res.*, 22(3): 389-392

Annadurai, G.; Juang, R.S. and Lee, D.J. (2002): Use of cellulose based wastes for adsorption of dyes from aqueous solutions, *J. Haz. Mat.*, B92: 263-274.

APHA (1998): Standard methods for the examination of water and waste water, *American Public Health Association*, 19th edition, 1015, Fifteenth Street, NW, pp: (1-1) – (10-150).

Aslam, M.M.; Baig, M.A.; Hassan, I.; Qazi, I.A.; Malik, M. and Saeed, H. (2004): Textile wastewater characterization and reduction of its COD and BOD by oxidation, *Electron. J. Environ. Agri. Food Chem.*, 3(6): 804-811.

Ather, M. and Vohra, S.B. (1985): Heavy metals and environment, *New Age International Publisher Limited, Wiley Eastern Limited, New Delhi*, pp: 635.

Aurangabadkar, K.; Swaminathan, K.; Sandhya, S; Uma, T.S.; Jothikumar, N. and Paramasivam, R. (2001): Groundwater quality around a municipality solid waste dumping site at Chennai, *IJEP*, 21(4): 323-327.

Bachmat, Y. (1994): Groundwater as part of the water system. In: Groundwater contamination and control, ed. V. Zoller. Marcel Dekker, Inc, New York, pp: 1-560.

Bachmat, Y. (1994): Groundwater as part of the water system. In: Groundwater contamination and control, Ed. V. Zoller. *Marcel Dekker, Inc.* New York, pp: 560.

Bae, W.; S.H. Lee; and G.B. Ko (2004): Evaluation of predominant reaction mechanisms for the Fenton process in textile dyeing waste. *Water Sc. and Tech.* 49 (4): 91-96.

Baruah N.K.; Kotoki, P.; Bhattacharya, K.G. and Borah, G.C. (1996): Metal speciation in Jhanjhi river sediments. *Sci. Total Environ.*, 193: 1-12.

Basu, A.K.; Rao, C.G.S.; Dhaneshwar, G; Mukharjee, M.K.A.; Kutty, D. Ray and Trivedi, R.C. (1973): Study on Hooghly estuaries pollution in the vicinity of tissue mill, *Proc. Symp. on Environ. Poll.*, pp: 24-26.

Beven, K. (2000): On the future of distributed modeling in hydrology, *Hydrological Processes*, 14: 3183-3184.

Bhakuni, T.S. and Bopardikar, M.V. (1967): Method of recovery Zinc from spinning bath waste of Viscos reyon factory by ion exchange process, *Env. Health*, 9(4): 327-338.

Bhargava, G.P.; Singhla, S.K. and Abrol, I.P. (1972): Characteristics of some typical saline sodic soils occurring in Karnal district Haryana state, Report No. 2, Division of soils and agronomy; *CSSRI, Karnal*, pp: 35.

Bhat, R. and Kulkarni, R. (2005): COD reduction of dye industry effluent, *J. Ind. Poll. Control*, 21 (1): 147-150.

Bhattacharya, A.K. (2010): Artificial groundwater recharge with a special reference to India, IJRRAS 4 (2): 214-221.

Bordas, S, and Bourg, C.M. (1998): A critical evaluation of sample pretreatment of contaminated sediments to be investigated for the potential mobility of their heavy metal load, *Water, Air and Soil Pollution*, 103: 137-149.

Bousselmi, L.; Gelsson S.V. and H. Schroeder (2004): Textile wastewater treatment and reuse by solar catalysis: results from a pilot plant in Tunisia, *Water Sc. and Tech.*, 49(4): 331-337.

Brady, N.C. (1995): The nature and properties of soils, Prentice Hall of India Pvt. Ltd., New Delhi, pp: 621.

Cances, B.; Ponthieu, M.; Castrec-Rouelle, M.; Aubry, E. and Benedatty, M.F. (2003): Metal ion speciation in a soil and its solution: Experimental data and modal results, *Geoderma*, 113: 341-355.

Canter, L.W. (1987): Groundwater quality protection, *Lewis publications*. Inc., Chelsea, Ml, pp: 1-650.

Canter, L.W. (1987): Groundwater quality protection, *Lewis publications. Inc.*, Chelsea, Ml, pp: 650.

Castro Dentros, T.S. Dentos Neto, A.A. Moura, M.C., P.A. Barros Neto, E$.I., Forte K.R., Leite, R.H.L. (2003): Heavy metals extraction by micromulsion, *Wat. Res.*, 37: 2709-2717.

CGWB (1994): Manual on Artificial Recharge of Groundwater 1994. Technical Series – M, No. 3, Central Groundwater Board, Faridabad, March 1994, 215 p.

CGWB (2000): Guide On Artificial recharge To Groundwater, Central groundwater board, Ministry of water resources, New Delhi, May, 2000.

Chao, Keh-Ping; Tsai, Ching-Tsan; Wang, John H.C.; Lin, Shaw-Tao and Chiang, Chow-Feng (2005) Health risk assessment of a heavy metal contaminated site in Taiwan. *Jr. Practice Periodical of Hazardous, Toxic, and Radioactive Waste Management*, pp: 167-171.

Christie, S.L. (1995): Speciation, In: Fitfield, F.W., Haines. P.J. (Eds). *Environmental Analytical Chemistry*, Chapman and Hall, UK, pp: 245-273.

Chung, K.T. (1983): The significance of azo-reduction in the mutagenesis and carcinogenesis of azo dyes, *Mutation Research*, 114: 269-279.

Considine, D.M. (1974): Chemical and process technology encyclopedia, *McGraw Hill Book Co.*, New York, pp: 655.

CPCB (2003): Parivesh: Groundwater, *Central Pollution Control Board*, Delhi-32, July, pp: 40.

CRIDA (2011): Groundwater Recharging Techniques, Central Research Institute for Dryland Agriculture Santoshnagar, Hyderabad.

CSE (2001): A rainwater harvesting manual for urban areas – Case studies from Delhi, *Centre for Science and Environment publication*, pp: 1-35.

Darra, B.L.; Mehta, K.M. and Pareek, B.L. (1964): Quality of irrigation water in Rajasthan, *J. Indian Soc, Soil Sc.*, 12: 121-130.

Dash, S.K. and Sahoo, H.K. (1998): Quality assessment of groundwater in a part of Sundargarh district, *Indian J. Environmental Protection*, 19(4): 273-278.

Davidson, C.M., Thomas R.P., McVey, S.E., Perala, R., Littlejohn, D. and Ure, A.M. (1994): Evaluation of a sequential extraction procedure for the speciation of heavy metals in sediments. *Anal.Chim. Acta.*, 291: 277-286.

Dayama, O.P. (1987): Influence of dyeing and textile water pollution on nodulation and germination of gram, *J. Acta. Ecol.*, 9(1-2): 34-37.

De, A.K. (2002): Environmental Chemistry, *New Age International (P) Limited Publishers*, pp: 392.

De, A.K. (2005): Adsorption of cadmium and zinc on coal fly ash, *J. Ind. Poll. Control*, 21 (1): 27-30.

Desh, D. (1981): Activated sludge treatment of liquid waste- A review, *J. IAWPC Tech.*, Vol-VII, pp: 69-72.

Dev Goel, (2005): "A political-economic analysis of India's river interlinking project" (August 30, 2005) *Florida State University D-Scholarship Repository*, Article #132. (http://dscholarship.lib.fsu.edu/undergrad/132)

Dhar, N.R.; Khoda, A.K.M.B.; Khan, A.H.; Bala, P. and Karim, M.F. (2005) A study of effect of acid activated saw dust on the removal of different dissolved tannery dyes (Acid dye) from aqueous solutions. *Journal of Environ. Sci. and Engg.* 47 (2): 103-108.

Doneen, L.D. (1954): Stalinization of soils of salts in irrigation waters, *Trans. Geophys. Union*, 35: 943-952.

Dowedy, R.H. and Larson, W.E. (1975): The availability of sludge borne metals in various vegetable crops, *J. Env. Qual.*, 4: 278-282.

Dulka, J.J. and Risby, T.H. (1976): Ultra trace metals in some environmental and biological systems, *Analytical Chemistry*, 48(8): 640-653.

Dutta, P.S. (1999): Groundwater situation in Delhi- Red alert, Nuclear research laboratory, *IARI, New Delhi*, pp: 39.

Dutta, P.S. (2005): Groundwater ethics for its sustainability, *Current Science*, 89 (5): 812-817.

Dwivedi, A.K.; Shashi and Singh, J. (2005): Water pollution and groundwater recharging, *Current Science*, 91 (4): 407-408.

Eaton, F.M. (1950): Significance of carbonates in irrigation waters, *Soil Sc.*, 39: 123-133.

ECIL methods manual (2004) Methods Manual, Atomic Absorption Spectrophotometer, AAS 4129, *Electronic Corporation of India Limited*, Hyderabad-500062, pp: 85.

Eckenfelder, W.W. and Bornad, J.L. (1971): Treatment cost relationship for industrial waste, *Chemical Engg. Progress*, 67(9): 76.

Fakayode, S.O. and Onianwa, P.C. (2002): Heavy metal contamination of soil, and bioaccumulation in Guinea grass (*Panicum maximum*) around Ikeja industrial Estate, Lagos, Nigeria, *Environmental Geology*, 43: 145-150.

Fetter, C.W. (1994): Applied Hydrology, 3rd edition, Macmillan, New York.

Florence, T.M. (1982): The speciation of trace elements in waters, *Talanta*, 29: 345-369.

Forstner, U. (1985): chemical forms and reactivities of metals in sediments in chemical methods for assessing bioavailable metals in sludge and soils, In: Leschber, R., Davies, R.D. and Hermite, L.P. (Eds), *Elsevier, London*, pp: 1-30.

Forstner, U. and Wittman, G.T.W. (1981): Metal pollution in the aquatic environment, second ed. *Springer, Berlin*, pp: 486.

Forstner, U.; Ahlf, W.; Calmano, W.; Kersten, M. and Schoer, J. (1990): Assessment of metal mobility in sludge and soild wastes, In: Metal speciation in the environment (Eds.- Broeckaert, J.A.C; Gucer, S. and Adams, F.) Springer, Berlin, pp: 1-41.

Fransson, Åsa (2007): A case study to verify methods for estimating transmissivity distributions along boreholes, *Hydrogeology Journal*, 15: 307–313,

Fraser, B.G. and Williams, D.D. (1998): Seasonal boundary dynamics of a groundwater/surface-water ecotone, *Ecology*, 79(6): 2019-2031.

Frostner, U., and Wittman, G.T.W. (1979) Metal pollution in the aquatic environment, *Berlin Germany, Springer- Verlag.*, pp: 545.

Gardner, W.R. (1957): Some steady state solutions of the unsaturated moisture flow equation with application to evaporation from a water table, *Soil Sci.*, 85: 228-232.

Garg, V. K; Sharma, I.S. and Bishnoi, M.S. (1998): Fluoride in under groundwater of Uklana town, District Hisar, Haryana, *Poll. Res.* 17(2): 149-152.

Garg, V.K. and Kaushik, P. (2006): Influence of short-term irrigation of textile mill wastewater on the growth of chickpea cultivars, *Chemistry and Ecology*, 22(3): 193-200.

Garg, V.K.; Chaudhary, A.; Deepshikha and Dahiya, S. (1998): An appraisal of groundwater quality in some villages of district Jind, *Indian J. Environmental Protection*, 19(4): 267-272.

Gharaibeh, M.A.; Eltaif, N.I. and Bayan Al-Abdullah (2007): Impact of Field Application of Treated Wastewater on Hydraulic Properties of Vertisols, *Water Air Soil Pollut*, DOI- 10.1007/s11270-007-9423-z.

Girma T. (2005): Extent and significant use of low quality water in Agriculture.

Golia, E.E.; Dimirkou, A. and Mitsios, I.K. (2007): Accumulation of Metals on Tobacco Leaves (Primings) Grown in an Agricultural Area in Relation to Soil, *Bul.l Environ. Contam. Toxicol.*, DOI 10.1007/s00128-007-9111-0.

Goltenboth, F. (1994): Impact of textile factory in Salatiga on Ledok river system, Central Java, *J. Environ. Toxicol.*, South East Asia, pp: 301-317.

Gomez-Serrano, Garcia-Macias, A., Espinosa-Mansilla, A. and Valenzuela-Calahorro (1998): Adsorption of mercury, cadmium and lead from aquoes solution on heat treated and sulphurized activated carbon. *Wat. Res.*, 32:1-4.

GoogleEarth (2006): Software for satellite imagery, available at http://www.google.com.

Gopal, B. (1994): Conservation of inland water in India: An overview. Verh. Internet. Verein. *Hydrobiologia*, 384: 267.

Govindan, V.S. and Sundarlingam, V.S. (1979) Studies on treatment of textile mill waste water by stabilization pond method. *J. Pollution Control*, 5 (2):137-145.

Gray, C. W. and Mclaren, R. G. (2006): Soil factors affecting heavy metal solubility in some New Zealand soils, *Water, Air and Soil Pollution*, 175: 3-14.

Groff, K.A. (1993): Textile waste, *Environmental Research*. 65: 421.

Groff, K.A. (1993): Textile waste. *Environmental Research*. 65: 421.

Gupta, R.K., Singh, R.R. and Abrol, I.P. (1989): Influence of simultaneous changes in sodicity and pH on hydraulic conditions of an alkali soil, *Soil Science*, 147: 28-33.

Harper, H.H.; Yusuf, Y.A. and Wanielista, M.P. (1984): Fate of heavy metals in stromwater management system, In: *Lake and Reservoir Management, USEPA, Washington*, pp: 329-334.

Hart, B.T. (1982): Trace metals in natural waters, *Speciation Chem. Australian*, 49: 260-265.

Hedge, V.S.; Shalini, G. and Kanchanagouri, D.G. (2006): Provenance of heavy minerals with special reference to Ilmenite of the Honnevar beach, central west coast of India, *Current Science*, 91 (5): 644-648.

Helena, B.A.; Vega, M.; Barrado, E.; Parado, R. and Fernandez, L. (1999): A case of hydro-chemical characterization of an alluvial aquifer influenced by human activities, *Water, Air and Soil Pollution*, 112: 365-387.

Hesse, P.R. (1994): A textbook of soil chemical analysis, *CBS Publishers and distributors*, 485, Bholanathnagar, Shahdhra, Delhi-110032, pp: 520.

Hitz, H.R.; Huber, W and Rud, R.H. (1978): The absorption of dyes on activated sludge, *Journal of society of dyers and Colorists*, February: 71-76.

Horing, R.H. (1976): Characterization and treatment of textile dyeing wastewaters, In: Proceedings of national technical conference, *American association of textile chemists and colorist*, pp: 100-104.

Hoston, A.K. (1965): An index number system for rating water quality, *J. Wat. Poll. Cont. Fed.*, 37(3): 300-306.

http//:www.engg.ksu.edu as access on 16 november, 2006

http//www. mapsofindia.com, as access on 12 October 2006.

http://www. boulder.com as access on 07 June 2007

http://www. cpcb.nic.in as accessed on 22 February 2007

http://www. Earth&table.com as accessed on August 2006.

http://www. epa.gov/safewater/mcl.html

http://www. haryanaonline.com as access on 21 March, 2006.

http://www. holar.is as access on 29 June, 2007

http://www. lef.org as accessed on August 2006.

http://www. lenntech.com/aquatic/metal.htm as accessed on May 2007.

http://www. tuberose.com as accessed on August 2006.

http://www. vistamagonline.com as accessed on August 2006.

http://www. who.in as accessed on 25 May 2007.

http://www.appliedhydrology.org

http://www.en.wikipedia.org as access on 18 October 2006.

http://www.indiatravelogue.com as access on 21 March, 2006.

http://www.iwmi.cgiar.org/assessment.

http://www.parliament.uk/post/home.htm

http://www.yearofplanetearth.org

Huang, J.; Huang, R.; Jiao, J.J. and Chen, K. (2007): Speciation and mobility of heavy metals in mud in coastal reclamation areas in Shenzhen, China, *Environ. Geol.*, DOI 10.1007/s00254-007-0636-7.

Hynes, H.B.N. (1970): The ecology of running waters, *Liverpool University Press, Liverpool, 4th impression*: 1-555.

Ireland, M.P. (1983): Heavy metals uptake and tissue distribution, In: Earthworm ecology- from Darwin to vermiculture (Ed.- Satchell, J.E., *Chapman and Hall*), pp: 135-147.

IS 1172: Indian Standard Code of basic requirement for water supply, drainage and sanitation.

IUPAC (1994): Atomic weights of the elements, 1993, International Union of Pure and Applied Chemistry, *Pure Appl. Chem.*, 66: 2423.

Jain, C.K. (2004): Metal fractionation study on bed sediments of river Yamuna, India, *Wat. Res.* 38: 569-578.

Jayabaskeran, K. J. Sree Ramulu U. S. (1996): Distribution of heavy metals in soil of various sewage farms in Tamil Nadu, *J. Indian Soc. Soil. Sci.*, 44: 401-404.

Jha, M.N. and Pandey, P. (1984): Impact of growing eucalyptus and soil monocultures on soil in natural sal area of Doon valley, *Ind. For.*, 110: 16-18.

Joshi, B.D.; Sharma, S.D.; Joshi, K.D. and Sengupta, S. (1998): Some physico-chemical properties of soil from different regions in relation to Eucalyptusization in Himalayan foothills, *Him.J. Env. Zool.*, 2(10): 58-60.

Judlins, J.F. and Hornsby, J.S. (1978): Color removal from textile dye waste using magnesium carbonate, *Journal of Water Pollution Control Federation*, 50: 2446-2456.

Kalra, Y.P. and Maynarol, D.G. (1991): Methods manual for forest soil and plant analysis. *For. Can., Northwest Reg. North. For. Cent. Edmonton, Alberta. Inf. Rep. Nor. X-319*, pp: 1-65.

Kanwar, J.S. (1961): Quality of irrigation water as an index of suitability for irrigation purposes, *Potash Review*, 13: 1-13.

Karle, K.K.; Bhusal, S.S.; Gunjal, P.S. and Kuchekar, S.R. (1992): Studied on groundwater quality in Pravaranagar area of Ahmednagar district, *Poll. Res.* 11(2): 65-68.

Kashem, M.A. and Singh, B.R. (1999): Heavy metal contamination of soil and vegetation in the vicinity of industries in Bangladesh, *Water, Air and Soil Pollution*, 115: 347-361.

Kataria, H.C. (1996): BOD and COD contents in bore well water of Bhopal (M.P.), *Natcon*, 8(1): 69-72.

Kataria, H.C.; Gupta, S.S. and Jain, O.P. (1995): Water quality of bore wells in B.H.E.L. area of Bhopal, *Poll. Res.* 14 (4): 455-462.

Katz, M. (1975): The effect of heavy metals on fish and aquatic environment. (Ed.-Krenkel, P.A.), *Pregamon Press, New York*, pp: 637-645.

Khan T.I., Marwari Richa, Singh N. (2003): Impact of textile wastewater on *Solanum melongena* var-FI- Hybrid Kanhaiya in pot experiment with special emphasis on analysis of heavy metals. *Dimensions Polln*, 2: 108-116.

Khanna, D.R. and Bhutiani, R. (2004): Water analysis-at a glance, ASEA, Rishikesh, pp: 108.

Khurshid, Zaheeruddin and Mohd. Usman Shabeer (1997): Degradation of water quality due to heavy metals pollution in Faridabad district, Haryana, India, *Poll. Res.* 16(1): 41-43.

Korfali, S.I. and Davies, B.D.E. (2004): The relationship of metals in river sediments (Nahr-Ibrahim, Lebanon) and adjacent floodplain soil, *the CIGR J. of scientific research and development*, manuscript LW 04 010, 6: 1-22.

Krebs, R.; Gupta, S.K.; Furrer, G. and Schulin, R. (1999): Gravel sludge as an immobilizing agent in soils contaminated by heavy metals: A field study, *Water, Air and Soil Pollution*, 115: 465-479.

Krishna, A. K. and Govil, P. K. (2004) Heavy metal contamination of soil around Pali industrial area, Rajasthan, India, *Environmental Geology*, 47: 38-44.

Krull, R. and E. Dopkens (2004): Recycling of dye house effluents by biological and chemical treatment, *Water Sc. And Tech.* 49(4): 311-317.

Kudesia, V.P. (1992): Water Pollution, *Pragati Prakashan, Meerut*, pp: 407.

Kumar, Rakesh; Singh, R.D. and Sharma, K.D. (2005): Water resources of India, *Current Science*, 89 (5): 794-811.

Kumar, S.; Bhatacharjee, J.W. and Sharma, R.K. (1992): Relationship between fluoride, total hardness and total alkalinity in the groundwater of Barmer Dist. (Rajsthan), *Poll. Res.* 11(2): 111-116.

Kumar, S; Kushwaha, R.; Sapra, S. Gupta, A.B. and Bhargava, A. (2001): Impact of textile industry on groundwater quality of Sanagar, Jaipur, *J. Indian Water Works Association*, 33(4): 321-326.

Lagas, P.; Verdam, B and Loch, J.P.G. (1989): Threat to Groundwater quality by pesticides in the Netherlands, Groundwater management: quantity and quality, IAHS Publ. no. 188, *IAHS Press Walling ford, United Kingdom*, pp.171-180.

Lee, K.K.; A.M. Kassim and H.K. Lee (2004): The object of nitrogen supplementation on the efficiency of colour and COD removal by Malaysian white rot fungi in textile dying effluent, *Water Sc. and Tech.* 50 (50): 73-77.

Lofts, S.; Spurgeon, D.J.; Svendsen, C. and Tipping, E. (2004): Deriving soil critical limits for Cu, Zn, Cd, and pH: A method based on free ion concentration, *Environ. Sci. Tech.*, 38: 3623-3631.

Lokeshwari, H. and Chandrappa, G.T. (2006): Impact of heavy metal contamination of Bellandur Lake on soil and cultivated vegetation, *Current Science*, 91(9): 622-627.

Lokeshwari, H., and Chandrappa, G.T. (2006): Imapct of heavy metal contamination of Bellandur lake on soil and cultivated vegetation. Current Science, 91(5), pp.622-27.

Loska, K. and Wiechula, D. (2002): Speciation of cadmium in the bottom sediment of rybnik Reservoir, *Water, Air Soil Pollut.*, 141: 73-89.

Lung, W. (1990): Speciation analysis – why and how? *Fresenius J. Anal. Chem.* 337: 557-564.

Mahesha, N.N. and Prasad, N.R.R. (2004): Physico-chemical characteristics of bore well water in Arsikara taluk, Hassan, *IJEP*, 24(12): 897-904.

Malik, D.S. and Bharti, P. K. (2007): Soil quality of irrigated agricultural fields in textile industrial area of Panipat city, *Asian Journal of Experimental sciences*, 21 (2): 445-451.

Malik, D.S.; Bharti, P.K. and Sumit Grover (2006): Alteration in surface water quality near textile industries at Panipat (Haryana), *Environment Conservation J.*, 7(2): 65-68.

Malik, D.S.; Bharti, P.K; Kamboj, N. and Yadav, R. (2007): Quantification of heavy metals migration in groundwater regime due to discharge of textile industrial effluents in Panipat area, Haryana, *Pollution Research*, 26 (4): 123-125.

Malik, D.S.; Yadav, Rashmi and Bharti, P.K. (2004) Accumulation of heavy metals in crop plants through irrigation of contaminated groundwater in Panipat region. *Environ. Conserv. J.*, 5 (3): 101-104.

Manahan, S. (1984): Environmental Chemistry, Brooks/Colei, CA, USA, pp: 638.

Manchanda, H.R. (1990): Significance of the type of salinity for growing pulses under saline conditions, *Indo-Pak workshop on Soil Salinity and Water Management*, Feb, 10-14, pp: 2-3.

Mani, V.; Kaur, H. and Mohini, M. (2005): Toxic metals and environmental pollution, *J. Ind. Poll. Cont.*, 21(1): 101-107.

Martin, J.M. and Whitfield, M. (1983): The significance of the river input of chemical elements to the ocean, In: Wong, C.S.; Boyle, E.; Bruland, K.W.; Burton, J.D. and Goldburg, E.D. (Eds.), Trace metals in sea water, *Plenum Press, New York*, pp: 324-331.

Martin, M.H. and Cougherty, P.J. (1982): Biological monitoring of heavy metals pollution, *Applied Science Publishers*, pp: 463.

Masters, G.M. (1998): Introduction to environmental engineering and science, *Prentice-Hall India*, pp: 460.

Mathess, G. (1974): Heavy metals as trace constituents in natural and polluted groundwater, *Goel mijnbouw, New Jersy, USA*, 53: 149-155.

Mathur, R.P. (1993): Water and wastewater testing (A lab manual). *Nemchand and Bros. Pub.*, Roorkee, pp: 45.

McBride, M., Sauve, S. and Hendershot, W. (1997): Solubility control of Cu, Zn, Cd, and Pb, in contaminated soils, *Euro. J. Soil Science*, 48: 337-346.

McKay, G. (1979): Waste color removal from textile effluents, *American Dyestuff Reporter*, 68: 29-36.

Meier, W., and Mull, R. (1989), Nitrate in Groundwater, in Groundwater management: Quantity and quality, IAHS, Publ. no.188, *IAHS Press, Wallingford, United Kingdom*, pp: 181-190.

Michaels, G.B. and Lewis, E.L. (1985): Sorption and toxicity of azo and triphenyl methane dues to aquatic microbial populations, *Environmental Toxicology and Chemistry*, 4: 45-50.

Mico, C; Recatal, L.; Peris, M. And Sanchez, J. (2007): A comparison of two digestion methods for the analysis of heavy metals by flame atomic absorption spectroscopy, *Spectroscopy Europe*, 19 (1): 23-26

Mido, Y. and Satake, M, (1995): Chemicals in the environment, *Discovery Publishing House, New Delhi*, pp: 491.

Millar, C.E. and Turk, L.M. (2002): Fundamentals of soil science, Biotech Books, Delhi-35, pp: 462.

Minhas, P.S. and Gupta, R.K. (1992): Quality of irrigation water – assessment and management, Publication and Information Division, ICAR, *Krishi Anusandhan Bhawan, Pusa, New Delhi*, pp: 123.

Minhas, P.S. and Khosla, B.K. (1986): Solute displacement in a silt loam soil as affected by the method of water application under different evaporation rates, *Agric. Wat. Mgmt*, 12: 63-75.

Mishra, E; Sharma, D. and Malkania, U. (1990): Fish mortality as affected by liquid effluents from Raja Textile Ltd., Rampur (U.P.), *Int. J. Ecol. Env. Sc.*, 16 (2-3): 119-123.

Mishra, N.K. and Sahoo, H.K. (2003): Evaluation of groundwater quality in and around Deogarh, *IJEP*, 23 (6): 667-672.

Mohan, Devendra and Yogesh Sharma (2002): Trace metals in a few water bodies of Pali, Rajsthan, *J. Natcon*. 14 (2): 363-366.

Mohan, R.; Chopra, N. and Chowdhary, G.C. (1998): Heavy metals (Fe, Pb, Cd, Zn) in the groundwater of Naini industrial area, Dist. Allahabad, U.P., *Poll. Res.* 17(2): 167-168.

Mohanasundaram, S. (2003) Affordable and effective textile processing effluent treatm entplants. *South India's Premier Magazine on Environment Sc. and Engg.*, pp 76-82.

Moon, C. H.; Lee Y. S. and Yoon, T. H. (1991): *Environmental Technology*; 12: 413.

Mor, S.; Bishnoi, M.S. and Bishnoi, N.R. (2003): Assessment of groundwater quality of Jind city, *IJEP*, 23(6): 673-679.

MPCA (2001): Effects of Land Use on Groundwater Quality, St. Cloud Area, Minnesota – Short Report, *Minnesota Pollution Control Agency*, Groundwater Monitoring and Assessment Program, pp: 1-29.

Muller, G. (1979):Schwermetalle in den sedimenten des Rheinsveranderungen seit, *Umschau*, 79: 778-783.

Mustafa, W.; Somasundaram, S.S.N.; Shahul, P.H. and Palaniappan, R. (1998): Evaluation of groundwater quality in Tiruchirapalli city, *Indian J. Environmental Protection*, 19(4): 284-289.

Narayan, A.C. and Suresh, G.C. (1989): Chemical quality of groundwater of Mangalore city, Karnataka, *Indian J. Env. Hlth.*, 131: 220-226.

Nasr, S.M.; Okbah, M.A. and Kasem, S.M. (2006): Environmental assessment of heavy metal pollution in bottom sediments of Aden port, Yemen, *International Journal of Oceans and Oceanography*, 1(1): 99-109

National Research Council (NRC) (1989): Contaminated marine systems- assessment and remediation, *National Academy Press, Washington*, D.C. pp: 185.

Navarro, A. and Font, X. (1993): Discriminating different sources of groundwater contamination caused by industrial waste in the Besos River Basin, Barcelona, Spain, *J. Applied Biochemistry*, APPGEY, 8: 277.

Nawar, S.S. and Doma, H.S. (1989): Removal of dyes from effluents using low-cost agricultural byproducts, *The Science of Total Environment*, 79: 271-279.

Nedunuri, K.V.; Govindaraju, R.S.; Erickson, L.E. and Schwab, A.P. (1995): Modeling of heavy metal movement in vegetated, unsaturated soils with emphasis on geochemistry, In: Proceedings of the 10th Annual Conference on Hazardous Waste Research, pp: 57-66.

Neelima Rajvaidya and Dilpi Kumar Markandey (1998). Advanced in Environmental Sciences and Technology. *A.P.H. Publishimg Corporation*, New Delhi, 6: 231-249.

Nemerow, N.L. (1971): Industrial water pollution: origins, characteristics and treatment, Addision, *Wesley Publishing* Co., pp: 532.

Nightingale, H. I. (1987): *Wat. Res. Bull.*, 23: 663.

Nongkynrih, P.; Dkhar, P.S. and Khathing, D.T. (1996): Micronutrients elements in acid alfisols of Meghalaya under rice cultivation, *J. Soil Si.*, 44(3): 455-457.

Nriagu, J.O. (1989): A global assessment of natural sources of atmosphere trace metals, *Nature*, 338: 47-49.

Nriagu, J.O. and Pacyna, J.M. (1988): Quantitative assessment of worldwide contamination of air, water and soil with trace metals, *Nature*, 333: 134-139.

Numberg, H.W. (1984): The volumetric approach in trace metal chemistry of natural waters and atmospheric precipitation, *Analyst. Chim. Acta*, 164: 1-21.

Obiri, Samuel (2007): Determination of Heavy Metals in Water from Boreholes in Dumasi in the Wassa West District of Western Region of Republic of Ghana, *Environ Monit Assess*, 130: 455–463

O'Hare, M.P., Fairchild, D.M., Hajali, P.A., Canter, L.W. (1986): Artificial Recharge of Groundwater. Proceedings of the Second International Symposium on Artificial Recharge of Groundwater. pp: 56-67.

Okonwo, J.O.; Lwenje, S.M.; Mtetwa, V.S.B.; and Mkhweli, T.B. (1999): Measurement of lead concentrations in the hair of school children in Manzini region, Swaziland, *Int. J. Environ. Stud.* 56: 419-428.

Okonwo, J.O.; Lwenje, S.M.; Mtetwa, V.S.B.; Gumedge, P.N. and Shilongonyane, M.M. (2001): Determination of urinary lead in school children in Manzini region, Swaziland, South Africa, *Environmentalist*, 21: 205-209.

Padmavathiamma, P.K. and Li, L.Y. (2007): Phytoremediation Technology: Hyper-accumulation Metals in Plants, *Water Air Soil Pollut.*, DOI- 10.1007/s11270-007-9401-5.

Palanivelu, K.; Priya, M.N.; Selvan, A.M. and Natesan,U. (2006): Water quality assessment in the tsunami affected coastal areas of Chennai, *Current Science*, 91 (5): 583-584.

Pathe, P.P.; Biswas, A.K.; Rao, N.N. and Kaul, S.N. (2005): Physico-chemical treatment of wastewater from clusters of small-scale cotton textile units, *Environmental Technology*, 26: 313-327.

PAU (2005): Ken Betwa river link to submerge parts of Panna TR. In: Protected Area Update, October, 2005, (No. 57) Vol-XI, No-5, pp: 10.

Pfafflin, J.R. and Ziegler, E.N. (2006): Encyclopaedia of Environmental Science and Engineering, *Taylor and Francis*, pp: 1408.

Pisharoty, P.R. (1986): Meteorology for the Indian Farmers, Indian Space Research Organisation, Bangalore, pp: 19.

Poots, V.J.; Mckay, G. and Heakt, J.J. (1976): The removal of acid dye from effluent using natural absorbents-II, *Water Research*, 10: 1067-1070.

Porter, J.J. (1970): The changing nature of textile processing and waste treatment technology, *Textile chemist and Colourists*, 2: 336.

Porter, J.J. (1972): Treatment of textile waste with activated carbon, *American Dyestuff Reporter*, 8: 2427.

PPCB (1993): A report on groundwater quality of Ludhiana city, Punjab Pulution control Board, pp: 50.

Prakash, G. and Prakash, J. (2001): Water- present, past and future, *Science Reporter-* cover story, July, pp: 10-14 and 62-63.

Prasad, B.V. and Chandra, P.R. (1997): Groundwater quality in an industrial zone, *Poll. Res.* 16(2): 105-107.

Prasad, S. (2003): Fundamentals of biostatistics (biometry), *Emkey Publication, Delhi-51*, pp: 168.

Pujari, G.K. and Sinha, B.K. (1999): Studies on the water and soil quality of some villages of Attabira area irrigated by Bargarg main canal originated from Hirakund reservoir of Orissa, *J. of Env. and Poll.*, 6(1): 71-76.

Ramani, K.V. and Srivastava, M.S. (1989): Effect of flyash from thermal power station on soil, *BHEL J.* 10: 1-4.

Rao, K.V.G.K.; Gupta R.K. and Kamra, S.K. (1987): Reclamation of waterlogged high SAR saline soil, CSSRI, Karnal, A feasibility report for *CIRB, Hissar, CSSRI, Karnal*, pp: 21.

Rao, N.S. and Rao, V.V.S.G. (1999): Pathlines of pollutants migration in groundwater of the Visakhpatanam urban area, India, *Hydrological Process*, 13: 1381-1389.

Reddy, K.J. and Jianping Lin (2000): Nitrate removal from groundwater using catalytic reduction, *Water Res.* 34 (3): 995-1001.

Reshma, S. and V.R. Prakasam (2003): Potability of dug wells of Mayyand Panchayat, Kerla, *Indian J. Environ. and Ecoplan.* 7(3): 471-476.

Rhoades, J.D. (1987): Use of saline water for irrigation, *Wat. Qual. Bull.*, 12: 14-20.

Richards, L.A. (1954): Diagnosis and improvement of saline and alkali soils, US Deptt. Agri., edited Handbook, No. 60: 160.

Rizk, Z.S.; Alsharhan, A.S. and Wood, W.W. (2007): Sources of dissolved solids and water in Wadi Al Bih aquifer, Ras Al Khaimah Emirate, United Arab Emirates, *Hydrogeology Journal*, DOI 10.1007/s10040-007-0188-7.

Royee, M.K.P. and Prakasham (2003): Water characteristics of dug and tube wells of Kollam municipality, *IJEP*, 23(6): 607-612.

Ruhela, Mukesh, R. Bhutiani and Aradhana Anand (2005): Rainwater Harvesting, Env. Conserv. J. 5(1-3): 21-34.

Saed, K.; Noor, M.M.M. and Yusuf, B. (2005): Sugarcane bagasse as an adsorbent for dye removal, *J. Ind. Poll. Control*, 21 (1): 1-10.

Saksena, R.K.; Sharma, M.L. and Jodha H.R. (1966): Quality of groundwaters for irrigation in Ahor developmental block, Jalore, *Ann. Arid Zone*, 5: 204-218.

Samy, D.I.A. and Gananarethinam, J.L. (1980): Effect of distillery effluents on the growth of three aquatic macrophytes, *J. Comp. Physiol. Ecol.*, 5(4): 290-295.

Sastry, K.V. and Pratima Rathee (1999): Groundwater quality in three villages of Rohtak district. *J. Natcon*, 11(2): 175-182.

Sastry, K.V. and Rathee, P. (1999): Groundwater quality in three villages of Rohtak district, *J. Natcon*, 11(2): 175-182.

Saxena, M.M. (1994): In: Environmental analysis water, soil and air, *Agro Botanical Publishers*. pp: 1-180.

Schroeder, W.H. (1989): Development in the speciation of mercury in natural waters, *Trends Anal. Chem.* 8: 339-342.

Seeber, P.R. (1962): Cation hydrological facies of groundwater in the English town Formation, New Jersey, In: Short paper in geology, hydrology and topography, USGC, Profes. Paper, 450B: 124-126.

Senthinathan, S. and Azeez, P.A. (1999): Influence of dyeing and bleaching industries on groundwater of Tripur, Tamilnadu, India, *Bull. Environ. Contam. Toxicol.*, 62: 330-335.

Seshadri, S.; Bishop, P.L. and Agha, A.M. (1994): Anaerobic and aerobic treatment of selected azo dyes in waste water, *Waste Management*, 15: 127-137.

Sharma, D.R. (1978): Testing of a model for prediction sodium hazards of irrigation waters, *J. Indian Soc. Soil Sci.*, 27: 204-208.

Sharma, D.R. and Parihar, S.S. (1973): Effect of depth and salinity of groundwater on evaporation and soil salinization, *Indian J. Agric. Sci.*, 43: 582-586.

Sharma, K. and K.S. Patel (1996): Spectrophotometric determination of Copper in water, *Journal of Indian Chemical Society*. 73, pp: 443-444.

Sharma, K.P.; Sharma, K.; Bhardwaj, S.M. and chaturvedi, R.K. (1999): Environment impact assessment of textile printing industries in Sanganer, Jaipur: A case study, *J. Ind. Bot. Soc.* 78:71.

Sharma, R.C.; Abrol, I.P. and Bhumbla, D.R. (1975): Quality of groundwaters of Jind district, Haryana, Bulletin No. 3 (ICAR), *Central Soil Salinity Research Institute (BKAP), Karnal*, pp: 63.

Sharma, R.C.; Abrol, I.P. and Bhumbla, D.R. (1976): Quality of groundwaters of Karnal district, Haryana, Report No. 3 (ICAR), *Central Soil Salinity Research Institute (BKAP), Karnal*, pp: 47.

Sharma, S.; Jain, P.C. and Mathur, R. (1995): Quality assessment of groundwater in municipal and fringe areas near Gwalior, *IJEP*, 15(7): 534-538.

Sheth, K.N. and Desai, A.P. (2005): Study of bio-kinetics of textile wastewater by designing a Bench Scale Completely Mixed Activated Sludge Reactor Model, *J. Ind. Poll. Control*, 21 (1): 11-16.

Sheth, K.N. and Patel, M.R. (2001): Characterization, treatment and comparative cost analysis studies of textile processing wastewater of Vatva industrial complex, *J. Engg. and Tech., S.P. University*, 14: 235-241.

Shivakumar, K.; Pandey, A.K. and Bhiksham, G. (1977): Toxic trace element pollution in groundwater around Patancheru and Bollaram Industrial area, A.P., India: a graphical approach, *Env. Monitor. Assess.*, 45 (1): 57-80.

Shrivastava V.S. and Patil B.H. (2003): Metallic and some physico-chemical studies of soil and aquatic sediments, *Eco Env Conserv*, 9(1): 75-77

Sial, R.A.; Chaudhary, M.F.; Abbas, S.T.; Latif, M.I. and Khan, A.G. (2006): Quality of effluent from Hatter Industrial Estate, *Journal Zhejang Univ. Science B*, pp: 974-980

Siddiqui, Z.M. and Pathania, D. (2002): Studies on heavy metals in surface and groundwater of Jalandhar and Ludhiana districts, *IJET*, 22(2): 201-206.

Singh, A.K. (2006): Chemistry of arsenic in groundwater of Genges-Brahmaputra river basin, *Current Science*, 91 (5): 599-606.

Singh, A.K.; Jaiswal, R.K. and Mukharjee, S. (1996): Groundwater quality assessment of Varanasi city, *Hydrology Journal*, 19(4): 23-31.

Singh, B. and Bhumbla, D.R. (1968): Effect of quality of irrigation water on soil properties, *J. Res.* (Punjab Agri. Univ.), 5: 166-171.

Singh, B. Rana, D.S. and Bajwa, M.S. (1977): Salinity and sodium hazards of underground irrigation waters of Bhatinda district (Punjab), *Indian J. Ecol.*, 4: 32-41.

Singh, K.N.; Bains, S.S. and Dayanand (1969): Salinity problem in high water table areas- An appraisal, *Indian J, Agron.*, 14: 31-34.

Singh, K.P.; Takroo, R. and P.K. Roy (1987): Pesticides and heavy metal residue analysis in water, ITRC Manual. *ITRC*, Lucknow, pp: 1-160

Singh, K.S. and Sharma, R.P. (1971): Studies on the effects of saline irrigation waters on physico-chemical properties of some soils of Rajasthan, *J. Indian Soc. Soil Sci.*, 18: 345-356.

Singh, T.B.; Jadon, S.P.S. and Mishra, G.J. (1994): Degradation of water and soil quality of Parwanoo area with respect to heavy metals, *IJEP*, 14 (4): 282-287.

Singh, V.K. (2006): Studies on distribution of heavy metals in Gomati river and development of low cost adsorbents for their removal, *Ph.D. Thesis, Gurukula Kangri University, Hardwar*, pp: 296.

Soltan, M.E. (1999): Evaluation of groundwater quality in Dakhla oasis (Egyptian Western Desert), *Environmental Monitoring and Assessment*, 57: 157-168.

Sophocleous M. (2004): Groundwater Recharge, in *Groundwater*, [Eds. Luis Silveira, Stefan Wohnlich, and Eduardo J. Usunoff], in *Encyclopedia of Life Support Systems (EOLSS)*, Developed under the Auspices of the UNESCO, Eolss Publishers, Oxford,UK, [http://www.eolss.net].

Souther, R.H. and Alsapaugh, T.A. (1957): Biological treatment of mixture of textile wastes and domestic sewage. *Textile*, 2 (1): 135-139.

Srinivas, C.; Piska, R.S. and Reddy, R. (2002): Groundwater pollution due to the industrial effluents in Kothur industrial area, Mahaboonagar, A.P., *Asian J. Micobiol. Biotech. Env. Sci.*, 4(3): 39-42.

Srinivasan, M. and Murali, M. (1996): Some studies on effect pollutants on properties of soils, *IJEP*, 16(7): 522-523.

Stetzenbach; Klaws, J.; Irene M. Farnham; Vernon F. Hodge and Kevin H. Johannesson (1999): Using multivariate stastical analysis of groundwater major cation and trace element concentrations to evaluate groundwater flow in a regional aquifer, *Hydrol. Process.* 13: 2655-2673.

Tan, K.H. and Nopamornbodi, O. (1981): Electron microbeam analysis and scanning electron microscopy of soil-root interfaces, *Soil Sci.*, 131: 100-106.

Taylor, S.R. (1964): Abundance of chemical elements in the continental crust – A new table, *Geochim. Cosmochim. Acta.* 28: 1273-1275.

Thorat, P.R. and Pathade, G.R. (2001): Textile waste: Characterization and treatment, In: Environmental Pollution and management of wastewaters by microbial techniques (Eds.- Pathade, G.R. and Goel, P.K.), ABD Publishers, Jaipur, India, pp: 316-325.

Todd, D.K. (1980): Groundwater hydrology, John Wiley, New York: 554.

Trevors, J.T. and Saier Jr., M.H. (2007): Regulation of Pollution, *Water Air Soil Pollut*, DOI 10.1007/s11270-007-9344-x.

Trivedi, R.K. and Goel, P.K. (1984): Chemical and biological methods for water pollution studies Karad, *Environmental publication*, pp: 1-251.

Tyagi, P. and Budhi (2000): Degradation of groundwater quality due to heavy metals in industrial area of India- A review, *Indian J. Env. Prot.*, 20 (3): 174-181.

Umar, R. and Ahmad, M.S. (1999): Groundwater quality in parts of Central Ganga Basin, India, *Environmental Geology*, 39 (6): 673-678.

USEPA (1990): Operation and quality control manual, Environmental Protection Agency (EPA), Athens, GA 30613.

Va´zquez, N.N.; Gil, M.A.; Esteves, J. L. and Narvarte, M. A. (2007): Monitoring Heavy Metal Pollution in San Antonio Bay, Rio Negro, Argentina, *Bull. Environ. Contam. Toxicol.*, DOI 10.1007/s00128-007-9084-z.

Vaidge, A.A. and Datye, K.V. (1982): Environment pollution during chemical processing of synthetic fibers, *Colourage*, 14: 3- 10.

Vates, M.V. (1986): Septic tank density and groundwater contamination, *Groundwater*, 23(5): 586-590.

Vazquez, N.N.; Gil, J.L.; Esteves, and Narvarte, M.A. (2007): Monitoring heavy metal pollution in San Antonio Bay, Rio Negro, *Argentina, Bull. Environ. Contam. Toxicol.*, DOI- 10.1007/s001 28-007-9084-z.

Verma, N.K. and Kharat, D.S. (2000): Textile Industry, *Central Pollution Control Board*, New Delhi, pp: 82.

Verma, S.R. and Mathur, R.P. (1974): Studies on the toxicity of industrial wastes to macrobranchium deyanum, *Indian J. Environ. Hlth.*, 16(1): 1-11.

Vijith, H. and Satheesh, R. (2007): Geographical Information System based assessment of spatiotemporal characteristics of groundwater quality of upland sub-watersheds of Meenachil River, parts of Western Ghats, Kottayam District, Kerala, India, *Environ Geol*, DOI 10.1007/s00254-006-0612-7.

Vishwanath, G. and Ananthmurthy, K.S. (2002): Assessment of groundwater quality around a solid waste dumpsite, *Nat. Env. Poll. Tech.*, 1(4): 411- 413.

Wainwright, John and Mulligan, Mark (2004): Environmental modeling, *John Wiley and Sons Ltd.* pp: 408.

Walker, D.J.; Bernal, M.P. and Correal, E. (2007): The Influence of Heavy Metals and Mineral Nutrient Supply on *Bituminaria bituminosa*, *Water Air Soil Pollut*, DOI 10.1007/s11270-007-9422-0.

Walker, R. (1970): The metabolism of azo compounds: a review of the literature, *Food Cosmetics Toxicology*, 8: 659-661.

Ward, N.I. (1995): In: Environmental analytical chemistry-Trace elements. (Eds.- F.W. Fifield, and P.J. Haines.), Blackie Academic and Professional, UK, pp.320-328

Watler, J.K. and Wint, M. (1981): Industrial effluent treatment, *Applied Science, UK*, pp: 548.

Wetzel, R.G. (1975): Limnology, *W.B. Saunders Co. Philadelphia*, pp: 743.

WHO (1984): Guideline for drinking water quality, Recommendations, *World Health Organization, Geneva*, pp: 130.

WHO (1988): International standards for drinking water. Word Health Organization, Geneva. pp: 142.

WHO (2006) Standards for drinking water, available at http//:www.lenntech.com

Widyanto, L.S. (1975): The effect of industrial pollutants on the growth of water hyacinth (Eicchornia crassipes Mart Solm.), In: *Proceedings of the third Indonesian Weed Science Conference*, Bandung, pp: 328.

Williums, D.R. (1972): Metals, Ligands and Cancer, *Chemical Review*, 72 (3): 203-213.

Wint, A. (1981): The disposal of toxic wastes, In: Industrial Effluent Treatment Vol-I (Eds.- Watler, J.K. and Wint, M.), pp: 1-19.

Wong, P.K. (2000): Application of enhanced photocatylytic oxidation in the treatment of azo dyes in textile waste water, In: Advances in Wastewater Treatment Technologies (II), (Eds.- Trivedi, R.K. and Kaul, S.N., *Global Science Publications, Aligarh*, pp: 302.

Yadav, A.K; P.K. Jain and Jyoti Sharma (2003): Assessment of groundwater quality of Behror textile of Alwar Dist., Rajasthan, *Aquacult*, 4(2): 265-270.

Yadav, J. P. and Lata, S. (2003): Pollution of fluoride in groundwater in Bahadurgarh block of district Jhajjar, Haryana, *Indian J. Environmental Protection*, 23(6): 680-686.

Yadav, R.K.; Goyal, B.; Sharma, R.K.; Dubey, S.K. and Minhas, P.S. (2002): Post-irrigation impact of domestic sewage effluent on composition of soils, crops and groundwater- a case study, *Environment International*, 28: 481-486.

Yu, F-Y; Li, C-W and Kang, S-F. (2005) Color, dye and doc removal, and acid generation during fenton oxidation of dyes, *Environmental Technology*, Vol-26: 537-544.

Yuandong, Z.; Shirong, L. and Jiangming, M. (2006): Water-holding capacity of ground covers and soil in alpine and sub-alpine shrubs in western Sichuan, China, *ACTA Ecologica Sinica*, 26(9): 2775-2782.

Yusuf, Y.A.; Wanielista, M.P.; Harper, H.H. and Hvitved-Jacobsen, T. (1986): Best Management practices- effectiveness of Retention and Detention Pond for control of contamination in Highway Runoff, *Final Report, University of Florida, Orlendo*, pp: 151.

Yusuff, R.O. and Sonibare, J.A. (2004): Characterization of textile industrial effluents in Kaduna, Nigeria and pollution implications, *Global nest: Int. J.*, 6(3): 212-221.

Zhang, J; Crittenen, J.C. and Hand, D.W. (1994): The solar photocatlytic decontamination of water, *Chemistry and Industry*, 19(1): 714-717.

Zheng, G.; Yue, L.; Li, Z and Chen, C. (2006): Assessment on heavy metals pollution of agricultural soil in Guanzhong District, *J Geographical Sciences*, 16, (1): 105-113.

Zilliox, Lothaire (1989): Industrial impact on the quality of groundwater in a large Basin: Case of the Rhine aquifer, *Water International*, 14(2): 62-68.

Zollinger, H. (1987): Colour chemistry synthesis properties and application of organic dyes and pigment, *New York VCH*, pp: 275.

Index

E

F

G

H